Contributors

Charles E. Barr, DDS
Director
Department of Dentistry
Beth Israel Medical Center
Professor of Dentistry
Mt Sinai School of Medicine
New York

Barbara Gerbert, PhD
Assistant Professor
Department of Dental Public
  Health and Hygiene
School of Dentistry
University of California
San Francisco

Markus Grassi, DDS, Dr Med Dent
Department of Comprehensive
  Dentistry
School of Dental Medicine
University of Berne
Switzerland

Deborah Greenspan, BDS
Associate Clinical Professor of
  Oral Medicine
Department of Stomatology
School of Dentistry
University of California
San Francisco

John S. Greenspan, BSc, PhD,
  BDS, FRCPath
Director, Oral AIDS Center
Professor and Chair of Oral
  Biology Division
Professor of Pathology
Department of Stomatology
School of Dentistry
University of California
San Francisco

Stanley Holt, PhD
Professor
Department opf Periodontology
Dental School
University of Texas
Health Science Center
San Antonio

Robert S. Klein, MD
Co-Director, AIDS Center
Montefiore Medical Center
Associate Professor
Department of Medicine and
  Department of Epidemiology
  and Social Medicine
Albert Einstein College
  of Medicine
New York

Mary Logan, JD
Associate General Council
The American Dental
  Association
Chicago

Laurence McCullough, PhD
Adjunct Professor
Department of Community
  Dentistry
Georgetown University
Senior Research Scholar
Kennedy Institute of Ethics
Washington, DC

John A. Molinari, PhD
Professor and Chairman
Department of Microbiology
  and Biochemistry
School of Dentistry
University of Detroit

Patricia A. Murray, DMD, PhD
Assistant Professor of
  Periodontology
Department of Stomatology
School of Dentistry
University of California
San Francisco

Jens J. Pindborg, DDS, Dr
  Odont
Professor of Oral Pathology
Royal Dental College
Copenhagen, Denmark

Paul B. Robertson, DDS
Dean
Faculty of Dentistry
University of British Columbia
Professor
Department of Stomatology
School of Dentistry
University of California
San Francisco

James R. Winkler, DDS, PhD
Assistant Professor of
  Periodontology
Department of Stomatology
School of Dentistry
University of California
San Francisco

Joseph J. Zambon, DDS, PhD
Associate Professor of
  Periodontology
Departments of Oral Biology
  and Periodontology
School of Dental Medicine
State University of New York
Buffalo

Perspectives on
Oral Manifestations of AIDS
Diagnosis and Management
of HIV-Associated Infections

Proceedings of a symposium held
January 18-20, 1988 in San Diego, California
Funded by an educational grant from
The Procter & Gamble Oral Health Group

PSG PUBLISHING COMPANY, INC.
LITTLETON, MASSACHUSETTS

Published by PSG Publishing Company, Inc., 545 Great Road, Littleton, Massachusetts 01460.

Printed in Hong Kong.

International Standard Book Number: 0-88416-592-2

Contents

Introduction

Previous studies of primary immunodeficiency diseases suggest that the oral consequences of immune disorders depend upon the nature of the host defect. Primary immune disorders of the B-cell system, particularly selective IgA deficiency and hypogammaglobulinemia, have not been associated in general with oral or craniofacial pathology as long as the other arms of the immune system remain functional. In stark contrast, severe oral changes are common in patients with phagocytic cell defects, T-cell defects such as mucocutaneous candidiasis and DiGeorge syndrome, and combined immunodeficiency diseases such as severe combined immunodeficiency, Nezelof's syndrome, ataxia-telangiectasia, and Wiskott-Aldrich syndrome. Phagocytic defects characteristic of chronic granulomatous disease may result in severe gingivostomatitis, and a growing body of evidence suggests that impaired neutrophil function is associated with rapidly progressing periodontal diseases, especially localized juvenile periodontitis. In addition, therapeutically induced immunosuppression by chemotherapy or radiation has long been associated with severe oral complications.

Thus, we should not have been surprised by the oral consequences of *acquired* immunodeficiency resulting from human immunodeficiency virus (HIV) infection. Nor is it surprising that infections secondary to HIV infection, often caused by organisms that are a minor component of the microflora, would be substantial problems in these patients. However, I admit to being totally unprepared for the frequency and severity of oral lesions in HIV-infected patients. Many of these patients present to the dental clinics with acute pain, with spontaneous oral bleeding, or with extensive oral soft tissue pathology without any knowledge of their HIV status. With estimates of the number of HIV-infected individuals extending well into the millions, the dental profession faces a major responsibility for the diagnosis of HIV infection and the treatment of HIV-associated oral lesions.

The HIV epidemic raises major questions for dental education and dental practice, including questions concerned with infection control that should have been addressed long before the AIDS crisis. These questions include: What are the implications of the epidemiology, virology and transmission of HIV infection for dental practice as conducted both in the community and in schools of dentistry? What are the oral soft tissue and periodontal effects of acquired severe immunosuppression? How does HIV infection affect the very delicate balance between the oral environment, oral microorganisms and the host? What approaches are effective in managing oral soft tissue and periodontal lesions in the HIV-infected patient? What are the ethical and legal considerations for students, faculty, and community practitioners of providing health care to the HIV-infected patient? How does the HIV epidemic, as well as other infectious diseases, affect infection control procedures in the delivery of dental care? And what is our role in educating the student and the graduate in these areas?

Benjamin Disraeli observed that questions are never settled by ignorance. And so, through an educational grant provided by Procter & Gamble Oral Health Group, and the efforts of Deborah Greenspan and John Greenspan at the University of California San Francisco, Matt Kinnard of the National Institute of Dental Research, and Cynthia Weeks from Procter & Gamble, we have invited to this workshop a select group representing investigators involved in AIDS research, educators located in geographic areas with high HIV prevalence, direct dental care providers, and leaders of professional organizations. We will hear a number of presentations, dealing primarily with the questions I have listed, as the basis for discussion in which to share this group's experience, raise other questions, and identify future strategies for research and delivery of oral health care in both educational and community environments.

Dr Paul B. Robertson

1

AIDS: Challenges and Opportunity

John S. Greenspan

The response of dentistry to the current challenge of AIDS will be an important consideration when future generations judge the profession's contributions to society. An appropriate response must be based on an adequate understanding of the disease processes involved. This presentation summarizes some of the current knowledge of the virology, immunology and epidemiology of HIV infection and AIDS.

Many of us who have been involved in studying the implications of the AIDS epidemic for dentistry during the last seven years have dreamed of having a meeting where we could exchange experiences. We are very grateful to Procter and Gamble for sponsoring this meeting. Where are we in the AIDS epidemic? Many of you are familiar with the description documented by Boccaccio and taken up by Camus in *The Plague* concerning the response of human societies to an epidemic. First, the epidemic is denied or not taken seriously. There follows a phase of overreaction and hysteria, and then people may try to find someone to blame for their problems. However, most of us are here today because we seek to understand the problem in order to deal with it. As Dr Robertson said, the only way to handle this, or for that matter any problem that we face as a profession, is to analyze it, determine its extent and thus find ways to control it. I hope that we will not lapse into a phase of complacency when the epidemic has reached a steady state or plateau, as we pray that it will.

In recent years we have neglected epidemiology and have tended to minimize the dangers of infectious diseases because so many have been controlled by vaccination, antibiotics and hygiene measures. Let me remind you of the size of the last major pandemic, which was the influenza pandemic following the First World War. During the period from 1918 to 1921 perhaps one-third of the world's population contracted influenza, and there were about twenty million deaths from "flu." When the AIDS epidemic started, I doubt if any of us in our most pessimistic moments dreamed that AIDS might achieve a comparable size, but it now seems possible unless research finds some kind of effective intervention measure before long. Gallo[1] and others have suggested that a number of factors may be responsible for the problem of new viral diseases that have appeared and become widespread in the last quarter of a century or so. These include the ready availability of travel, the use of blood and blood products for therapeutic purposes, blood transfusions to treat hemophiliacs, abuse of illicit substances with sharing of needles, and occupational needlesticks. Also contributing are changes in sexual practices, consistent with the general increase in prevalence of many sexually transmitted diseases.

This meeting is about a group of acute and chronic conditions that are due to infection with HIV. The more severe forms, the tip of the iceberg, represent AIDS and are fatal, for at present there is no cure and no vaccine. HIV is an RNA virus,[2] the genetic material of which is in the form of RNA message. On infection, this messenger RNA is converted by the cell into DNA, which then encodes for the various viral proteins. The RNA in the viral particle carries with it reverse transcriptase, an enzyme that is the secret of this virus's life cycle. I am now going to identify two or three of the viral proteins because they are of importance in testing for antibodies to HIV and because they themselves are the subject of antigen tests. The proteins I want to mention are the P24 core protein and two of the molecules that together make up the envelope glycoprotein molecule, namely the GP120 component and the GP41 component. There are other proteins which are of significance, but those are the ones to which I want to draw your attention. The HIV genome is simple. In contrast to other pathogenic retroviruses in mammals, the human HIVs do not contain the

onc gene and thus far have not been shown to be directly oncogenic. The important genes are the *gag* gene, which encodes the
core, including P24; the *pol* gene, which encodes the reverse
transcriptase; and the *env* gene, which encodes the envelope glycoprotein, composed of the two molecules mentioned before,
GP41 and GP120. In addition, there are a number of other
important genes. These include regulatory genes such as *tat*,
which is capable of turning on major, almost explosive replication of HIV. I mention these molecular biology details because
they probably are the explanation for the extraordinary capacity
of this virus to infect and then remain latent for a prolonged
period of time, only to undergo very dramatic activation and
replication.

The modes of HIV infection[3] are quite clearly defined and
are confined to these three: sexual transmission; through blood
or blood products; and perinatal transmission from an infected
mother to the fetus or to the newborn at the time of birth. Once
inside the host, HIV seeks out its target cell. The major target
cell is the CD4-bearing T4 helper lymphocyte. HIV attaches by
specific interaction with the CD4 molecule, is internalized, and
becomes uncoated. The viral RNA, in conjunction with reverse
transcriptase, then produces double-stranded linear DNA. This
passes into the nucleus, becomes a closed circular form, unzips
part of one or more of the host chromosomes, and incorporates
itself into the host chromosome. There it remains, either for a
short period of time if activation and replication are to occur
soon, or for a very prolonged period. Thus, infection with HIV, at
least for the cells concerned, is for life. Because of the ability of
this virus to go from cell to cell, the latent virus can be virtually
undetectable, or at least not expressed in the clinical form. It
can go on to be expressed. That expression requires the production, through messenger RNA, of viral protein and genomic
RNA. The combination of these with plasma membrane components produces new viral particles. In the process, the virus
may kill the target cell or may make the target cell combine
with others to form a biologically ineffective giant cell. These
new viral particles may be released at the cell surface, or may
spread by direct cell-to-cell transmission with no significant
virus being released into the body fluids. This fact has implications for studies that attempt to culture HIV from cell-free fluids. The targets of infection of HIV are primarily the T4 helper
lymphocytes, but it is also clear that the macrophage can

become infected. Some believe this represents true infection of the macrophage, while others believe it is due to phagocytosis. There is a suggestion that endothelium can be infected, and there is no doubt that some brain components can be infected, possibly macrophages, possibly glial cells. It is even possible that epithelial cells can be infected. We know that is true of retroviruses in other animals. In feline leukemia virus infection and in the primate version of AIDS, for example, infection of salivary glands and transmission by biting and licking are common. Finally, there is the suggestion that Langerhans cells may be directly infected.

In the infection process there is, in most cases, viremia, with virus being present in the blood, certainly in cells, and to a lesser extent in plasma. Antigen is present in the bloodstream and can be detected. After a short period, the body produces antibodies to the virus infecting the T4 cells. That, of course, is the major means, the surrogate means, by which we detect infection. In addition, there is evidence that the host produces autoantibodies against the T4-infected cells, which may contribute further to the immunosuppression. Some think that the profound immunosuppression in AIDS cannot be explained purely on the basis of the number of infected cells, but that other mechanisms are killing helper cells, leading to immunosuppression. Autoantibodies represent one such mechanism, and cell-mediated immunity against the infected T4 cell is another possible mechanism.

Either fairly shortly after infection or after a more or less prolonged period, perhaps up to seven years, these processes reduce the helper T-cell numbers and other immunological functions enough to cause increased susceptibility to opportunistic infections and to the occurrence of those neoplasms that take advantage of the suppressed immune system. Whether the main variable that determines passage from a latent infection through an active infection to immunosuppression and clinically significant disease is time alone, or whether there are biologically significant cofactors, is a very important question. In our discussions today and tomorrow it is important that we consider the possible role of oral infections, which are themselves immunosuppressive, in further exacerbating the immunosuppression and leading to a downhill course.

HIV infection results in a wide range of diseases, and the Centers for Disease Control (CDC) classification is useful in categorizing this spectrum.[4,5] There is acute infection, a flulike or mononucleosislike episode in which the individual has an acute viral infection with malaise, fever and lymphadenopathy, shortly after suspected or known exposure to the virus. This was discovered originally by the group in Sydney and has since been confirmed in other places. Then the individual may either go on to manifest HIV disease or go into a period of asymptomatic infection, during which there are circulating antibodies to HIV and HIV is recoverable from peripheral blood.

Overt HIV disease can include a wasting syndrome, and can also include HIV neurological disease. Both of these have been added to the modified CDC definition of AIDS, increasing the reported case numbers. The neurological disease has become increasingly important clinically. First there are subtle cognitive changes, leading through a more or less prolonged clinical course to complete neurological impairment with dementia, failure of many neurological functions, and death. Both of these can occur without the more widely recognized expressions of HIV disease, or they can be combined with any of the others.

The secondary infectious diseases include all of the opportunistic infections, of which many are fatal (category C1). *Pneumocystis carinii* pneumonia is the major culprit. This is a potent opportunist which has long been known to take advantage of individuals with primary or secondary immunosuppression. Tuberculosis, an increasing problem in this population, is another opportunist which was recently added to the revised case definition. There are a whole range of other opportunistic infections, many of them oral, which can affect the profoundly immunosuppressed individual. Then there are the neoplasms that occur in association with immunosuppression, notably non-Hodgkin's lymphoma and Kaposi's sarcoma. Other conditions include the autoimmune manifestations and the idiopathic manifestations of HIV infection, whose mechanisms we do not understand. Again, these can be expressed in the mouth. Thus, the dental profession has a great part to play in the diagnosis and management of HIV disease.

I want to emphasize that in category C2 are the nonfatal infections. Six are recognized and several of them are oral: oral hairy leukoplakia; herpes zoster, which can be oral or facial; tuberculosis; and oral candidiasis. They require a degree of immunosuppression sufficient to allow these fairly ubiquitous organisms to take hold and cause disease. A final note: There are, I believe, three lesions that are unique to HIV infection. They are the ablation of the T4 lymphocyte; the neurological effects, which are histologically and clinically a new disease; and oral hairy leukoplakia, which had never been seen before the AIDS epidemic.

There are a number of approaches to staging HIV infection. The most useful, apart from the CDC classification, is the Walter Reed[6] system in which laboratory data and clinical manifestations are used in a multicriterion staging mechanism. Even the Walter Reed classification, with its poor understanding of the different oral features, recognizes the importance of oral infections as the first clinical signs of the disease. Although the oral manifestations are often the first clinical manifestations, they nevertheless occur at quite a late stage in the story which runs from infection through seroconversion and latency to the ultimate outcome.

The sources of HIV are important to us in dentistry because of infection-control implications. The major sources of HIV are those body fluids that contain high levels of the virus. Blood is the main one, semen is probably the only other of any significance. There are, at most, very low levels of HIV in saliva, and there is some HIV in cervical secretion, urine, sweat, feces and milk. This latter is probably a factor in perinatal transmission. Our opinion in regard to saliva is that for two reasons there are no grounds for alarm. Firstly, HIV is not consistently recovered from saliva. It is only present in the minority of samples, and then at very low titers. Secondly, epidemiological studies give no credence whatsoever to the notion that saliva can be a route for transmission of AIDS. I refer to studies of individuals in the context of sexual practices, particularly as regards kissing and oral sex.

I would like to describe briefly the tests[7] for HIV infection that are currently used, because in today's presentations and in tomorrow's we will be talking about testing, and we need to have some of the terminology at hand. The tests that are currently employed assay the presence of either antibody to HIV or HIV antigen. Of course, the "gold standard" is culture of infectious virus particles from blood or body fluids or tissue. This assay is extremely laborious and expensive. The ELISA test (enzyme-linked immunosorption assay) depends on the use of HIV antigen produced from HIV-infected cells. The cells are broken up, and the viral proteins are separated and used as target on beads or on plastic well dishes. More recent versions use specific viral antigens produced by recombinant DNA technology. Test serum is diluted and brought into contact with the viral antigens. If there are antibodies to HIV in the patient's serum, they react with the protein. They can then be visualized by a second step, in which goat antihuman antibody conjugated with horseradish peroxidase is added and the color is developed by an enzyme process. There are some variables, and the test must be performed in strict accordance with the manufacturer's recommendations. The kits have to be within the expiration date and must be interpreted in a standardized fashion, for there are a number of molecules that can interfere. For example, patients who have very high quantities of immunoglobulins or who have intercurrent infections or autoimmune disease may show nonspecific reactivity. The ELISA assay has a reasonable level of sensitivity and specificity, particularly in areas where there is a high prevalence of seropositivity. It falls short of perfection in populations where there is a very low prevalence, because in such circumstances false positivity significantly interferes with the values of the studies. We must bear this in mind when talking about testing large proportions of the population where we expect a very low rate of seropositivity.

There are other antibody tests, including indirect immunofluorescence and competitive assays. The gold standard for antibody tests is the Western blot. In this assay, HIV antigens are run out and are separated on paper strips by electrophoresis. When patient's serum is placed in contact with these strips, HIV antibody reacts with the antigen and is again visualized by means of an enzyme method. Western blot permits both detection of antibodies to HIV and determination of their specificity against known viral antigens. It is more sensitive and more specific than ELISA, but it too has its limitations. A recent study by the American College of Pathologists showed that the performance of laboratories using Western blot varied widely. There are a number of kits on the market, and these also vary in quality. The interpretation of this test requires skill, and yet even when the laboratory work is of a high standard, there are still cases where the results are equivocal. So even the Western blot, which is about as good as an antibody assay can be, is not 100% accurate. We have to bear that in mind as well when talking about large-scale testing.

The antigen assay depends not on the presence of antibody produced by the host but on the presence of HIV antigen. The key reagent is antibody to HIV. When it is exposed to a specimen, if there is HIV antigen present in that specimen, a reaction will occur that can be developed and measured. The antibody used can be specific to known viral antigens, so it is possible to determine not only that there is viral antigen present but which one it is. The antigen assay is thus a more direct test for the presence of HIV.

Both antibody and the antigen assays have been used to define the events occurring during the course of HIV infection. After initial infection, there is a period of viral replication when HIV is present on culture of peripheral blood mononuclear cells. Antigen can be detected for about six weeks on average before antibody becomes demonstrable. A controversial study done in Finland claimed that the period during which virus and antigen can be detected but no antibody is found can extend to as long as six months or even a year.[8] If that is confirmed, it presents a very serious problem for blood banks, where antibody assays are widely used. The accuracy of the ELISA assays used in the Finnish study and another in children has been questioned. Other uses proposed for the antigen and antibody assays include determining an individual's place in the clinical spectrum of disease. Thus, it has been suggested that certain antibodies fall off just before full-blown AIDS occurs, at which time the antigen level rises again. This has not yet been confirmed. Obviously this would be a very powerful tool, not only in epidemiological and screening studies, but also in the clinical management of the HIV-infected individual.

So where are we with the epidemic? By January of 1988, in the United States there had been just over 50,000 cases, of which just over half had died.[9] In California we are approaching 11,000 cases, while in San Francisco there have been over 4,000 cases. During the month of November 1987 in San Francisco there were reported 159 cases and 102 deaths. This represents three or more deaths a day in the city of San Francisco from AIDS. About one third of these November cases and deaths reflect the new definition of AIDS, a fact that must be borne in mind when charting the size of the epidemic. AIDS deaths in 1987 in the USA averaged 73 per day, and it is estimated that in 1991 there will be about 148 deaths per day, or 1 death every 10 minutes in this country. There is no reason to believe that 1991 will be the point at which the epidemic peaks and starts to fall off. We are dealing with a very substantial problem which the dental profession, along with others, is going to have to face.

I will now discuss the scope of the epidemic, not in terms of AIDS, but in terms of HIV infection.[10] The seropositivity rates in the groups that are at recognized risk are as follows. Most groups of gay men now have an antibody prevalence of between 20% and 50%, rising as high as 70% or more in the San Francisco City Clinic cohort. In very few cohorts of gay men has a seropositivity rate of less than 10% been found. Among intravenous drug abusers (IVDA) studied, 50% to 65% have HIV antibodies; the rate is higher in New York City and some other places in the world. In the United States, the high prevalence among IVDA is mostly an East Coast phenomenon. On the West Coast, the prevalence in this group is still 5% or less. Hemophiliac groups show a prevalence ranging from 30% to almost 70%. Younger hemophiliacs are no longer getting HIV-containing blood and so show a lower prevalence. Heterosexual partners of HIV-positive individuals have about the same prevalence of antibodies as do gay men. What about non-risk-group individuals? How far has the epidemic penetrated the general population? CDC figures as of December 1987 suggest that four in 10,000 people presenting to be blood donors have HIV antibodies. About 0.15% of military applicants are HIV seropositive. Job Corps entrants show a prevalence of 0.33%. About one in 300 hospital patients carry HIV antibodies. Among childbearing women in Massachusetts — some in risk groups, some not — about one in 500 are positive. The overall prevalence within our population was intensely studied and estimated at about 1.5 million in 1986, the Coolfont study, and there has really been no update since then. Until the next six months or year has passed, and the results of more studies in hospitals, antenatal clinics and other random groups in our population become available, we will not know what the current figure really is. Thus the best estimate is actually two years out of date. The epidemic of AIDS is now right in the middle of the original Coolfont predictions, which estimated that by 1991 there will have been over 250,000 reported cases of AIDS in the United States.

Now I would like to remind you of the questions we will be trying to answer in these presentations. First, we want to know the extent of the oral manifestations of HIV infection in the populations at risk and among those with known seropositivity. Second, we would like to know much more about the relation of the oral manifestations in HIV diseases to the progression of the infection and the ultimate outcome. Third, we seek to understand what is causing the oral manifestations, so that even if we cannot soon deal with HIV itself, we will at least have a good chance of dealing with its effects. Currently that is the only course available in treatment of HIV infection and AIDS.

There is a great deal to be learned from AIDS, for even such a catastrophe has some positive aspects. The experiment of nature which AIDS presents us is an opportunity which we cannot, in conscience, ignore. We have the opportunity to learn something about the pathogenesis of many oral diseases. I think that the periodontal lesion which Dr Winkler and others will discuss is one of the best examples of how the understanding of a disease can perhaps be improved through studies of it when it occurs in association with AIDS. Attention must be directed at means for the prevention and treatment of the oral manifestations of HIV infection. There will be no discussion at this meeting of the animal models of AIDS, but it may be possible for Dr Schiødt to say a few words about that work in one of the panel discussions. AIDS has drawn attention to the need for dealing with infection control in dental practice and to such questions as the right to refuse to treat; the degree, if any, to which treatment plans should be modified by HIV-antibody status; and whether that status should be revealed to the dentist. There are a myriad of legal and ethical issues which we will try to address. From all of this comes, I think, an obligation and an opportunity to educate ourselves, our profession and the coming generations of students, and indeed, the public, about those areas in which we have specific expertise.

REFERENCES

1. Gallo RC: The first human retrovirus. *Sci Am* 1986;255:88-98.
2. Fauci A: The human immunodeficiency virus: Infectivity and mechanisms of pathogenesis. *Science* 1988;239:617-622.
3. Curran JW, Jaffe H, Hardy AM, et al: Epidemiology of HIV infection and AIDS in the United States. *Science* 1988;239:610-616.
4. Centers for Disease Control: Revision of the CDC surveillance case definition for acquired immunodeficiency syndrome. *MMWR* 1987;36(Suppl):3-16.

5. Centers for Disease Control: Classification system for human T-lymphotropic virus type III/lymphadenopathy associated virus infection. *MMWR* 1986;35:334-339.
6. Redfield RR, Wright DC, Tramont EC: The Walter Reed staging classification for HTLV-III/LAV infection. *N Engl J Med* 1986; 314:131-132.
7. Schwartz JS, Dans PE, Kinosian BP: Human immunodeficiency virus test evaluation, performance and use. *JAMA* 1988;259:2574-2579.
8. Ranki A, Valley SL, Krohn M, et al: Long latency precedes overt seroconversion in sexually transmitted human immunodeficiency virus infection. *Lancet* 1987;2:589-593.
9. Centers for Disease Control: Monthly AIDS statistics. Feb 29, 1988.
10. Centers for Disease Control: Human immunodeficiency virus infection in the United States: A review of current knowledge. *MMWR* 1987;36:1-48.

2

Occupational Transmission of HIV

Robert S. Klein

The fact that AIDS is communicable and transmitted by routes similar to hepatitis B, combined with the recognized increased risk of hepatitis B in health care workers, has prompted considerable concern among these individuals about the risk of occupational transmission of HIV. This chapter reviews the information contributing to this concern, and the available data which permit a rational approach to identifying, quantifying and minimizing this risk.

Prior to identification of HIV as the etiological agent in AIDS, information about the likely routes of transmission was based on analysis both of the reported cases meeting the Centers for Disease Control surveillance case definition for AIDS and of other individuals with apparently AIDS-related conditions belonging to groups recognized to be at increased risk for this syndrome. First recognized in June 1981 among homosexual men,[1] AIDS was subsequently found to occur also among intravenous drug abusers,[2] Haitians,[3] hemophiliacs[4] and other recipients of blood or blood products,[5] infants born to mothers with or at risk for AIDS,[6] heterosexual partners of individuals with AIDS,[7] and Africans.[8] Among the factors associated with risk in these groups were the numbers of sexual partners among homosexual men,[9] receipt of blood products from large numbers of donors or from individuals at increased risk for AIDS,[10] sharing of needles and syringes contaminated with blood — often from many individuals — among intravenous drug abusers,[11]

12

perinatal transmission,[12] and heterosexual sexual intercourse with persons at high risk.[13] Therefore, it appeared that AIDS was a communicable disease, transmissible by routes similar to those important in transmission of hepatitis B.[14-16] When HIV was identified as the causative agent of AIDS,[17-18] seroepidemiologic studies supported the conclusion that these routes are important in transmission.[19]

Because of the transmission of HIV by exposure to infected blood, its similar routes of transmission as hepatitis B, and the well-recognized occupational risk of hepatitis B among health care providers,[20] AIDS has generated a great deal of concern among these professionals. Much of this concern is magnified because of the general perception that HIV infection is universally fatal, a perception which at this time is not yet supported by fact. In order for the health care professional to rationally approach the question of how best to render care while minimizing personal risk, it is important to review the available data regarding occupational risk of HIV infection among health care professionals.

OCCUPATIONAL TRANSMISSION OF HIV INFECTION TO HEALTH CARE WORKERS

In June 1986, it was estimated that there were between 1,000,000 and 1,500,000 individuals infected with HIV in the United States alone.[21] It is likely that whatever the true number of individuals infected at that time, the number is higher today. As of January 1988, there have been 13 well-documented episodes of HIV transmission to individuals by virtue of their being engaged in health care.

Among these episodes have been six accidental parenteral inoculations with sharp instruments contaminated with blood from a known infected individual.[22-26] These accidents all have been due to needlestick injuries, which have been shown to be potentially preventable by routine adherence to recommended infection control procedures in approximately 40% of accidents.[26] Two workers became infected after a blood splash or spill on skin or mucous membranes,[27] one after blood contaminated ungloved chapped hands,[27] and two after extensive contact with blood or body fluids in the absence of recommended barrier precautions.[28-29] Finally, one laboratory worker regularly handling large amounts of concentrated HIV became infected in the absence of a documented specific spill, splash or inoculation incident leading to this infection, although undetected skin contact with virus culture supernatant might have occurred.[30] It is important to note in this last case that the laboratory worker was working on a regular basis with material containing large amounts of virus, considerably greater than the amounts likely to be present in the body fluids of infected patients. Another laboratory worker infected as a result of parenteral needlestick exposure to concentrated HIV has been noted briefly, but full details of the case are not yet available.[30]

These events clearly demonstrate that an occupational risk for HIV transmission to health care workers does exist. It is possible that additional as yet unrecognized or unreported cases have occurred. However, with possibly several million HIV-infected individuals in the United States alone, it is likely that tens of thousands or more health care workers have been exposed to HIV-infected persons. While anecdotal reports can show that an event occurs, they cannot define a rate of risk. Only population-based studies examining a sample of a population at risk can help to define this rate. Fortunately such studies are becoming available and will be discussed below.

DETERMINING WHERE RISK OF HIV EXPOSURE EXISTS

Before attempting to determine the magnitude of risk for occupational transmission of HIV infection, it is important to consider where that risk lies. Information about demographics and the factors likely to reflect routes of acquisition of HIV infection are most complete for individuals who have been reported to have AIDS. In the United States, as of January 18, 1988, these have included 51,361 individuals.[31] Of the 50,583 adults, 65% have been homosexual or bisexual men, 17% heterosexual intravenous drug abusers, 8% both intravenous drug abusers and homosexual or bisexual men, 4% men or women believed to have acquired infection via heterosexual sex, and 3% who became infected via transfusion of blood or blood components, including coagulation factors. Nearly 50% of cases have been reported from New York and California. However, it is important to understand that the incubation period of AIDS is prolonged. It has been estimated that the median incubation period from time of HIV infection to AIDS is 4.5 years.[32]

Therefore, cases of AIDS represent transmission events that occurred, on average, years ago. Although it seems very likely that HIV infection still involves predominantly individuals in the groups at risk enumerated above, the proportions in any geographic location have been changing over time. The location of these individuals is also slowly changing, as the epidemic spreads from the handful of large metropolitan centers where the first cases occurred. Until seroprevalence studies of populations not yet ill due to HIV infection become available to determine where HIV infection exists today, reliance on information derived only from individuals with HIV-induced illness will provide information about transmission events outdated by several years. Therefore, if the proportion of HIV-infected individuals with any particular type of exposure leading to acquisition of their infection is changing substantially over time, reliance on the proportion of high risk behaviors associated with AIDS in an attempt to determine who may be infected at present may be misleading.

HIV has been isolated from most body fluids, including blood,[17,18] semen,[33,34] saliva,[35,36] vaginal secretions,[37,38] cerebrospinal fluid,[39] breast milk,[40] tears,[41] serum,[42] urine,[43] and alveolar fluid.[44] However, it is important to recognize that the isolation of HIV from a particular body fluid does not necessarily mean that the fluid is important in transmission of the virus. The proportion of infected individuals having virus in a particular body fluid as well as the concentration of virus in that fluid are important, and only epidemiologic studies can define the importance of a body fluid in transmission. For example, although HIV has been isolated from saliva, it is infrequently found in infected individuals, and when present it is at a much lower concentration than found in blood or semen.[36] There is no epidemiologic evidence, as yet, demonstrating that saliva is important in HIV transmission.

Serological testing of patients for the presence of HIV antibodies is currently the most widely used laboratory test for identifying HIV-infected persons. The tests most commonly employed are an ELISA screening test, with a confirmatory procedure, such as the Western blot assay, used on specimens reactive on the screening test. In combination, these tests are highly sensitive and specific.[45] However, there would be distinct problems in implementing serological testing on a routine basis in an attempt to identify all HIV-infected patients. Educating patients sufficiently to obtain truly informed consent would require substantial resources. Although the cost of the ELISA tests is not excessive, confirmatory test costs can be substantial. Despite good sensitivity and specificity, use of the test in groups where the prevalence of infection is low may lead to a large proportion of positive results being false positives. Considerable resources are necessary for posttest counseling and care of seropositives. Results of the tests, especially confirmatory tests, are likely to take some time to obtain. False negative test results occur, most often among individuals recently infected who have not yet developed an antibody response.[46] Therefore, a negative test result does not assure absence of infection and the infectious state. Finally, serological testing only conveys information relevant to the point in time at which the specimen was taken. Subsequent infection could occur, necessitating repeated examinations to determine serological status for subsequent patient-provider interactions. It should be clear that attempts to implement routine serological screening for HIV infection for all patients would be impractical, expensive and unlikely to achieve the desired result, the identification of all HIV-infected persons.

Because it is not possible currently to identify all HIV-infected patients by history, physical examination, or laboratory testing, it has been recommended that health care workers practice as if all patients are infected, by the implementation of universal precautions to reduce risk of HIV transmission.[47]

RISK OF TRANSMISSION BY CLOSE NONSEXUAL CONTACT

There is now abundant evidence supporting the conclusion that with the exception of sexual and perinatal transmission, close personal contact with an HIV-infected individual results in transmission of HIV infection rarely, if at all, in the absence of parenteral exposure to infected blood or other body fluids. Among the more than 51,000 cases of AIDS reported in the United States, none are reported to be individuals without high risk behavior who are household members of another AIDS patient, excluding sexual partners and infants born to infected mothers. Additionally, the rate of AIDS among health care workers is not significantly higher than that in the general population in the United States[48] or Africa.[49] More directly, studies have now contributed substantial knowledge about the prevalence of HIV infections among household contacts of patients with AIDS and health care workers exposed to such patients or to specimens from them.

In studies of household contact of patients with AIDS, nearly 500 family members have been reported.[50-56] Included have been adult and child family members of intravenous drug users, transfusion recipients, Haitians, persons infected by heterosexual sex, and hemophiliacs. These family members engaged in the expected types of family interactions with their infected family member, often including sharing household facilities, such as beds, toilets, kitchens, and bathing facilities, as well as items likely to be soiled by the patient's saliva or other body fluids such as plates, drinking glasses, eating utensils and towels. Personal interactions including hugging and kissing on the lips or cheeks had occurred frequently where studied. Because of the prolonged incubation period of AIDS, contact with the infected patient likely occurred on average for months or years before the patient became ill, when it first could be recognized that the patient might be infectious and specific precautions instituted. In no study was a family member found to be infected with HIV in the absence of sexual or perinatal transmission.

There have now been more than 1800 health care workers studied who had contact with AIDS patients or specimens from such patients (Table 2-1). Included in these studies have been physicians, including endoscopists, surgeons, and pathologists, nurses, research scientists, laboratory technicians, aides, paramedics, dentists, dental hygienists and dental assistants. All subjects studied had determination of serum antibody to HIV measured by ELISA with Western blot or viral isolation confirmation of reactive specimens. Three (0.16%) of the 1,827 subjects studied were found to be HIV-positive without behavioral risk factors for AIDS. One was a laboratory worker who regularly worked with concentrated HIV.[30] This worker regularly dealt with greater amounts of virus than would be encountered in routine medical contact with AIDS patients or their body fluids. Although there was no specific episode recalled in which contamination of the worker's skin or mucous membranes was known to have occurred and recommended precautions were routinely followed, it appears likely that an inapparent exposure led to occupational infection with HIV in this case. A second infected health care worker had received an accidental parenteral inoculation of material from a patient with AIDS,[58] a route of transmission now well documented to occur and which

Table 2-1
Studies of the Risk of HIV Infection Associated with Exposure to Patients with AIDS or Specimens from Such Patients

Study	No. of Subjects Tested	No. of Subjects Positive	No. Positive Without Other Risk Factor
Hirsch et al[57]	85	0	0
Weiss et al[58]	359	8	2*
Henderson et al[59]	442	2	0
Gerberding et al[60]	270	0	0
Gerberding et al[61]	72	0	0
Klein et al[62]	199	0	0
Weiss et al[30]	255	1†	1†
Kuhls et al[63]	145	0	0
Total	1,827‡	11	3

*Includes one subject in whom accidental parenteral inoculation of material from a patient with AIDS occurred and one in whom the epidemiologic investigation was incomplete.
†Includes one of 99 subjects who were laboratory personnel working with concentrated HIV-1.
‡Includes 394 subjects with accidental parenteral or mucous-membrane exposure to body fluids of patients with HIV infection (included in Table 2-2) and 1,433 subjects without such exposure.
Adapted and updated from Friedland and Klein.[64]

will be discussed further below. For the third infected health care worker, epidemiological information was incomplete.[58] Therefore, analysis of these health care workers who were in contact with AIDS patients or their specimens leads to the conclusion that for those workers in whom information was complete, occupational transmission of HIV occurred only with parenteral exposure or when working with concentrated virus.

PARENTERAL OR MUCOUS MEMBRANE EXPOSURE

In addition to studies looking at risk of HIV infection for all health care workers exposed to AIDS patients or their specimens, there have been 800 health care workers studied with known accidental parenteral inoculation or mucous membrane contamination with body fluids of HIV-infected patients (Table 2-2). This possible route of infection has been of major concern to health care professionals since early in the AIDS epidemic when it was recognized that AIDS was communicable with routes of transmission similar to those of hepatitis B. It had been known that seroconversion occurs in 12% to 17% of health care workers after accidental percutaneous injection of blood or serum from patients who are positive for hepatitis B surface antigen, even after passive immunization of recipients by immune serum globulin.[65,66] In contrast, only three (0.38%) of 800 subjects exposed to HIV by parenteral inoculation or mucous membrane exposure were found to be seropositive, all after parenteral inoculation. Furthermore, in a nationwide study of health care workers with parenteral or mucous membrane exposure to potentially HIV-infected specimens, 40% of 938 exposures were considered preventable if recommended infection control precautions had been followed. Deviations from these recommendations which led to exposure included recapping of a used needle (in 41%), injury from an improperly disposed-of needle or sharp object (32%), contamination of an open wound (25%), and using a needle-cutting device (2%).

Therefore, even after direct parenteral inoculation or mucous membrane exposure of a health care worker, seroconversion appears to occur in less than one percent of cases. In addition, nearly 40% of such exposures appear potentially preventable by routine adherence to recommended infection control precautions.

OCCUPATIONAL RISK FOR DENTAL PROFESSIONALS

Studies have suggested that dentists are among the health care providers at greatest risk of occupational acquisition of hepatitis B infection.[67,68] The similarity in routes of transmission between hepatitis B and HIV and the recognized occupational risk of hepatitis B infection among dental professionals suggested that this would be an important group in which to assess risk of HIV infection not only for this profession, but also because this group could be considered a "sentinel" population that is likely to indicate the maximal anticipated rate of occupational risk for health care workers in general.

Dental professionals share with other health care workers the risk of exposure to HIV-infected patients from close nonsexual contact and accidental parenteral inoculations. However, dental professionals are at additional risk for frequent aerosolization of and splashes from blood and saliva. Furthermore, they are likely to be exposed repeatedly to persons

Table 2-2
Studies of the Risk of HIV Infection Associated
with Parenteral or Mucous-Membrane Exposure

Study	No. of Subjects Tested	No. of Subjects Positive	No. Positive Without Other Risk Factor
Hirsch et al[57]	33	0	0
Weiss et al[58]	42	1	1
Henderson et al[59]	150	0	0
Gerberding et al[60]	94	0	0
McCray et al[26]	451	2	2
Gerberding et al[61]	5	0	0
Kuhls et al[63]	25	0	0
Total	800	3	3

Adapted and updated from Friedland and Klein.[64]

infected with HIV, often for months or years before these persons become ill or know that they have an HIV infection. Recommended infection control precautions designed to reduce these risks are inconsistently used.[62] Therefore, if substantial occupational risk of HIV infection for health care workers exists, it is likely to be reflected among dentists and other dental professionals.

There have now been reported nearly 4,000 dental professionals evaluated for risk of HIV infection (Table 2-3). Of 3,396 dentists and 347 other dental professionals studied, only one (0.025%) was positive for HIV antibody without other risk. Although a minority of subjects were reported to have treated known AIDS patients, many practiced in geographic locations where AIDS is common and most had individuals at increased risk for AIDS among their patients.

The most complete information available about types of exposures encountered by these dental professionals is from a study of 1309 subjects without other risk for HIV infection.[62] Forty-seven percent practiced in geographic locations where large numbers of AIDS cases have been reported. One hundred ninety-nine (15%) treated known AIDS patients and 949 (72%) treated persons at risk for AIDS, including homosexual or bisexual men, intravenous drug abusers, and persons with hemophilia. Nearly all (94%) reported receiving accidental inoculations from instruments which had been used on patients. Only one-third of subjects wore gloves for all procedures.

Table 2-3
Studies of the Risk of HIV Infection Among Dentists and Other Dental Personnel

Study	Year	Location	No. of Subjects Studied			No. of Subjects Who Treated Known AIDS Patients	No. of Subjects Positive	No. of Subjects Positive Without Other Risk
			Dentists	Other	Total			
Klein et al[62]	1985-7	USA*	1145	177	1322	199	5	1
ADA†[69]	1987	USA	1195	0	1195	NA‡	0	0
Ebbesen et al[70]	1985	Denmark	961	0	961	NA	0	0
Flynn et al[71]	1985	California	89	166	255	NA	0	0
Gerberding et al[61]	1986	California	NA	NA	181	72	0	0
Lubick et al[72]	1986	California	6	4	10	NA	0	0
Total			3396	347	3924	> 271	5	1

* 47% of subjects studied practiced in metropolitan locations reporting large numbers of patients with AIDS.
† American Dental Association
‡ NA = Data not available

Despite the frequent occupational exposures to persons at increased risk for HIV infection, frequent accidental parenteral inoculations with sharp instruments, and infrequent compliance with recommended infection control precautions, only a single subject without other risk was found to be seropositive for HIV antibody. This subject was a male dentist who practiced in New York City, treated individuals in risk groups but never a person known to have AIDS, had received several accidental inoculations over the preceding five years at a rate typical of the entire study population, and used recommended barrier precautions intermittently. It appeared likely that the infection in this dentist was acquired occupationally, illustrating that risk does exist, even when no known AIDS patients are treated. However, the magnitude of the occupational risk is defined by the finding of 1/1309 (0.08%) subjects seropositive (95% confidence interval, 0 to 0.004). Although a single episode of occupational transmission of HIV infection should prompt appropriate measures to minimize risks where possible, it is reassuring that the observed rate is as low as it is.

CONCLUDING REMARKS

Occupational transmission of HIV infection does occur via parenteral exposure to infected body fluids. However, occupationally acquired infection is uncommon even after accidental parenteral exposure. Many occupational exposures probably could be avoided by routine adherence to recommended infection control procedures. At present, there is no practical way to routinely identify all infected individuals who might present a risk of HIV transmission. Therefore, routine adherence to recommended infection control guidelines for all patients will minimize the risk of occupational transmission of HIV infection.

REFERENCES

1. Pneumocystis pneumonia: Los Angeles. *MMWR* 1981;30:250-252.
2. Update on Kaposi's sarcoma and opportunistic infections in previously healthy persons: United States. *MMWR* 1982;31:294-301.
3. Opportunistic infections and Kaposi's sarcoma among Haitians in the United States. *MMWR* 1982;31:353-361.

4. Update on acquired immune deficiency syndrome (AIDS) among patients with hemophilia A. *MMWR* 1982;31:644-652.

5. Possible transfusion-associated acquired immune deficiency syndrome (AIDS): California. *MMWR* 1982;31:652-654.

6. Unexplained immunodeficiency and opportunistic infections in infants: New York, New Jersey, California. *MMWR* 1982;31:665-668.

7. Immunodeficiency among female sexual partners of males with acquired immune deficiency syndrome (AIDS): New York. *MMWR* 1983;31:697-698.

8. Clumeck N, Mascart-Lemone F, deMaubeuge J, et al: Acquired immune deficiency syndrome in black Africans. *Lancet* 1983;1:642.

9. Jaffe HW, Choi K, Thomas PA, et al: National case-control study of Kaposi's sarcoma and *Pneumocystis carinii* pneumonia in homosexual men. Part 1. Epidemiologic results. *Ann Intern Med* 1983;99:145-151.

10. Curran JW, Lawrence DN, Jaffe H, et al: Acquired immunodeficiency syndrome (AIDS) associated with transfusions. *N Engl J Med* 1984;310:69-75.

11. Friedland GH, Harris C, Butkus-Small C, et al: Intravenous drug abusers and the acquired immunodeficiency syndrome (AIDS): Demographic, drug use, and needle-sharing patterns. *Arch Intern Med* 1985;145:1413-1417.

12. Rubinstein A, Sicklick M, Gupta A, et al: Acquired immunodeficiency with reversed T4/T8 ratios in infants born to promiscuous and drug-addicted mothers. *JAMA* 1983;249:2350-2356.

13. Harris C, Butkus Small C, Klein RS, et al: Immunodeficiency in female sexual partners of men with the acquired immunodeficiency syndrome. *N Engl J Med* 1983;308:1181-1184.

14. Acquired immune deficiency syndrome (AIDS): Precautions for clinical and laboratory staffs. *MMWR* 1982;31:577-580.

15. Landesman SH, Vieira J: Acquired immune deficiency syndrome (AIDS): A review. *Arch Intern Med* 1983;143:2307-2309.

16. Ravenholt RT: Role of hepatitis B virus in acquired immunodeficiency syndrome. *Lancet* 1983;2:885-886.

17. Barre-Sinoussi F, Chermann JC, Rey F, et al: Isolation of a T-lymphotrophic retrovirus from a patient at risk for the acquired immune deficiency syndrome (AIDS). *Science* 1983;220:868-871.

18. Gallo RC, Salahuddin SZ, Popovic M, et al: Frequent detection and isolation of cytopathic retroviruses (HTLV-III) from patients with AIDS and at risk for AIDS. *Science* 1984; 224:500-503.

19. Antibodies to a retrovirus etiologically associated with acquired immunodeficiency syndrome (AIDS) in populations with increased incidences of the syndrome. *MMWR* 1984;33:377-379.

20. Snydman DR, Bryan JA, Dixon RE: Prevention of nosocomial viral hepatitis, type B (hepatitis B). *Ann Intern Med* 1975;83:838-845.

21. Coolfont report: A PHS plan for prevention and control of AIDS and the AIDS virus. *Public Health Rep* 1986;101:341-348.

22. Needlestick transmission of HTLV-III from a patient infected in Africa. *Lancet* 1984;2:1376-1377.
23. Stricof FL, Morse DL: HTLV-III/LAV seroconversion following a deep intramuscular needlestick injury. *N Engl J Med* 1986; 314:1115.
24. Oksenhendler E, Harzil M, LeRoux J-M, et al: HIV infection with seroconversion after a superficial needlestick injury to the finger. *N Engl J Med* 1986;315:582.
25. Neisson-Vernant C, Arfi S, Mathez D, et al: Needlestick HIV seroconversion in a nurse. *Lancet* 1986;2:814.
26. McCray E: The cooperative needlestick surveillance group. Occupational risk of the acquired immunodeficiency syndrome among health care workers. *N Engl J Med* 1986;314:1127-1132.
27. Update: Human immunodeficiency virus infections in health-care workers exposed to blood of infected patients. *MMWR* 1987;36:285-289.
28. Grint P, McEvoy M: Two associated cases of the acquired immune deficiency syndrome (AIDS). *PHLS Commun Dis Rep* 1985;42:4.
29. Centers for Disease Control: Apparent transmission of human T-lymphotropic virus type III/lymphadenopathy-associated virus from a child to a mother providing health care. *MMWR* 1986;35:76-79.
30. Weiss SH, Goedert JJ, Gartner S, et al: Risk of human immuno-deficiency virus (HIV-1) infection among laboratory workers. *Science* 1987;239:68-71.
31. Centers for Disease Control: AIDS weekly surveillance report — United States. January 18, 1988.
32. Lui K-J, Lawrence DN, Morgan WM, et al: A model-based approach for estimating the mean incubation period of transfu-sion-associated acquired immunodeficiency syndrome. *Proc Natl Acad Sci USA* 1986;83:3051-3055.
33. Ho DD, Schooley RT, Rota TR, et al: HTLV-III in the semen and blood of a healthy homosexual man. *Science* 1984;226:451-453.
34. Zagury D, Bernard J, Leibowitch J, et al: HTLV-III in cells cul-tured from semen of two patients with AIDS. *Science* 1984; 226:449-451.
35. Groopman JE, Salahuddin SZ, Sarngadharan MG, et al: HTLV-III in saliva of people with AIDS-related complex and healthy homosexual men at risk for AIDS. *Science* 1984;226:447-449.
36. Ho D, Byington RE, Schooley RT, et al: Infrequency of isolation of HTLV-III virus from saliva in AIDS. *N Engl J Med* 1985;313:1606.
37. Vogt MW, Witt DJ, Craven DE, et al: Isolation of HTLV-III/LAV from cervical secretions of women at risk for AIDS. *Lancet* 1986;1:525-527.
38. Wofsy CB, Cohen JB, Hauer LB, et al: Isolation of AIDS-associ-ated retrovirus from genital secretions of women with antibodies to the virus. *Lancet* 1986;1:527-529.
39. Ho DD, Rota TR, Schooley RT, et al: Isolation of HTLV-III from

cerebrospinal fluid and neural tissues of patients with neurologic syndromes related to the acquired immunodeficiency syndrome. *N Engl J Med* 1985;313:1493-1497.

40. Thiry L, Sprecher-Goldberger S, Jonckheer T, et al: Isolation of AIDS virus from cell-free breast milk of three healthy virus carriers. *Lancet* 1985;2:891-892.
41. Fujikawa LS, Salahuddin SZ, Palestine AG, et al: Isolation of human T-lymphotrophic virus type III from the tears of a patient with the acquired immunodeficiency syndrome. *Lancet* 1985;2:529-530.
42. Michaelis BA, Levy JA: Recovery of human immunodeficiency virus from serum. *JAMA* 1987;257:1327.
43. Levy JA, Kaminsky LS, Morrow WJW, et al: Infection by the retrovirus associated with the acquired immunodeficiency syndrome. *Ann Intern Med* 1985;103:694-699.
44. Ziza J-M, Brun-Vezinet F, Venet A, et al: Lymphadenopathy-associated virus isolated from bronchoalveolar lavage fluid in AIDS-related complex with lymphoid interstitial pneumonitis. *N Engl J Med* 1985;313:183.
45. Weiss SH, Goedert JJ, Sarngadharan MG: Screening test for HTLV-III (AIDS agent) antibodies. Specificity, sensitivity, and applications. *JAMA* 1985;253:221-225.
46. Centers for Disease Control: Transfusion-associated human T-lymphotropic virus type III/lymphoadenopathy-associated virus infection from a seronegative donor. Colorado. *MMWR* 1986; 35:389-391.
47. Centers for Disease Control: Recommended infection-control practices for dentistry. *MMWR* 1986;35:237-242.
48. Lifson AR, Castro KG, McCray E, Jaffe HW: National surveillance of AIDS in health care workers. *JAMA* 1986;256:3231-3234.
49. Mann JM, Francis H, Quinn TC, et al: HIV seroprevalence among hospital workers in Kinshasha, Zaire: Lack of association with occupational exposure. *JAMA* 1986;256:3099-3102.
50. Saltzman BR, Friedland GH, Rogers MF, et al: Lack of household transmission of HTLV-III/LAV infection. Presented at the Second International Conference on AIDS, Paris, June 23-25, 1986.
51. Rogers MF, White CR, Sanders R, et al: Can children transmit human T-lymphotropic virus III/lymphadenopathy-associated virus (HTLV-III/LAV) infection? Presented at the Second International Conference on AIDS, Paris, June 23-25, 1986.
52. Fischl MA, Dickinson GM, Scott GM, et al: Evaluation of heterosexual partners, children, and household contacts of adults with AIDS. *JAMA* 1987;257:640-644.
53. Redfield RR, Markham PD, Salahuddin SZ, et al: Frequent transmission of HTLV-III among spouses of patients with AIDS-related complex and AIDS. *JAMA* 1985;253:1571-1573.
54. Thomas PA, Lubin K, Enlow RW, Getchell J: Comparison of HTLV-III serology, T-cell levels and general health status of children whose mothers have AIDS with children of healthy

26

inner city mothers in New York. Presented at the First International Conference on AIDS, Atlanta, April 14-17, 1985.

55. Lawrence DN, Jason JM, Bouhasin JD, et al: HTLV-III/LAV antibody status of spouses and household contacts assisting in home infusion of hemophilia patients. *Blood* 1985;66:703-705.

56. Jason JM, McDougal JS, Dixon G, et al: HTLV-III/LAV antibody with immune status of household contacts and sexual partners of persons with hemophilia. *JAMA* 1986;255:212-215.

57. Hirsch MS, Wormser GP, Schooley RT, et al: Risk of nosocomial infection with human T-cell lymphotropic virus III (HTLV-III). *N Engl J Med* 1985;312:1-4.

58. Weiss SH, Saxinger WC, Rechtman C, et al: HTLV-III infection among health care workers: Association with needle-stick injuries. *JAMA* 1985;254:2089-2093.

59. Henderson DK, Saah AJ, Zak BJ, et al: Risk of nosocomial infection with human T-cell lymphotropic virus type III/lymphadenopathy-associated virus in a large cohort of intensively exposed health care workers. *Ann Intern Med* 1986;104:644-647.

60. Gerberding JL, Bryant-LeBlanc CE, Nelson K, et al: Risk of transmitting the human immunodeficiency virus, cytomegalovirus, and hepatitis B virus to health care workers exposed to patients with AIDS and AIDS-related conditions. *J Infect Dis* 1987;156:1-8.

61. Gerberding JL, Bryant-LeBlanc CE, Greenspan D, et al: Risk to dentists from exposure to patients infected with AIDS virus, in *Abstracts of the 26th Interscience Conference on Antimicrobial Agents and Chemotherapy*, Sept 28-Oct 1, 1986. Washington, DC, American Society for Microbiology, 1986, p 283. Abstract No. 1015.

62. Klein RS, Phelan JA, Freeman K, et al. Low occupational risk of human immunodeficiency virus infection among dental professionals. *N Engl J Med* 1988;318:86-90.

63. Kuhls TL, Vicker S, Parris NB, et al: A prospective cohort study of the occupational risk of AIDS and AIDS-related infections in health care personnel, abstract. *Clin Res* 1986;34:124A.

64. Friedland GH, Klein RS. Transmission of the human immunodeficiency virus. *N Engl J Med* 1987; 317:1125-1135.

65. Werner BG, Grady GF: Accidental hepatitis-B surface-antigen-positive inoculations: Use of e antigen to estimate infectivity. *Ann Intern Med* 1983;97:367-369.

66. Seeff LB, Wright EC, Zimmerman HJ, et al: Type B hepatitis after needle-stick exposure: Prevention with hepatitis B immune globulin: Final report of the Veterans Administration Cooperative Study. *Ann Intern Med* 1978;88:285-293.

67. Mosley JW, Edwards VM, Casey G, et al: Hepatitis B virus infection in dentists. *N Engl J Med* 1975;293:729-734.

68. Smith JL, Maynard JE, Berquist KR, et al: Comparative risk of hepatitis B among physicians and dentists. *J Infect Dis* 1976; 133:705-706.

69. *ADA News*. Chicago, American Dental Association, December 21, 1987, pp 1, 9.

70. Ebbesen P, Melbye M, Scheutz F, et al: Lack of antibodies to HTLV-III/LAV in Danish dentists. *JAMA* 1986;256:2199.
71. Flynn NM, Pollet SM, Van Horne JR, et al: Absence of HIV antibody among dental professionals exposed to infected patients. *West J Med* 1987;146:439-442.
72. Lubick HA, Schaeffer, LD: Occupational risk of dental personnel survey. *J Am Dent Assoc* 1986;113:10-12.

3

Oral Candidiasis in HIV Infection

Jens J. Pindborg

Oral candidiasis is a common feature of HIV infection. Four major clinical types of candidiasis have been defined: pseudomembranous, hyperplastic, erythematous, and angular cheilitis. This review discusses the clinical features, oral distribution, and diagnosis of each type, with particular emphasis on candidiasis in patients with HIV infection.

In the first report on the disease in homosexuals which later became known as AIDS, oral candidiasis was mentioned as being present in four of the five patients.[1] In the same year, Masur et al reported on 11 patients (young men) with *Pneumocystis carinii* pneumonia, of whom four had oral candidiasis.[2]

Since then, oral candidiasis has been described in almost all papers dealing with the clinical aspects of AIDS, and oral candidiasis has been found in other risk groups such as hemophiliacs, transfusion recipients, heterosexuals, and intravenous drug abusers.

Most often, the term oral candidiasis is used, but occasionally terms like thrush, white lesions, and chronic oral florid candidiasis are applied. Thrush and pseudomembranous candidiasis are usually considered synonyms. Only very few papers from 1981 to 1985 referred to red areas of the oral mucosa as an expression of candidiasis.[3]

CLINICAL SUBDIVISION

In September 1986, the European Economic Common Market sponsored a meeting in Copenhagen for the purpose of identifying the various oral lesions associated with the HIV infection. At that time it was known that not only AIDS and AIDS-related complex (ARC) patients, but healthy individuals who were seropositive, presented with oral candidiasis in a number of cases.

With regard to oral candidiasis, four major types were recognized: (1) pseudomembranous, (2) hyperplastic, (3) erythematous (atrophic), and (4) angular cheilitis. The classification was presented as a poster at the Third International Conference on AIDS in Washington, DC.[4] In the 1986 monograph by Greenspan et al the various types were illustrated.[5]

The *pseudomembranous* type is characterized by the presence of creamy white or yellowish plaques on a red or normal-colored mucosa (Figure 3-1). Upon scraping, the white plaque can be removed to reveal a bleeding surface. This type of candidiasis may involve any part of the oral mucosa but most frequently affects the palatal, buccal and labial mucosa and dorsum of the tongue.

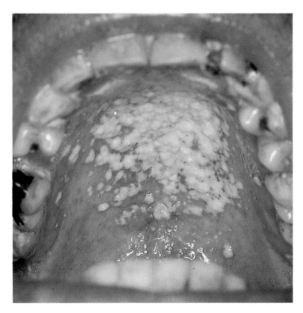

Figure 3-1 Pseudomembranous candidiasis in a man with AIDS.

The *hyperplastic* type is characterized by white plaques which cannot be removed by scraping. The most common location is the buccal mucosa (Figure 3-2). In contrast to patients not infected with HIV, in whom the hyperplastic candidiasis most often is located in commissures, this location is rarely affected in HIV-infected patients.

The *erythematous* (atrophic) type is characterized by a red appearance. The color intensity may vary from fiery red to a hardly discernible pink spot. Common locations are the palate (Figure 3-3) and dorsum of the tongue (Figure 3-4), as in the so-called multifocal candidiasis in patients who are not infected with HIV but who are heavy smokers. However, erythematous candidiasis may also appear as spotty areas of the buccal mucosa (Figure 3-5). This is a very characteristic feature of the HIV infection, but is quite often overlooked as erythematous candidiasis usually is without disturbing clinical symptoms.

In the elderly, angular cheilitis is not an unusual lesion and may be due to anemia, loss of occlusal vertical dimension, or vitamin deficiency. But it should be remembered that when it is observed in a young man, it could be the first indication of

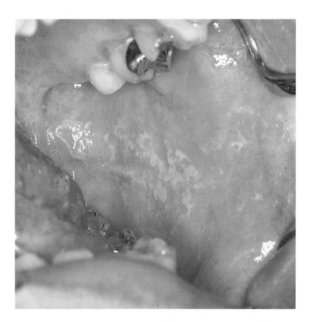

Figure 3-2 Hyperplastic candidiasis in a man with AIDS.

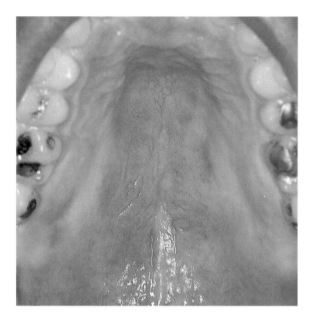

Figure 3-3 Palatal erythematous candidiasis in a man who is seropositive.

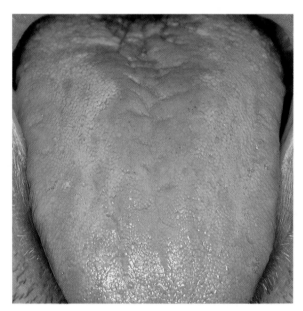

Figure 3-4 Lingual erythematous candidiasis in the patient in Figure 3-3.

an HIV infection. The lesion is characterized by fissures radiating from the angles of the mouth, often associated with small white plaques (Figure 3-6). Today it is generally recognized that the most important etiologic factor is *Candida albicans*. However, *Staphylococcus aureus* may also be present in some patients. The diagnosis of candidiasis relies on the clinical features and the presence of *Candida* hyphae on smears examined by potassium hydroxide, periodic acid-Schiff or Gram stain.

All four types were illustrated in the monograph by Greenspan et al.[5]

FREQUENCY OF ORAL CANDIDIASIS
IN HIV-INFECTED PATIENTS

Surprisingly few epidemiologic studies have been carried out to determine the frequency of oral candidiasis in HIV-infected patients. Most information exists with regard to the occurrence of oral candidiasis in patients with AIDS.

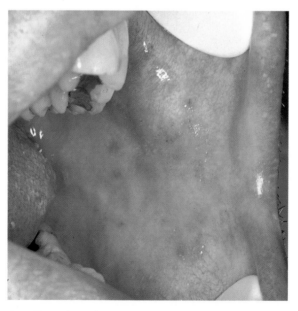

Figure 3-5 Buccal erythematous candidiasis in a man with AIDS.

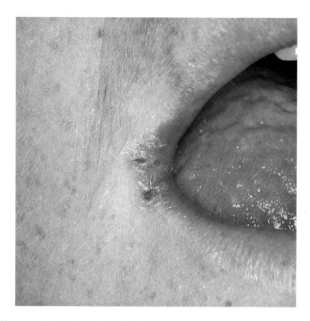

Figure 3-6   Angular cheilitis in a man who is seropositive.

In Table 3-1 an attempt has been made to tabulate the available information. Several investigators pool oral and pharyngeal candidiasis; such figures are not included in Table 3-1.

The largest sample of AIDS patients with information on the occurrence of oral candidiasis comes from the Centers for Disease Control.[12] From June 1983 to March 1985 information from 6,545 AIDS patients was analyzed. Oral candidiasis was recorded in a check-off box on the report form. Forty-five percent had oral candidiasis. From April 1985 to February 1987 there were no check-off boxes on the report form and the diagnosis of oral candidiasis had to be written down in longhand. Consequently, its prevalence dropped to 7%.

It is interesting to note the very marked differences in prevalence rates, especially among the seropositives. The differences may be due either to variations in the diagnostic criteria or to variations in the severity of the HIV infections among the samples.

However, some information is difficult to get into a table. Thus, Silverman et al reported that candidal organisms were cultured from 66% of 375 homosexual men studied and that 92% of these participants showed associated signs and symptoms.[17]

Table 3-1
Epidemiologic Studies on Oral Candidiasis
in HIV-Infected Patients

Investigator(s)	Country	Year	Diagnosis	Size of Sample	% with Candidiasis
Small et al[6]	USA	1983	AIDS	14	93
Barr & Torosian[7]	USA	1986	AIDS	73	91
Rindum et al (unpublished)	Denmark	1987	AIDS	39	90
Phelan et al[8]	USA	1987	AIDS	103	88
Rindum et al[9]	Denmark	1985	AIDS	13	77
Goudot et al[10]	France	1985	AIDS	46	54
Andriolo[11]	USA	1988	AIDS/ARC	50	53
Reichart et al[3]	FRG	1986	AIDS/ARC	58	51
Salik et al[12]	USA	1987	AIDS	6545	45
Shiødt et al[13]	Tanzania	1988	AIDS	59	43
Kenrad et al[14]	Denmark	1987	Sero+	23	48
Rindum et al (unpublished)	Denmark	1987	Sero+	281	27
Sindrup et al[15]	Denmark	1988	Sero+	150	7
Syrjänen et al[16]	Finland	1988	Sero+/ARC	14	93

The 375 participants comprised the following groups: AIDS, ARC, high risk, contact, and healthy.

Culture of *C albicans* from the oral cavity has been found to correlate with low helper-to-suppressor ratios in T-lymphocytes of Danish homosexual men.[18]

Torssander et al studied a sample of 225 Swedish homosexual men, of whom 44% had HIV antibodies, and 175 heterosexual men.[19] The prevalence of *C albicans* in the mouth, judged by culture (using a four-point scale) and smear, was increased in the homosexuals, and higher carrier rates as well as high density carriage correlated with HIV infection. Hyphae of *C albicans* were demonstrated in mucosal smears from all patients with oral mucosal lesions suspected for candidiasis. Unfortunately, the paper does not allow any conclusion as to the prevailing type of oral candidiasis and correlation with results from smear and culture. An interesting finding was the fact that 49% with positive smears had no clinical signs of oral candidiasis.

It would be desirable for investigators using culture of *C albicans* to apply the same grading of colonies so direct comparisons could be made.

ORAL CANDIDIASIS AS A PREDICTOR

Several case reports in the dental literature have demonstrated oral candidiasis preceding the development of AIDS[20,21]; It has also been postulated that oral candidiasis may precede the development of pharyngeal[22] and esophageal candidiasis.[23]

Oral candidiasis among risk groups may be of predictive value for the subsequent development of full-blown AIDS.[24] Klein et al compared 22 previously healthy adults having unexplained oral candidiasis, reversed T4/T8 lymphocyte ratios, and generalized lymphadenopathy with 20 similar patients who did not have oral candidiasis. Thirteen of the 22 patients with oral candidiasis (59%) developed a major opportunistic infection or Kaposi's sarcoma (and, thus, AIDS) in a median of 3 months compared with none of the 20 patients with lymphadenopathy and immunodeficiency but without candidiasis who were followed for a median of 22 months. Therefore, dentists should be aware of the implications of discovering oral candidiasis in otherwise apparently healthy persons.

Murray et al studied 81 men with persistent lymphadenopathy without (38) or with (43) oral candidiasis or constitutional symptoms.[25] After an observation period of 12.9 months, opportunistic infections developed in none of the patients with lymphadenopathy alone; however, 46% with lymphadenopathy accompanied by constitutional symptoms (14 patients) or oral candidiasis (10 patients) or both (4 patients) had opportunistic infections within the follow-up period, thus illustrating the value of oral candidiasis as a reliable predictor for the development of AIDS.

In a study from central Manhattan it was demonstrated that four years after diagnosis of herpes zoster, nearly half of the patients were found to have progressed to AIDS.[26] Manifestations that significantly increased the predicted incidence of AIDS were oral thrush and hairy leukoplakia.

REFERENCES

1. Gottlieb MS, Schanker HM, Fan PT, et al: Pneumocystis pneumonia. Los Angeles. *MMWR* 1981;30:250-252.
2. Masur H, Michelis MA, Greene JB, et al: An outbreak of community-acquired *Pneumocystis carinii* pneumonia. *N Engl J Med* 1981;305:1431-1438.

3. Reichart P, Pohle H-D, Gelderblom H: Orale manifestationen bei AIDS. *Dtsch Z Mund Kiefer Gesichts Chir* 1985;9:167-176.
4. Pindborg JJ, Rindum J, Schiødt M: Oral manifestations of the HIV infection: Suggested EEC classification and prevalence in a Danish sample. *Third International Conference on AIDS,* Washington, DC, Abstr MP 207.
5. Greenspan D, Greenspan J, Pindborg JJ, Schiødt M: *AIDS and the Dental Team.* Copenhagen, Munksgaard, 1986.
6. Small CB, Klein RS, Friedland GH, et al: Community-acquired opportunistic infections and defective cellular immunity in heterosexual drug abusers and homosexual men. *Am J Med* 1983; 74:433-441.
7. Barr CE, Torosian JP: Oral manifestations in patients with AIDS or AIDS-related complex. *Lancet* 1986;2:288.
8. Phelan JA, Saltzman BR, Friedland GH, Klein RS: Oral findings in patients with acquired immunodeficiency syndrome. *Oral Surg* 1987;64:50-56.
9. Rindum J, Sommer M, Pindborg JJ, Nielsen JO: Acquired immunodeficiency syndrome AIDS — A review of literature and report of 13 patients. (Danish, English abstract) *Dan Dent J* 1985;89:131-140.
10. Goudot P, Rozenbaum W, Princ G, Vaillant JM: Manifestations maxillo-faciales du syndrome d'immunodèpression acquise. *Rev Stomatol Chir Maxillofac* 1985;86:3-8.
11. Andriolo M: AIDS and AIDS related complex. Oral manifestations and treatment. *Third International Conference on AIDS,* Washington, DC, 1987, Abstr F 3.5.
12. Salik RM, Starcher ET, Curran JW: Opportunistic diseases reported in AIDS patients: Frequencies, associations, and trends. *AIDS* 1987;1:175-182.
13. Schiødt M, Bygbjerg I, Bakilana P, et al: Oral manifestations of AIDS in Tanzania, abstract. *J Dent Res* (special issue) 1988; 67:201.
14. Kenrad B, Rindum JL, Pindborg JJ: Oral findings in 23 patients with antibodies against HIV (human immunodeficiency virus). *Tandlaegebladet* 1987; 91:100-102.
15. Sindrup J, Weismann K, Petersen CS, et al: Skin and oral mucosal changes in patients infected with human immunodeficiency virus. *Acta Dermato-Venereol* 1988, in press.
16. Syrjänen S, Valle S-L, Antouen J, et al: Oral candidal infections as a sign of HIV infection in homosexual men. *Oral Surg* 1988;65:36-40.
17. Silverman S Jr, Migliorati CA, Lozada-Nur F, et al: Oral findings in people with or at high risk for AIDS: A study of 375 homosexual males. *J Am Dent Assoc* 1986;112:187-192.
18. Schönheyder H, Melbye M, Biggar RJ, et al: Oral yeast flora and antibodies to *Candida albicans* in homosexual men. *Mykosen* 1984;27:39-44.
19. Torssander J, Morfeldt-Månson L, Biberfeld G, et al: Oral *Candida albicans* in HIV infection. *Scand J Infect Dis* 1987;19:291-295.

20. Babajews A, Poswillo DE, Griffin GE: Acquired immune deficiency syndrome presenting as recalcitrant *Candida*. *Br Dent J* 1985;159:106-108.
21. Chandrasekar PH, Molinari JA: Oral candidiasis: Forerunner of acquired immunodeficiency syndrome (AIDS)? *Oral Surg* 1985;60:532-534.
22. Romanowski B, Weber J: Oral candidiasis and the acquired immunodeficiency syndrome. *Ann Intern Med* 1984;101:400-401.
23. Tavitian A, Raufman J-P, Rosenthal LE: Oral candidiasis as a marker for esophageal candidiasis in the acquired immunodeficiency syndrome. *Ann Intern Med* 1986;104:54-55.
24. Klein RS, Harris CA, Small CB, et al: Oral candidiasis in high-risk patients as the initial manifestation of the acquired immunodeficiency syndrome. *N Engl J Med* 1984;311:354-358.
25. Murray HW, Hillman JK, Rubin BY, et al: Patients at risk for AIDS-related opportunistic infections. *N Engl J Med* 1985;313:1504-1510.
26. Melbye M, Grossman R, Goedert JJ, et al: Risk of AIDS after herpes zoster. *Lancet* 1987;1:728-731.

4

Oral Manifestations of HIV Infection

Deborah Greenspan

Oral lesions associated with HIV infection were included in some of the early descriptions of the epidemic. This paper describes some of the salient features of some of these lesions and emphasizes their importance in the diagnosis of HIV disease and AIDS.

HIV induces immunological defects that allow the development of opportunistic infections and neoplasms. The mouth is particularly susceptible to HIV-related disease, and a great variety of oral lesions, including some new ones, have been described in association with the epidemic.[1,2] The time from infection with HIV to the development of AIDS is unpredictable and epidemiological studies suggest that it may vary. The relationship between the time of infection with HIV and the appearance of the oral lesions is also unknown. The oral lesions may represent a diagnosis of AIDS or may be the first clinical feature of immunosuppression.[3,4] The types of oral lesions seen in HIV infection may be classified into neoplastic, viral, bacterial, fungal, and idiopathic lesions. Fungal diseases, the most common of which is candidiasis, are described in another chapter. Several diseases of bacterial origin have been described in association with HIV infection. These include case reports of oral lesions of *Mycobacterium avium intercellulare* and *Klebsiella pneumoniae*. Many of the oral lesions seen in HIV infection are not new, but in association with HIV infection, their clinical appearance, behavior, and response to treatment may be quite different. This is frequently the case with the neoplasms.

38

NEOPLASMS

Kaposi's Sarcoma

Kaposi's sarcoma (KS) was first described in the nineteenth century, as a neoplasm most commonly occurring in elderly middle-aged Jewish or Mediterranean men. More recently, it was seen in Africa where it is endemic, particularly in East Africa. The lesions in these groups were usually slow growing and responded readily to therapy. However, in association with HIV infection the lesions of KS may be more aggressive and sometimes quite resistant to therapy.

KS is a multicentric neoplasm. Intraoral lesions may occur either alone or in association with skin, visceral and lymph node lesions. Frequently the first lesions of KS appear in the mouth.[5,6] They can be red, blue or purple and may be flat or raised, solitary or multiple. The commonest oral site reported is the hard palate (Figure 4-1), although lesions may be found on any part of the oral mucosa including the gingiva (Figures 4-2 and 4-3), soft palate and buccal mucosa. KS lesions on the gingiva produce diffuse swelling of the gingival papilla, resembling periodontal disease or may sometimes resemble a parulis.[7] The gingival lesions may be associated with considerable gingival enlargement causing pocketing. The pockets may become secondarily infected because of poor oral hygiene, and superficially the mucosa may become superinfected with *Candida*. When the lesions occur on the tongue, usually in the midline, they may be paler in color, and several cases have been reported of KS presenting as a swelling of normal mucosal color.[8]

The KS lesion is thought to arise from either lymphatic or blood vessel endothelium. Histologically, early lesions show atypical vascular channels and chronic inflammatory cells; more advanced lesions contain a prominent spindle-cell component and mitotic figures as well as red blood cells and eosinophilic bodies.[9,10] The nature of the cofactors that cause KS in the presence of HIV immunodeficiency is unknown, although several agents have been implicated, including cytomegalovirus and carcinogenic nitrites. Treatment for aggressive lesions involves radiation therapy, laser surgery and/or the use of chemotherapeutic drugs. Radiation therapy is frequently associated with a rapid onset of severe mucositis, so severe that treatment is often interrupted. The lesions sometimes recur several months after treatment. Surgical debulking may be successful for small

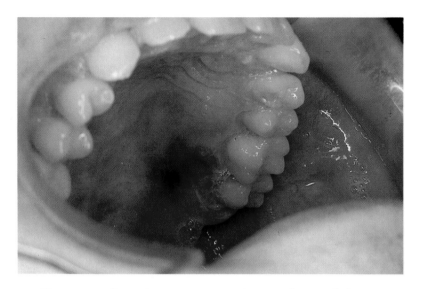

Figure 4-1 Kaposi's sarcoma appearing as a flat purple lesion.

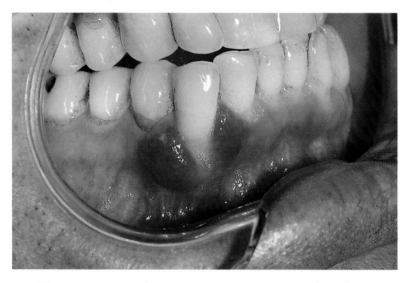

Figure 4-2 Kaposi's sarcoma appearing as gingival swelling.

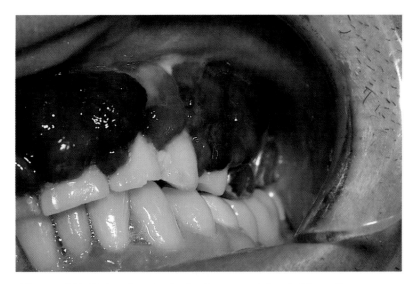

Figure 4-3 Extensive gingival enlargement due to Kaposi's sarcoma.

lesions, producing a very good esthetic result with few side effects; if the lesions recur the procedure can readily be repeated. Protocols involving the use of experimental drugs are presently undergoing investigation.

Lymphoma

The type of lymphoma most commonly seen in association with HIV infection is non-Hodgkin's lymphoma. Although cases of Hodgkin's lymphoma have been seen, none have been reported in the oral cavity. Non-Hodgkin's lymphoma may present as a firm painless swelling that can occur anywhere in the mouth. The swelling may be ulcerated, probably from trauma, or may be covered with intact normal-appearing mucosa. The oral lesions may be the first presentation of this malignancy and may not be accompanied by disseminated disease.

VIRAL LESIONS

In the same way that potentially pathogenic fungi are able to take advantage of the immune paralysis induced by HIV infection, several viruses become able to colonize or become reactivated in the mouth, producing lesions. These include herpes-group viruses and papillomaviruses.[11]

Human Papillomavirus

Human papillomaviruses cause warts, such as oral papillomas, condylomata and focal epithelial hyperplasia.[12] Immunosuppressed individuals show an increased tendency to develop skin warts, whereas anogenital warts occur as a sexually transmitted disease in male homosexuals and in heterosexual individuals of both sexes.[13] We have seen many cases of oral warts of varying clinical appearance in HIV-infected individuals. Some warts have a raised cauliflowerlike appearance, whereas others

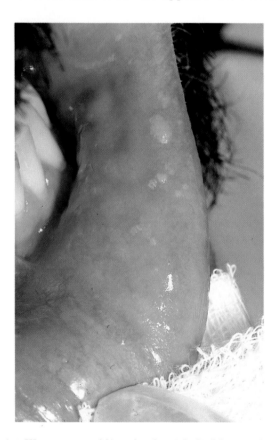

Figure 4-4 Warts, resembling focal epithelial hyperplasia, on the labial mucosa.

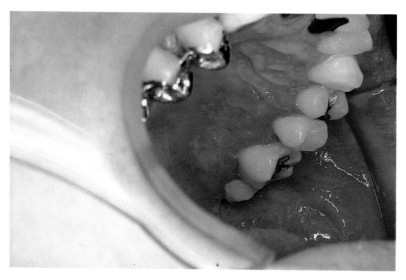

Figure 4-5 Ulcers and vesicles on the hard palate, due to herpes simplex virus.

are well circumscribed, have a flat surface and almost disappear when the mucosa is stretched (Figure 4-4). The histological appearance may show multiple fingerlike projections covered by hyperkeratotic epithelium with a prominent granular layer, blunt projections covered by parakeratotic epithelium, or solitary areas of focal acanthosis (focal epithelial hyperplasia). Some koilocytosis may be seen. The warts can be quite troublesome, in that many lesions may be scattered throughout the oral cavity and frequently recur after removal.

Herpes Simplex Virus

Herpes simplex virus can produce recurrent episodes of painful ulceration. Intraorally the lesions appear most commonly on the palate. The patient may report small vesicles that erupt to form ulcers[14] (Figure 4-5).

In association with HIV infection, these lesions may persist for several weeks, causing considerable pain. They may also take on an atypical appearance, looking like ulcers or slitlike lesions on the tongue or mimicking other diseases. Diagnosis can be made from culture, in the case of early lesions, or from cytologic smears showing characteristic viral giant cells. More accurate confirmation has become possible through the use of monoclonal antibodies, available in a commercial kit.

Varicella Virus

Herpes zoster caused by varicella, the chicken pox virus, another member of the herpes group, can produce oral ulcerations, usually accompanied by characteristic skin lesions. The lesions of herpes zoster involving the trigeminal nerve are of a unilateral distribution and may occur on both keratinized and nonkeratinized mucosa. The early lesions are vesicles that in the mouth rupture to form ulcers and heal uneventfully. On the skin, however, they become crusted and sometimes heal with scarring. The lesions are frequently painful. In some cases a complaint of tooth pain is one of the early symptoms, preceding the appearance of the lesions, even though there is no apparent dental cause.

Hairy Leukoplakia

Oral hairy leukoplakia (HL) is a white lesion that is found predominantly on the lateral margins of the tongue. Discovered in San Francisco in 1981, it was first seen in male homosexuals[15] and has been seen in members of all the other risk groups for AIDS,[16] including children.[17] Virtually all patients with HL are antibody-positive to HIV. Their clinical and laboratory profiles are similar to those of patients with asymptomatic HIV infection and ARC. Besides on the tongue, the lesion is occasionally also seen on the buccal or labial mucosa. It is white and does not rub off. The surface may be smooth, corrugated or markedly folded (Figure 4-6). The folds tend to run vertically, along the lateral surface of the anterior tongue. The surface may become so thick that hairlike projections appear (Figure 4-7). Microscopically there are characteristic changes, consisting of folds or "hairs," hyperparakeratosis, acanthosis, vacuolation of bands or clumps of prickle cells, and little if any subepithelial inflammation.

HL is probably a virally induced lesion. Studies have revealed the presence of Epstein-Barr virus (EBV) in HL tissue as EBV viral capsid antigen on immunofluorescence, as typical particles on electron microscopy, and as the complete linear form of EBV DNA in a very high copy number in Southern blot hybridization.[18] This is the first lesion in which EBV has been found in this prolific and fully replicating form. Intraepithelial Langerhans' cells are reduced or absent in the HL lesion, and this decrease correlates with the presence of viral antigens.[19] HL has not been found in the anal mucosa.[20]

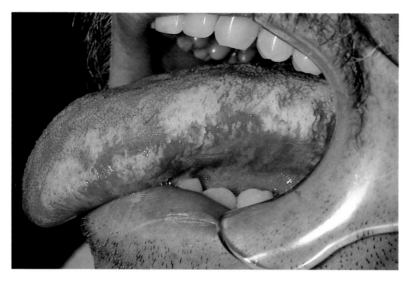

Figure 4-6 HL occurring on the lateral margin of the tongue.

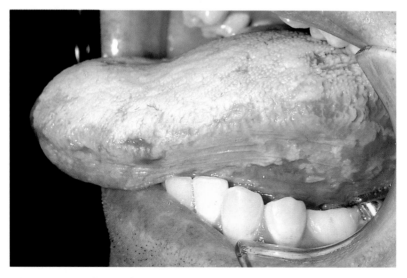

Figure 4-7 Extensive HL involving the lateral margins and dorsal surface of the tongue.

As regards the relationship of HL with the development of AIDS, data have been analyzed on 143 homosexual patients who had HL but not AIDS. The data indicate that over half of the patients with HL will develop AIDS, and that more patients with HL develop *Pneumocystis carinii* pneumonia as their first manifestation of AIDS than is seen in the general San Francisco AIDS population.[21] Recent studies showed that there was no relationship between the size and location of the lesions and the ultimate prognosis.[22] Studies are in progress, using acyclovir, to find an effective treatment for HL. It was noted that HL disappeared in patients who received high-dose acyclovir for herpes zoster. Preliminary trials with the experimental drug Desciclovir, an analogue of acyclovir, showed temporary elimination or almost compete resolution in the clinical extent of the lesion.[23]

HL is a remarkable lesion. It is unique to HIV-infected people, having never been seen before the AIDS epidemic. It serves as an excellent model of virally induced oral epithelial hyperplasia, presents new opportunities to study the biology of EBV infection, and is a significant clinical marker or early warning sign of HIV infection.[20]

IDIOPATHIC AND OTHER FEATURES

Oral Ulceration

Oral ulcers are being reported with increasing frequency in people with HIV infection. The ulcers resemble aphthous ulcers, a common oral lesion. The cause of recurrent aphthous ulceration is unknown but hormonal factors, food allergy, stress and viral factors have been implicated.[24] A role for cellular immune defects in the pathogenesis has been suggested. Perhaps the local and systemic host defects in HIV infection are the cause of these ulcers in this group of patients. The lesions often have the typical appearance of recurrent aphthous ulceration, appearing as well-circumscribed ulcers with an erythematous margin. Sometimes, patients exhibit extremely large, necrotic ulcers which are very painful and may persist for several weeks. Some cases of persistent lesions may require biopsy to exclude other diseases.

Salivary Gland Enlargement

Salivary gland swelling, usually involving the parotid glands, has been seen in both adults and children with HIV infection. This is often accompanied by complaints of xerostomia, which is generally the only complaint associated with the enlargement. The etiology of the swelling is unknown.[25,26]

Idiopathic Thrombocytopenic Purpura

Oral lesions may occur as a first presentation of this HIV-related autoimmune disorder, or may appear in conjunction with other cutaneous lesions. The oral lesions appear as small blood-filled purpuric lesions or ecchymoses. Spontaneous gingival bleeding may also occur and should not be confused with bleeding secondary to gingivitis.

CONCLUSION

The varied nature and important implications of the oral lesions associated with HIV infection are among the factors that make an understanding of oral soft tissue diseases increasingly important in health care.

REFERENCES

1. Greenspan D, Silverman S Jr: Oral lesions of HIV infection.*Calif Dent Assoc J* 1987;15:28.
2. Greenspan D, Greenspan JS, Pindborg JJ, Schiødt M: *AIDS and the Dental Team.* Copenhagen, Munksgaard, 1986.
3. Reichart PH, Pohle H-D, Gelderblom H: Oral manifestations of AIDS. *Dtsch Z Mund Kiefer Gesichts Chir* 1985;9:167.
4. Reichart PA, Gelderblom HR, Becker J, Kuntz A: AIDS and the oral cavity. The HIV-infection: Virology, etiology, origin, immunology, precautions and clinical observations in 110 patients. *Int J Oral Maxillofac Surg* 1987;16:129.
5. Keeney K, Abaza NA, Tidwel O, Quinn P: Oral Kaposi's sarcoma in acquired immune deficiency syndrome. *J Oral Maxillofac Surg* 1987;45:815-821.
6. Silverman S Jr, Migliorati CA, Lozada-Nur F, et al: Oral findings in people with or at high risk for AIDS: A study of 375 homosexual males. *J Am Dent Assoc* 1986;112:187-192.
7. Petit JC, Ripamonti U, Hille J: Progressive changes of Kaposi's sarcoma of the gingiva and palate. Case report in an AIDS patient. *J Periodontol* 1986;57:159-163.
8. Greenspan D, Greenspan JS: Oral mucosal manifestation of AIDS. *Dermatol Clin* 1987;5:733-737.

9. Green TL, Beckstead JH, Lozada-Nur F, et al: Histopathologic spectrum of oral Kaposi's sarcoma. *Oral Surg Oral Med Oral Pathol* 1984;58:306-314.

10. Kuntz AA, Gelderblom HR, Winkely T, Reichart PA: Ultrastructural findings in oral Kaposi's sarcoma (AIDS). *J Oral Pathol* 1987;16:372-379.

11. Kanas RJ, Jensen JL, Abrams AM, et al: Oral mucosal cytomegalovirus as a manifestation of the acquired immunodeficiency syndrome. *Oral Surg* 1987;64:153.

12. Scully C, Prime S, Maitland N: Papillomaviruses: Their possible role in oral diseases. *Oral Surg* 1985;60:166.

13. Owen WF: Sexually transmitted disease and traumatic problems in homosexual men. *Ann Intern Med* 1980;92:805.

14. Quinnan GV, Masur H, Rook AH, et al: Herpes virus infections in the acquired immunodeficiency syndrome. *JAMA* 1984;252:72.

15. Greenspan D, Greenspan JS, Conant M, et al: Oral "hairy" leukoplakia in male homosexuals: Evidence of association with papillomavirus and a herpes group virus. *Lancet* 1984;2:831.

16. Greenspan D, Hollander H, Friedman-Kien A, et al: Oral hairy leukoplakia in two women, a hemophiliac and a transfusion recipient, letter. *Lancet* 1986;2:978.

17. Greenspan JS, Mastrucci T, Leggott PJ, et al: Hairy leukoplakia in a child. *AIDS*, in press.

18. Greenspan JS, Greenspan D, Lennette ET, et al: Replication of Epstein-Barr virus within the epithelial cells of oral "hairy" leukoplakia, an AIDS-associated lesion. *N Engl J Med* 1985;313:1564.

19. Daniels TE, Greenspan D, Greenspan JS, et al: Absence of Langerhans cells in oral hairy leukoplakia, an AIDS-associated lesion. *J Invest Dermatol* 1987;89:178.

20. Hollander H, Greenspan D, Stringari S, et al: Hairy leukoplakia and the acquired immunodeficiency syndrome. *Ann Intern Med* 1986;104:892.

21. Greenspan D, Greenspan JS, Hearst N, et al: Relation of oral hairy leukoplakia to infection with the human immunodeficiency virus and the risk of developing AIDS. *J Infect Dis* 1987;155:475.

22. Schiødt M, Greenspan D, Daniels TE, Greenspan JS: Clinical and histologic spectrum of oral hairy leukoplakia. *Oral Surg Oral Med Oral Pathol* 1987;64:716-720.

23. Greenspan D, Greenspan JS, Chapman S, et al: Efficacy of BWA515U in treatment of EBV infection in hairy leukoplakia, abstract. *Third International Conference on AIDS*, Washington, DC, 1987.

24. Greenspan JS, Gadol N, Olson JA, et al: Lymphocyte function in recurrent aphthous ulceration. *J Oral Pathol* 1985;8:592.

25. Ammann, AJ: The acquired immunodeficiency syndrome in infants and children. *Ann Intern Med* 1985;103:734.

26. Leggott PJ, Robertson PB, Greenspan D, et al: Oral manifestation of primary and acquired immunodeficiency diseases in children. *Pediatr Dent* 1987;9:98-104.

5

Clinical Description and Etiology of HIV-Associated Periodontal Diseases

James R. Winkler, Markus Grassi, and Patricia A. Murray

Over the past several years an increased frequency and severity of periodontal disease in HIV-infected homosexual males has been observed. We have named these lesions HIV-associated gingivitis (HIV-G) and HIV-associated periodontitis (HIV-P) because of their unique features. For example, unlike conventional periodontal disease, they do not respond effectively to standard periodontal therapy. In addition, we have observed the rapid progression from mild gingivitis to advanced, painful and spontaneously bleeding periodontitis in a few months. Frequently, this periodontitis caused the exposure of bone and extended past the attached gingiva well into the mucosa. The end result of this rapid progression was frequently bone sequestration and the extraction of multiple teeth.

In this study, 113 HIV-seropositive homosexual males from San Francisco were given thorough medical and dental examinations. Complete periodontal indices including the plaque index, gingival index, probing depth, attachment loss, and a mucosal evaluation were done on all teeth present. The medical histories, dental histories and frequency of other HIV-associated signs and symptoms were related to the presence of HIV-G and HIV-P. In addition, T4/T8 ratios, humoral antibody levels to specific microbiota, and other host-response factors were evaluated for their role in the etiology of HIV-P and HIV-G.

Until now, only anecdotal observations have been available in the literature concerning HIV-G and HIV-P. The purpose of this study was to provide a classification and standardization of HIV-associated peri-odontal diseases on which future longitudinal, epidemiologic and treat-ment studies at different centers can be based.

Before the identification of HIV as the etiologic agent, clinical signs and symptoms were the only means to identify HIV-seropositive individuals.[1-3] Today, HIV antigen and antibody tests are readily available, but these tests pose difficult moral, ethical, and financial questions which make high risk group individuals hesitant to obtain confirmation of their HIV status.[4,5] Therefore, the early identification and presumptive diagnosis of seropositive individuals by clinical signs and symptoms continues to play a major diagnostic role.

An increasing number of HIV-associated signs and symptoms continues to be identified. These include a number of oral lesions, many of which are among the first signs of HIV infection.[6,7] In addition, an increased severity and frequency of periodontal lesions have been observed in HIV-seropositive individuals. Clinical observations over the past several years have demonstrated that HIV-associated periodontal diseases are an additional intraoral manifestation of HIV infection. In fact, periodontal disease may be one of the earliest signs and symptoms. However, these descriptions have been anecdotal and based on nonquantitative data.[8,9] The purpose of this study was to quantitatively define the nature and range of severity of HIV-associated periodontal diseases. Specifically, we wished (1) to describe the clinical features, (2) to describe the relationship to other intraoral and extraoral HIV-associated diseases, (3) to determine the predictive value for seroconversion, and (4) to investigate the pathogenesis of HIV-associated periodontal diseases. Furthermore, these data offer a classification and standardization of HIV-associated periodontal disease on which future longitudinal, epidemiologic, and treatment studies at different centers can be based.

HISTORICAL PERSPECTIVE

Since 1983, we have observed an increasing number of HIV-seropositive individuals who presented for treatment with severe periodontal disease. On initial examination, these painful, bleeding lesions resembled acute necrotizing ulcerative gingivitis superimposed upon rapidly progressive periodontitis. Frequently, even with immediate treatment these cases progressed from mild to severe periodontitis requiring extraction of teeth in a matter of months. At the same time we began to observe an increasing number of HIV-infected individuals with an unusual gingivitis. This gingivitis was unusual in that it did not respond in a typical fashion to conventional therapy and was frequently seen in the presence of good plaque control. Subsequently, several of these HIV-associated gingivitis (HIV-G) cases progressed to HIV-associated periodontitis (HIV-P) in a short period of time.

Interestingly, only 21% of the high risk group individuals who presented with only HIV-G at their initial visit were aware of their HIV serostatus. On the other hand, nearly 85% of the individuals with HIV-P lesions at their initial visit were aware of their serostatus.

Most of the early cases of HIV-G and HIV-P were referred to us from Oral Medicine Clinic where they were being seen for other HIV-associated intraoral lesions. At present, however, most patients coming to us are by self-referral from San Francisco Bay Area dentists and the many cohorts that are involved in all aspects of the Oral Aids Project at the University of California San Francisco.

METHODS

As of January 1988, 384 HIV-seropositive individuals have been treated in the Periodontology Clinical Research Center at the University of California, San Francisco, for HIV-associated periodontal lesions. Of these patients, 113 males ranging in age from 24 to 41 years (mean age = 34 yr) agreed to participate in longitudinal studies to evaluate disease progression and effectiveness of treatment. At the initial visit, all patients completed comprehensive medical and dental health histories which were verified by thorough questioning and correlated with their physicians' history, dental school records, and hospital records. It was determined that 42 of these patients had been previously diagnosed as having AIDS, 23 with ARC, and 48 with no previous AIDS/ARC diagnosis or known HIV-seropositive status.[10]

All of the AIDS and ARC patients allowed the investigators complete access to their HIV status and medical records. Forty-four of the undiagnosed individuals voluntarily agreed to HIV testing and medical evaluations. HIV-positive patients were confirmed to be positive by enzyme-linked immunosorbent assay (ELISA) and by Western blot.[4,5] However, four of the undiagnosed individuals did not wish to be tested and were diagnosed as being an "AIDS case" by Centers for Disease

Control surveillance case definition.[10] This classification scheme allows for the diagnosis of an AIDS case in the absence of laboratory evidence by ruling out disqualifying immunodeficient states and by using indicator diseases that have been definitely diagnosed.

As part of the oral examination, the plaque index[11] and gingival index[12] were assessed on facial, lingual and proximal surfaces of all teeth. A score of 3 was recorded for the gingival index if a site showed the presence of a blood clot or bled in response to air drying. Pocket depth from the gingival margin and attachment loss from the cementoenamel junction were measured on six surfaces of all teeth. In addition, HIV-associated periodontal lesions consistently showed widespread inflammation that extended from the free gingival margin into the mucosa. Consequently, the gingiva and alveolar mucosa adjacent to each tooth were assessed for the presence or absence of a linear band of free gingival erythema, diffuse erythema of gingiva or mucosa, and punctate or "petechialike" erythema of gingiva or mucosa. Full mouth intraoral photographs were taken on all patients. Radiographs were taken when no recent films were available (>2 years) and as needed for diagnosis and treatment.

In addition, serial dilutions of serum from 35 of the 113 HIV-seropositive male homosexuals, 35 HIV-seronegative male homosexual controls, and 20 HIV-seronegative male heterosexual controls were analyzed by ELISA[13] to determine IgG titers against *Bacteroides gingivalis, Bacteroides intermedius, Fusobacterium nucleatum, Eikenella corrodens, Actinobacillus actinomycetemcomitans, Capnocytophaga sputigena,* and *Streptococcus sanguis.* Alkaline phosphatase–conjugated goat antihuman IgG F(ab')$_2$ was used as the secondary antibody for visualization of host IgG to these whole bacterial antigens.

RESULTS

Chief Complaints

The chief complaints of the patients in this study ranged from a distinctive redness of the gingiva and mucosa to severe oral pain, rapidly progressing gingival necrosis, and exposure of bone. Patients complained that the redness seen in the free gingival margin was unaesthetic and characteristically occurred in a very short period of time. Gingival bleeding when brushing, or in more severe cases spontaneous bleeding, was a common complaint (Figure 5-1). The spontaneous bleeding frequently manifested itself as nocturnal gingival bleeding, with individuals complaining of blood stains on their pillow cases and blood clots in their mouth.

Clinical Features

A consistent finding among the individuals examined was the presence of periodontal lesions, which ranged from a mild but distinctive gingivitis to a severe and rapidly progressive periodontitis. In many cases, however, clinical healthy periodontium was juxtaposed to periodontally involved regions. For the sake of discussion and data analysis, individual teeth and their associated periodontal tissues were diagnosed as having HIV-G, HIV-P, or as being clinically healthy (HIV-H). HIV-G was defined as lesions confined to the soft tissues which showed the distinctive erythema of the free gingiva, attached gingiva and alveolar mucosa (Figure 5-2). HIV-P was defined as sites with the signs described for HIV-G and, in addition, extensive soft tissue necrosis and severe loss of periodontal attachment.

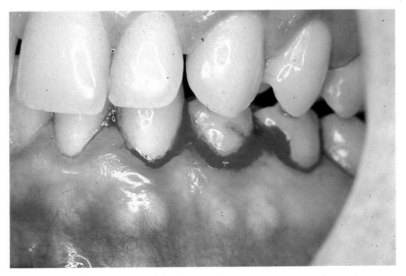

Figure 5-1 Spontaneous bleeding. Note the presence of spontaneous bleeding in the incisor bicuspid region.

HIV-G was initially noticed because of its lack of response to conventional therapy. Previous studies in the general population have shown that gingivitis is reversible, that is, the removal of plaque and maintenance of good oral hygiene results in the return of gingival health.[14] However, in these patients extensive scaling and root planing in conjunction with improved oral hygiene did little to improve free gingival erythema.

Rapid Destruction

The most distinguishing features of HIV-P are its severe soft tissue necrosis and rapid destruction of the periodontal attachment and bone (Figure 5-3). In HIV-P lesions more than 90% attachment loss was seen in some teeth in as little as in 3 to 6 months and resulted in exodontia. Soft tissue cratering, interproximal necrosis and ulceration are seen in direct relationship to the regions of bone loss. Areas affected by HIV-P did not show deep pocket formation. This is in definite contrast to chronic inflammatory periodontal diseases where the loss of attachment precedes the loss of overlying periodontal tissues and results in the formation of pockets. In HIV-P, loss of crestal alveolar bone

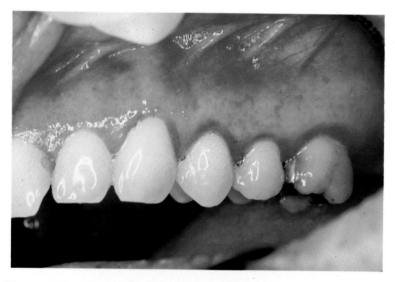

Figure 5-2 HIV-G. The gingivitis in this patient did not respond to conventional therapy. The free gingival erythema and the punctate lesions of HIV-G are clearly seen.

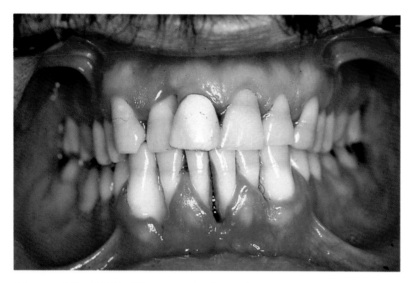

Figure 5-3   HIV-P. The extensive loss of attachment in this patient occurred in a matter of months.

coincided with necrosis of the gingival margin which sometimes led to exposure of alveolar bone and subsequent interseptal bone sequestration (Figure 5-4). This sequestration of bone in conjunction with soft tissue necrosis extending into the vestibular mucosa (Figure 5-5) or palate (Figure 5-6) was suggestive of necrotizing stomatitis. In HIV-P, it appears that periodontal and alveolar bone may be rapidly destroyed, which is in contrast to the lesions of acute necrotizing ulcerative gingivitis (ANUG) which are normally self-limiting to the soft tissue of the periodontium.[15-17] Although bone loss can be seen in some cases of recurrent severe ANUG, this is usually the result of multiple attacks over many years. Individuals with HIV-P, on the other hand, typically report no previous long term ANUG history.

Pain

Severe pain is also a distinguishing feature of HIV-P. In fact, this was the chief complaint of many patients and the reason they sought dental treatment. Unlike the ANUG patient in whom pain is located in the "gums,"[18] the pain of HIV-P was described as being localized to the "jaw bones," or as being a

56

"deep, aching" pain. Frequently, patients report that it feels as if their teeth are hitting the "jaw bone" when chewing. Often this deep pain preceded the development of the clinically obvious HIV-P lesion. The cause of this pain is not clear but is probably the result of rapid bone destruction seen in HIV-P.

Distribution

HIV-G most frequently involves the entire mouth, and is usually distributed equally to all quadrants. In some mouths, however, it is found in limited regions involving one or two teeth. Severe cases of HIV-P can affect all of the teeth and surrounding periodontium. More frequently, HIV-P affects several localized areas independently, resulting in islands of severely involved periodontium surrounded by relatively normal tissue. In fact, it is frequently observed that only one surface of the tooth, for example the distal, is severely involved with HIV-P while the remaining surfaces are only slightly involved. The reason for such discrete localization is unclear. On the other hand, all regions of the mouth appear to have similar chances of being affected.

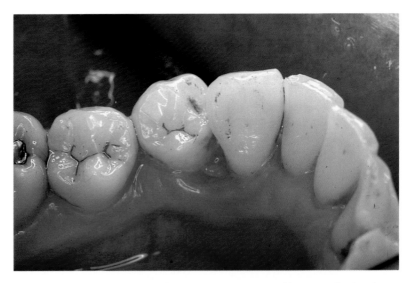

Figure 5-4 Interseptal bone sequestration. Frequently in these patients, interseptal bone begins to be exposed during healing.

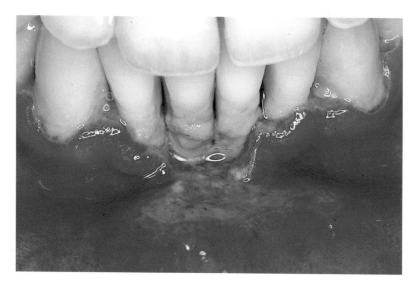

Figure 5-5 The extension of soft tissue necrosis into the mucosa can be seen in the mandibular incisor region.

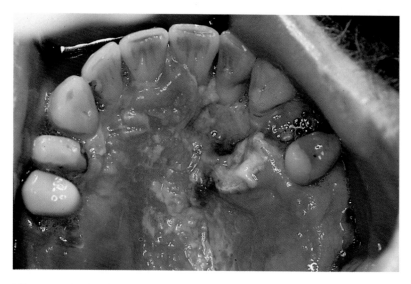

Figure 5-6 In this patient osseous and soft tissue necrosis extended into the palate.

Periodontal Indices

The full mouth mean plaque index, gingival index, probing depth and attachment loss were 1.38 (SD 0.8), 1.93 (SD 0.6), 3.38 (SD 1.1) mm, and 3.66 (SD 1.5) mm, respectively. More than 90% of facial, lingual, and proximal sites in these patients showed either HIV-G or HIV-P.

Gingival and Mucosal Evaluation

Erythema was observed to be a consistent clinical feature of both HIV-P and HIV-G. The unique features of these lesions made it necessary to develop a semiquantitative basis to evaluate longitudinal changes and effectiveness of treatment (see chapter 9).

Free gingival erythema. Free gingival erythema was observed in essentially all sites of HIV-G and HIV-P. In greater than 50% of the cases this erythema could be described as an intense red linear band that extended 2 to 3 mm apically from the free gingival margin into attached gingiva. In the remainder of cases, free gingival erythema was considerably more diffuse. Whether bandlike or diffuse, the erythema was often associated with spontaneous bleeding or bleeding on probing. The percentage of sites that showed gingival index scores of 2 or 3 is 24.3. Furthermore, this erythema did not satisfactorily respond to the removal of plaque by intensive scaling and root planing and improved plaque control measures. No significant improvement in clinical features or indices was observed in one month of treatment when compared to conventional gingivitis (see chapter 9). In fact, the disease had a tendency to become progressively more severe.

Attached gingival erythema. Both HIV-G and HIV-P were found to have either punctate gingival erythema or diffuse gingival erythema of the attached gingiva in direct association with the free gingival erythema. Very infrequently were punctate or diffuse gingival erythema present in the absence of free gingival erythema. In most cases, punctate gingival erythema involved the entire attached gingiva from the free gingival margin to the alveolar mucosa. In other regions the petechialike lesions gave the appearance of coalescing, making the entire attached gingiva bright red. Clinical impression suggested that punctate gingival erythema was a precursor to diffuse gingival erythema and that a correlation might exist between these two lesions.

Mucosal erythema. Diffuse erythema of the mucosa was seen in approximately three fourths of the sites. Diffuse mucosal erythema was seen more often in HIV-P than in HIV-G. Punctate gingival erythema was observed more frequently than punctate mucosal erythema and punctate changes were seen more often in HIV-G than HIV-P.

Relationship to *Candida*

It is not clear what relationship erythema of the gingiva and mucosa has to *Candida*. The small areas of bleeding ulceration that result from the removal of *Candida* colonies from the mucosa by wiping with a gauze are distinct from these non-bleeding areas characteristic of the punctate lesions. Clinical observations suggest that successful treatment of HIV-G or HIV-P is frequently dependent on the successful treatment of intraoral candidiasis. In these successfully treated individuals the characteristic features of HIV-G or HIV-P disappear, such as the involvement of the attached gingiva and alveolar mucosa. In addition, the presence of subgingival *Candida* is a frequent finding in subgingival plaque of HIV-G and HIV-P (see chapter 8). This is an interesting finding because *Candida* is not a common inhabitant of plaque in conventional periodontal disease. The relationship of *Candida* to these lesions is not established but deserves further consideration.

Relationship of HIV-Associated Periodontal Disease to other Systemic and Intraoral Lesions

The relationship of HIV-G and HIV-P to systemic or intra-oral manifestations of HIV-infection was determined by correlating the medical histories or clinical findings obtained at the baseline visit to the periodontal manifestations seen at the baseline visit. For purposes of this analysis, patients were classified as falling into the HIV-G class (N = 43) if they had only lesions of the HIV-G type or were placed into the HIV-P category (N = 70) if they had one or more lesions that were consistent with a diagnosis of HIV-P.

The most common systemic histories included *Pneumocystis carinii* pneumonia (PCP), Kaposi's sarcoma (KS), recurrent

60

herpes simplex virus lesions (HSV), human papilloma virus lesions (HPV), systemic candidiasis, night sweats, and lymphadenopathy. With the exception of lymphadenopathy, no significant relationship between the presence of HIV-G or HIV-P could be seen for any of these systemic features (Figure 5-7).

HIV-G and HIV-P were then related to the presence or history of other intraoral lesions seen in HIV-seropositive individuals including hairy leukoplakia (HL), intraoral candidiasis, HPV, HSV, and abscesses (periapical or periodontal). Both HIV-G and HIV-P appeared to occur most frequently with HL and candidiasis but this relationship was only significant for HIV-P. No significant relationship was seen to the other intraoral manifestations observed (Figure 5-8).

Relationship to habits. The presence of HIV-G and HIV-P as related to smoking, the consumption of alcohol, and the use of recreational drugs is seen in Figure 5-9. In this population greater than 80% of the individuals smoked and consumed

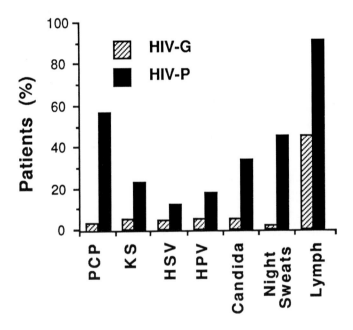

Figure 5-7 The baseline percentage of patients with HIV-G and HIV-P that had other HIV-associated extraoral lesions. Individuals with both HIV-G and HIV-P were not included in this analysis.

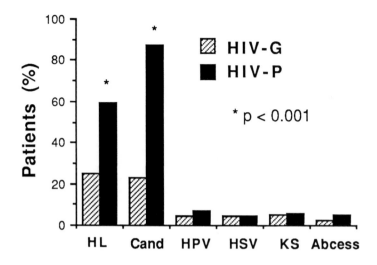

Figure 5-8 The baseline percentage of patients with HIV-G and HIV-P that had other HIV-associated intraoral lesions. Individuals with both HIV-G and HIV-P were not included in this analysis.

alcohol on a regular basis and greater than 60% used recreational drugs. The presence or absence of these habits did not seem to influence whether or not an individual had HIV-G or HIV-P.

T4/T8 ratios. The relationship of HIV-G and HIV-P to T4/T8 ratios was determined by point prevalence. As above, individuals were classified as having HIV-G (N = 25) or HIV-P (N = 43) at the baseline examination. The T4/T8 ratios were then obtained from the most recent blood assay, which was in all cases within 2 days of the periodontal examination. T4/T8 ratios for HIV-G fell within the low normal range, 0.9 to 1.7, whereas the ratios associated with in HIV-P were significantly lower, in the range of 0.1 to 0.9 (Figure 5-10).

Serum antibody levels. *B gingivalis, B intermedius, F nucleatum, E corrodens,* and *A actinomycetemcomitans* showed significantly higher antibody titers ($P < 0.001$) in the HIV-seropositive homosexuals than in HIV-seronegative homosexuals and HIV-seronegative heterosexuals. No significant difference was found between the groups for *C sputigena* or *S sanguis* (data not shown).

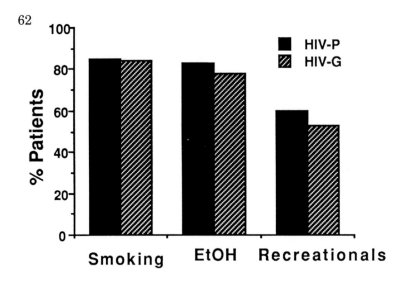

Figure 5-9 The relationship of smoking, drinking, and use of recreational drugs to the appearance of HIV-G and HIV-P in patients at the baseline examination. Individuals with both HIV-G and HIV-P were not included in this analysis.

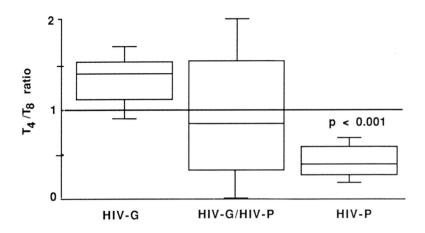

Figure 5-10 Point prevalence data relating T4/T8 ratios to HIV-G, HIV-P and the combination of HIV-P and HIV-G in individuals at baseline.

DISCUSSION

The oral cavity represents a unique microenvironment where the host is continuously defending against microbial infection.[19,20] Evidence suggests that the host's immune system plays a critical role in preventing microbial colonization of these tissues.[19-21] It is well recognized that the development of periodontal disease depends upon the interaction between the resident oral microbiota found in the dentogingival plaque and the host response.[19] Since HIV-infection can cause severe immunosuppression, an increased frequency and severity of periodontal disease in HIV-infected individuals is not unexpected.

For clarity in discussion and data analysis we have described two clinically distinct lesions, HIV-G and HIV-P, but the relationship of these diseases to each other is not clear. One suggestion is that HIV-G is the precursor to HIV-P. For example, HIV-P lesions are always associated with areas of preexisting or coexisting HIV-G. Longitudinal data on a number of cases have documented the progression from a mild gingivitis to a rapidly progressive and severe periodontitis in a short period of time. In fact we have observed as much as 10 mm of bone loss in as little as three months. On the other hand, HIV-G may be a mild form of HIV-P. In this case we would be observing the progression from a mild periodontitis at one end of the spectrum to HIV-P and necrotizing stomatitis at the other end of the spectrum. This concept is supported by the finding of identical flora in the HIV-G and HIV-P lesions and is consistent with the rapid progression from a mild-appearing HIV-G to HIV-P (see chapter 8).

The etiology of HIV-P and HIV-G remains unclear. Investigations of the microbiota associated with these lesions demonstrate species of bacteria qualitatively similar to those seen in other forms of periodontal disease. Importantly, however, there is a significant increase in some of the more virulent species such as *Eikenella* spp, *Wolinella* spp, and *Bacteroides* spp. These organisms possess sufficient virulence factors to cause direct tissue damage, especially when they are seen in high numbers. This quantitative increase in virulent organisms which possess tissue damaging properties may be the major factor leading to rapid progression. Thus, it can be proposed that the HIV-infected individual's compromised immune system allows for a shift in virulence potential of the oral microbiota, allowing the overgrowth of specific pathogens during periods when the tissue defense mechanisms have been compromised; this may occur in a manner analogous to that found in previous studies on ANUG.[22]

Available data suggest that there may be geographic differences in the prevalence and severity of HIV-G and HIV-P.[23-25] Some investigators have reported the absence of these manifestations in their respective patient populations while others have reported findings identical to ours. Whether or not these differences are real or artifactual is not clear at this time. These differences might be attributed to the lack of well-documented data to provide a basis for classification and standardization. Until now only scattered anecdotal clinical observations have been available, making it impossible to address the significance of these differences. A major purpose of this study was to provide well-documented clinical data as a baseline for future longitudinal, epidemiologic, and treatment studies at different centers.

Furthermore, an evaluation of the prevalence and severity of periodontal disease in any population requires consideration of the socioeconomics of the population being investigated, as well as the influence that diet, the dental "IQ," availability of dental care, age, endocrine disorders, and habits can have on the periodontium.[24] It stands to reason that, in a population of individuals with a high level of periodontal disease (for example intravenous drug abusers), differences superimposed by additional etiologic factors such as HIV might go unnoticed or be underestimated.

In addition, the route of HIV infection needs to be considered because of the potential for exposure to a variety of other diseases and documented differences in disease patterns between the different risk groups.[25-28] The data in this study were derived from male homosexuals whose primary risk factor was homosexual sexual practices. Only one individual had a history of intravenous drug abuse as the potential route of exposure. In general, the individuals in this population were college educated, had received regular dental care throughout their lives and were very concerned about their oral health and aesthetics. Of the 113 patients only 9 had a previous history of periodontal disease, but in all cases this disease had been successfully treated and maintained for more than one year before entry into this study. None of the patients in our study population were malnourished for lack of food, although several of the patients in the later stages of AIDS were underweight due to illness and medications.

This San Francisco patient population is considerably different from those seen in other study areas. For example, the patient population in New York City is largely drawn from the intravenous drug abusers and prostitutes, while others have investigated primarily hemophiliac populations or Africans. There is insufficient data available to suggest that these patient populations have a different baseline level of periodontal disease, but it should be considered as a factor which might mask the observation of subtle changes. In San Francisco, we may have been able to detect more subtle periodontal changes because the population under study has relatively low baseline levels of moderate to advanced periodontitis.

Most studies on AIDS focused on the generalized profound immune suppression caused by the reduction in number and function of CD4 lymphocytes.[29] In contrast to immune deficiency, HIV infection also induces immune stimulation of CD8 T-cells and B-cells. B-cell activation and formation is the result of the absence of CD4 cells which normally act as a constraint on B-cell activation/maturation.[30] This activation leads to inappropriate nonspecific polyclonal responses to antigens.

Interestingly, in HIV-seropositive individuals we were able to detect significantly increased antibody levels to a number of putative periodontal pathogens such as *B gingivalis, B intermedius, F nucleatum, E corrodens,* and *A actinomycetemcomitans.* These studies were based on the concept that serum antibody titers frequently reflect the microbiota involved in the pathogenesis of periodontal lesions and might allow us to rapidly identify the specific microflora involved in HIV-associated periodontitis.[31,32] In these studies the differences in levels were not limited to those with periodontal disease but were related to the serostatus of the individuals involved. How the finding of significantly increased antibody levels to periodontopathic organisms is related to the progression of HIV-associated periodontal diseases is not clear at this time. However, the demonstration of elevated antibody levels combined with the microbiological data obtained from culture and indirect immunofluorescence may provide valuable information on the microbiota directly involved in HIV-G and HIV-P.

In addition, previous studies have demonstrated that decreased polymorphonuclear leukocyte (PMN) function is frequently associated with rapidly progressing and severe periodontal lesions.[33,34] Therefore, we evaluated several functional capacities of PMNs[35-37] isolated from HIV-positive individuals with HIV-P and candidiasis. Interestingly, we found significantly increased phagocytosis, oxidative burst and F-actin formation in the HIV-positive individuals when compared to HIV-negative controls.[38] This is in contrast to the decreased activity typical of previous studies on periodontal disease.

Initially, the finding of increased phagocytic activity and oxidative burst may seem contradictory to the prevalence of candidiasis and bacterial infection seen in the HIV-infected individuals. In fact, it is these functional capacities that are frequently impaired in seronegative individuals with aggressive bacterial and fungal infections.[39] The HIV-infected individual, in contrast to the normal situation, is unique in that the immune system has become virtually unregulated due to the dramatic decrease in number and function of T4 lymphocytes.

The PMN normally is the primary line of defense against acute microbial invasion, and is rapidly replaced by lymphocytes and macrophages. In the HIV-positive patient this sequence of events is not maintained. The prolonged presence of PMNs in resisting bacterial and fungal invasion may be required because the CD4 lymphocyte response and macrophage response is severely altered or absent. Consequently, the PMN now may have the capacity to cause severe host tissue damage.

The concept of a subpopulation of PMNs that are hyperresponsive or primed by virtue of acute bacterial or fungal infection has recently arisen from earlier studies on toxic PMNs.[40,41] It appears that the primed population of PMNs has a marked increase in oxidative metabolism and phagocytosis in host tissues such as the pulmonary vascular endothelium during bacteremia. A similar phenomenon may be occurring in the HIV-infected individuals. Since HIV-infected individuals frequently have intraoral bacterial and fungal infection, it can be proposed that one site of priming for the PMNs may be in the mouth. In the case of the rapidly progressive intraoral lesions, transient bacteremias caused by chewing or toothbrushing could easily give rise to such a primed PMN population. Under normal circumstances, the PMN response to invasion is short-lasting and modulated by the ensuing lymphocyte and macrophage infiltration to the site of action. In the HIV-infected individual this loss of regulation results in the PMN playing a more major role in the protection against invasion and having a greater potential for host tissue destruction.

The finding of increased phagocytosis, oxidative burst, and actin polymerization in PMNs isolated from the peripheral blood of HIV-infected individuals is in agreement with some previous reports and in disagreement with others.[42-44] Since our population of patients all had documented periodontal disease and intraoral candidiasis, we suspect that what we are observing is "priming" due to bacteremia. The existence of a large subpopulation of primed PMNs may have a localized detrimental effect on host tissues such as the periodontium.

These results suggest that PMN "priming," ie, hyperresponsive PMNs, may result from the transient bacteremia and fungemia seen in HIV-seropositive patients. These hyperresponsive PMNs may play a direct role in the rapidly progressive periodontal disease seen in HIV-seropositive patients, or may be a protective mechanism which compensates for other defects in the host immune response.

In summary, the importance of diagnosing HIV-G and HIV-P is twofold. First, this lesion may represent one of the first signs of HIV infection and consequently aid in the identification of HIV-seropositive individuals. HIV-G seems to be a fairly early disease manifestation of HIV infection, appearing before many other intraoral and extraoral HIV manifestations. In addition, the data presented here suggest that HIV-G is frequently seen before a dramatic decrease in T4 cell number occurs, as evidenced by relatively normal T4/T8 ratios. HIV-P seems to occur later because it is more frequently associated with other intraoral and extraoral manifestations and significantly decreased T4/T8 ratios. Secondly, HIV-P is a rapidly progressive, painful, and locally destructive disease. Conventional treatment has proven to have only limited success in controlling this lesion. On the other hand, proper diagnosis and the concomitant appropriate therapy has been shown to be highly effective in controlling HIV-G and HIV-P. Therefore, the early identification of HIV-associated lesions, including HIV-G and HIV-P, is a particularly important role for the dental professional.

REFERENCES

1. Gottlieb MS, Schroff R, Sehanker HM, et al: *Pneumocystis carinii* pneumonia and mucosal candidiasis in previously healthy homosexual men. *N Engl J Med* 1981;305:1425-1431.

68

2. Masur H, Michelis MA, Greene JB, et al: An outbreak of community-acquired *Pneumocystis carinii* pneumonia: Initial manifestation of cellular immune dysfunction. *N Engl J Med* 1981;305:1431-1438.
3. Mildvan D, Mathur U, Enlwo RW, et al: Opportunistic infections and immune deficiency in homosexual men. *Ann Intern Med* 1982;96:700-704.
4. Weiss SH, Goedert JJ, Sarngadharan MG, et al: Screening test for HTLV-III (AIDS agent) antibodies: Specificity, sensitivity and applications. *JAMA* 1985;253:221-225.
5. Esteban JI, Tai CC, Kay JWD, et al: Importance of Western blot analysis in predicting infectivity of anti-HTLV/LAV-positive blood. *Lancet* 1985;2:1083-1086.
6. Klein RS, Harris CA, Small CB, et al: Oral candidiasis in high-risk patients as the initial manifestation of the acquired immunodeficiency syndrome. *N Engl J Med* 1984;311:354-358.
7. Greenspan D, Greenspan JS, Hearst N, et al: Oral "hairy" leukoplakia — AIDS retrovirus status and risk of development of AIDS. *J Infect Dis* 1987;155:475-481.
8. Winkler JR, Murray PA: Periodontal disease — A potential intraoral expression of AIDS may be a rapidly progressive periodontitis. *Calif Dent Assoc J* 1987;15:20-24.
9. Silverman S Jr, Migliorati CA, Lozada-Nur F, et al: Oral findings in people with or at high risk for AIDS: A study of 375 homosexual males. *J Am Dent Assoc* 1986;112:187-192.
10. Revision of the CDC surveillance case definition for acquired immunodeficiency syndrome. *MMWR* 1987;36:1s-15s.
11. Silness J, Löe H: Periodontal disease in pregnancy. II Correlation between oral hygiene and periodontal conditions. *Acta Odontol Scand* 1964;22:112-135.
12. Löe H, Silness J: Periodontal disease in pregnancy. I. Prevalence and severity. *Acta Odontol Scand* 1963;21:533-551.
13. Engvall E, Perlmann P: Enzyme linked immunosorbent assay, ELISA. III. Quantitation of specific antibodies by enzyme labelled anti-immunoglobulin in antigen-coated tubes. *J Immunol* 1972;109:129-135.
14. Löe H, Theilade E, Jensen SB: Experimental gingivitis in man. *J Periodontol* 1965;36:177-178.
15. Barnes GP, Bowles WF, Carter HG: Acute necrotizing ulcerative gingivitis: A survey of 218 cases. *J Periodontol* 1973;44:35-42.
16. Johnson BD, Engel D: Acute necrotizing ulcerative gingivitis: A review of diagnosis, etiology, and treatment. *J Periodontol* 1986;57:141-150.
17. Pindborg JJ: Gingivitis in military personnel with special reference to ulceromembranous gingivitis. *Odontologisk Tidskrift* 1951;59:407.
18. Johnson BD, Engel D: Acute necrotizing ulcerative gingivitis: A review of diagnosis, etiology, and treatment. *J Periodontol* 1986;57:141-150.

19. Slots J, Genco RJ: Black-pigmented *Bacteroides* species, *Capnocytophaga* species, and *Actinobacillus actinomycetemcomitans* in human periodontal disease: Virulence factors in colonization, survival, and tissue destruction. *J Dent Res* 1984;63:412-421.

20. Genco RJ, Slots J: Host responses in periodontal diseases. *J Dent Res* 1984;63:441-451.

21. Taubman MA, Yoshie H, Ebersole JL, et al: Host response in experimental periodontal disease. *J Dent Res* 1984;63:455-460.

22. Loesche WJ, Syed SA, Laughon BE, et al: The bacteriology of acute necrotizing ulcerative gingivitis. *J Periodontol* 1982;53:223-230.

23. Pape JW, Liautaud B, Thomas F, et al: Characteristics of the acquired immunodeficiency syndrome (AIDS) in Haiti. *N Engl J Med* 1983;309:945-950.

24. Jaffe HW, Bergman DJ, Selik RM: Acquired immunodeficiency syndrome in the United States: The first 1,000 cases. *J Infect Dis* 1983;148:339-345.

25. Haverkos HW, Drotman DP: Prevalence of Kaposi's sarcoma among patients with AIDS. *N Engl J Med* 1985;313:1518.

26. Peterman TA, Jaffe HW, Rerorino PM, et al: Transfusion-associated acquired immunodeficiency syndrome in the United States. *JAMA* 1985;254:2913-2917.

27. Eyxter ME, Goedert JJ, Sarngadharan MG, et al: Development and early natural history of HTLV-III antibodies in persons with hemophilia. *JAMA* 1985;253:2219-2223.

28. Goeder JJ, Biggar RJ, Weiss SH, et al: Three-year incidence of AIDS in five cohorts of HTLV-III-infected risk group members. *Science* 1986;231:992-995.

29. Klatzman D, Barre-Sinoussi F, Nugeyre MT, et al: Selective tropism for the helper inducer T lymphocyte subset of a new human retrovirus (LAV) associated with the acquired immunodeficiency syndrome. *Science* 1984;225:59-63.

30. Palacios R, Martinez-Maza O: IFN-gamma-mediated suppression of Epstein-Barr-virus-induced activation of B lymphocytes by OKT4+ lymphocytes. *Interleukins Lymphocytes Cytokines* 1983;1:375-380.

31. Tew JG, Marshall DR, Moore WC, et al: Serum antibody reactive with predominant organisms in the subgingival flora of young adults with generalized severe periodontitis. *Infect Immun* 1985;48:303-311.

32. Ebersole JL, Taubman MA, Smith DJ, Frey DE: Human immune response to oral microorganisms: Patterns of systemic antibody levels to *Bacteroides* species. *Infect Immun* 1985;51:507-513.

33. Tempel TR, Kimball HR, Kakehashi J, et al: Host factors in periodontal disease: Periodontal manifestations of Chediak-Higashi syndrome. *J Periodont Res* 1972;7(Suppl10):26-27.

34. Rabson AR, Anderson R, Glover A: Defective neutrophil motility and recurrent infection. In vitro and in vivo effects of levamisole. *Clin Exp Immunol* 1978;33:142-149.

70

35. Dunn PA, Tyrer HW: Quantitation of neutrophil phagocytosis using fluorescent latex beads. *J Lab Clin Med* 1981;98:374-381.
36. Bass DA, Parce JE, Dechatelet LR, et al: Flow cytometric studies of oxidative product formation by neutrophils: A graded response to membrane stimulation. *J Immunol* 1983;130:1910-1917.
37. Nagel JE, Han K, Coon PJ, et al: Age difference in phagocytosis by polymorphonuclear leukocytes measured by flow cytometry. *J Leukocyte Biol* 1986;39:399-407.
38. Ryder MI, Winkler JR, Weintrub PS: Elevated phagocytosis, oxidative burst, and F-actin formation in PMNs from individuals with intraoral manifestations of HIV-infection. *J AIDS,* submitted for publication.
39. Walker SM, Urbianka SJ: A serum-dependent defect of neutrophil function in chronic mucocutaneous candidiasis. *J Clin Pathol* 1980;33:370-372.
40. Bass DA, Olbrantz P, Szejda P, et al: Subpopulations of neutrophils with increased oxidative product formation in blood of patients with infection. *J Immunol* 1986;136:860-866.
41. Hill HR, Gerrard JM, Hogan NA, et al: Hyperactivity of neutrophil leukotactic responses during active bacterial infection. *J Clin Invest* 1974;53:996-1001.
42. Poli G, Foppa CU, Cinque P, et al: Mononuclear and polymorphonuclear phagocyte functions in AIDS and prodromal syndrome. *International Conference on AIDS,* Paris, June 23-25, 1986, p 86, poster 341.
43. Sumersgill JT, Johnson JD: Enhanced phagocytosis in patients with acquired immunodeficiency syndrome. *International Conference on AIDS,* Paris, June 23-25, 1986, p 87, poster 342.
44. Martin LS: Assessment of monocyte and polymorphonuclear leucocyte chemotaxis and oxidative metabolism following incubation with HTLV-III/LAV. *International Conference on AIDS,* Paris, June 23-25, 1986, p 87, poster 343.

Dr John Greenspan introduced the Session I speakers and welcomed additional members to the panel:

Dr Philip Fox, Clinical Investigation and Patient Care Branch, National Institute of Dental Research

Dr Sandra Melnick, Department of Dental Public Health, Seattle, Washington

Dr Sol Silverman, University of California, San Francisco

Dr Frank Lucatorto, University of California, Los Angeles

Dr Penny Leggott, University of California, San Francisco

Dr Peter Reichart discussed oral Kaposi's sarcoma. About 21 cases of Kaposi's sarcoma have been observed in Berlin, 18 of which showed oral involvement. Most of these lesions appeared in the palate and were located at sites where the palatal artery leaves the palatal bone. Most of the lesions were seen in homosexual men. Dr Reichart showed slides of "nonblue" Kaposi's sarcoma and observed that these lesions clinically resembled lymphoma. Slides of Kaposi's sarcoma affecting the gingiva showed extensive destruction of alveolar bone and displacement of the teeth.

Dr Lucatorto noted that macular, papular and nodular forms of Kaposi's sarcoma had been seen in patients at UCLA. In addition, a number of ulcerative lesions had been observed. He described a lymphoma of the mucobuccal fold as an example of areas of ulceration that form as small, innocuous lesions and rapidly progress within several weeks to reach 2.5 to 3.0 centimeters in diameter. Herpetic lesions are also a major problem in HIV-infected patients. In many cases, herpetic lesions do not present as typical vascularlike lesions, but become large and erosive.

Dr Silverman agreed that many HIV-infected patients showed "old" lesions with greater severity and frequency than immunocompetent patients. Moreover, there were a number of "new" lesions seen in HIV-infected patients. This new test of oral pathology puts an additional burden on the dental profession to take a prominent role in the diagnosis and management of HIV infection. Dr Silverman stressed the importance of diagnosis, particularly of secondary infections by organisms not normally seen in the oral cavity. He noted that approximately 10% of UCSF patients complain of xerostomia resulting from either the disease process or related medications. He described a number of HIV-infected patients who presented with lichenoid lesions in the mouth. Often, these patients had corresponding skin lesions consistent with erythema multiforme. He pointed out that 30% to 40% of individuals initially infected with HIV have central nervous system infection and these patients have reduced levels of adrenal cortex cortisol. Dr Silverman noted that Kaposi's sarcoma remained a major problem for HIV-infected patients. Over 50% of those with skin lesions have oral manifestations and about 10% have only oral lesions. He referred to the periodontal implications of HIV infection, and suggested that carefully conducted epidemiological studies be performed to assess the importance of HIV-associated gingivitis and periodontitis.

Dr Stanley Holt observed that microorganisms that may be important in HIV-associated periodontal disease included species of *Wolinella* and *Eikenella*. These organisms are producers of very high levels of cytokines responsible for inflammation. He also noted that when his group examined the lipopolysaccharides of the members of the genus *Wolinella*, they found that they produced interleukin-1 at the highest levels of any gramnegative microorganisms investigated to date; *Wolinella* and *Eikenella* also appear to make very high levels of tumor necrosis factor, a very strong correlate of inflammatory conditions. Dr Holt asked Dr James Winkler to comment on what role these microorganisms might play in the PMN hyperresponses his research has uncovered.

Dr Winkler noted that there was very little research done on the effect of these two organisms on PMN function. He noted that other organisms, such as *Candida albicans* and many of the *Streptococcus* species, are important organisms in the priming phenomenon that has been seen in diseases other than periodontal disease, and that *Wolinella* and *Eikenella* may be involved in this activation, or priming concept, as well.

Dr Mark Schubert posed a question to the panel on expression of hairy leukoplakia in the drug-using population. Since Epstein-Barr virus (EBV) is more common in lower socioeconomic groups than in higher socioeconomic groups, he asked why practitioners or researchers were not seeing more hairy leukoplakia in the drug-using population.

Dr Deborah Greenspan stated that the relationship of development of hairy leukoplakia to the time since seroconversion is still not well understood, and that because of the small IV drug-using population in San Francisco, her experience is very limited. She noted that the UCSF group had found that EBV infection ranged across the whole spectrum of socioeconomic and racial groups and that the prevalence of EBV infection in HIV positive populations was similar to that in the non-HIV-infected gay population and only slightly higher than in the heterosexual population. She felt that the occurrence of hairy leukoplakia might be more highly correlated with time since seroconversion than with prior exposure to EBV.

Dr Morton Schiødt posed a question concerning the classification of candidiasis in relation to hairy leukoplakia. In order to promote a classification system that would be useful for the future comparison of prevalences in different studies, he asked the panel whether they would classify a candidiasis superimposed on hairy leukoplakia as a pseudomembranous candidiasis or erythematous candidiasis.

Dr Jens Pindborg responded that in Copenhagen they had done 80 biopsies of hairy leukoplakia, and that they showed an enormous amount of hyphae when stained with periodic acid-Schiff stain.

Dr Pindborg was not sure whether this is a superimposed infection. He stated that in order to keep the classifications clear, hairy leukoplakia should be treated as a separate phenomenon.

Dr Deborah Greenspan agreed with this statement. She stated that she would like to see it classified as hairy leukoplakia with or without *Candida*, particularly in light of the fact that if treated with antifungal medication, the lesion itself rarely responds.

Dr Silverman and Dr Lucatorto both agreed that what is classified as hairy leukoplakia never disappears with treatment of antifungal medications.

Dr Philip Fox discussed the work his group has done with salivary functions and fungal forms in the oral cavity. He stated that although HIV has been isolated in saliva, he thought it should be noted that the virus has yet to be demonstrated in gland saliva. He stated that research into the presence of HIV in saliva had been done with whole saliva, and that whole saliva contained more bronchial and bacterial secretions and more blood than gland saliva. He stated that his group had been unable to identify the presence of HIV in the gland secretions of seven patients. Dr Fox outlined work that is being done on parotid and submandibular secretions in collaboration with Dr Chih-Ko Yeh. This study found no change in unstimulated secretions but a significant decline in stimulated secretions, the opposite of what is usually found in autoimmune conditions. He stated that the saliva chemistries of these patients showed no elevations in their electrolytes, but there was detectable albumen in their secretions. He felt this demonstrated that there was not a great deal of serum contamination in inflamed glands. In the fungal studies being conducted at NIH, he noted that as many as 75% of the AIDS patients had cytopathological abnormalities that included the presence of hyphae, hyperkeratosis, and epithelial abnormalities, signaling manifestations of HIV infections that are unique from other types of infections.

Dr John Greenspan noted that his group has been able to culture HIV from both cells and cell-free duct saliva.

Dr Chrispian Scully asked if the panel would comment on squamous carcinoma and comment on the oral manifestations of AIDS in pediatric cases. He asked if anyone could define what type of transmission was responsible, perinatal or intrauterine.

Dr Penny Leggott responded to the question concerning the oral manifestations of pediatric AIDS. She stated that the majority of cases were through transmission directly in utero from mother to child. She stated that as with adult AIDS, oral candidiasis is the most common feature of pediatric AIDS. Her group and Dr Gwen Scott's group in Florida have seen pediatric manifestations of HIV-associated gingivitis (interestingly the conditions did not progress over a period of two years), herpes simplex, herpes zoster, and a number of cases of parotid enlargement. She noted that there are no cases of pediatric Kaposi's sarcoma, and that HIV-associated periodontal disease is also not seen. She also stated that they had found no cases of pediatric neoplasms, and that an interesting question was one of a possible dysmorphic syndrome. She stated that Dr Rubenstein of New York had a hypothesis that children infected in utero present with a very characteristic dysmorphic syndrome.

Dr Robert Klein commented on the issue of perinatal versus transplacental transmission of pediatric AIDS. Dr Klein stated that it is virtually impossible to separate exposure at the time of delivery from intrauterine exposure, and that to date, there are no definitive answers. He stated that until a study is conducted where uninfected babies in utero are identified, and the method of delivery is compared (Cesarean section v vaginal), a definitive answer as to how and at what point in time HIV is transmitted would not be forthcoming.

Dr Silverman then responded to the portion of Dr Scully's question dealing with squamous carcinoma. He stated that carcinomas in general are the third most common malignancy seen in individuals infected with the AIDS virus. His group has seen ten individuals with squamous carcinoma; the point of interest was that the mean age was 32 years, whereas before the advent of AIDS, the mean age of individuals presenting with oral cancers was more likely to be near 60 years. He stated that there is some evidence that hairy leukoplakia is a mature keratin, so the assumption that carcinoma is not related to hairy leukoplakia should not be made. He also stated that it is unclear whether oral cancer is positively correlated with the presence of *Candida*.

Dr Pindborg also commented on squamous cell carcinomas. He stated that if there was a correlation between squamous cell carcinoma and hairy leukoplakia, one would expect to see cases of epithelial dysplasia appear in a biopsy. He stated that in the 80 biopsies his group had done, they had not seen a single case of epithelial dysplasia. He related a case where Dr O'Malley of Eastman Dental Hospital in London had a young man with hairy leukoplakia who developed squamous cell carcinoma in the same area; this would be the first example of an association.

Dr Deborah Greenspan stated that she had one patient that she had biopsied over four years, and that the last biopsy of his hairy leukoplakia showed epithelial dysplasia.

Dr John Greenspan commented that to substantiate claims concerning the coexistence of hairy leukoplakia and squamous cell carcinoma, or claims of the development of squamous cell carcinoma in hairy leukoplakia, one must confirm that the hairy leukoplakia contains EBV and is true nairy leukoplakia. He also expressed an opinion that the HIV-positive population had matured to the point where we may begin to establish links between oral cancers and nonlymphoma malignancy with HIV-induced immunosuppression.

Dr Klein commented that findings of squamous cell carcinoma in homosexual men and initial associations of papilloma virus and hairy leukoplakia had prompted his group to study papilloma virus in HIV-positive women. He stated that by doing

Pap smears on HIV-positive women who are sexual partners of HIV-positive men, and HIV-negative women who are sexual partners of HIV-positive men, they found there is a very strong correlation between squamous abnormalities as high as grade 3 cervical intraepithelial neoplasia with HIV positivity, but that the numbers are still small. He stated that the preliminary conclusions are that the rapidity of the changes and the aggressiveness of the neoplasia are much greater in the HIV-positive women, and that this is not totally explicable by sexual history differences.

Dr John Greenspan noted that the papilloma virus, both as the cause of warts and as an oncogenic agent, will be an area for more investigations in the future.

Dr Robert Koch of the US Navy posed a question to the panel concerning whether there was a positive correlation in the advancement of HIV-related diseases in those patients who were also hepatitis B–positive.

Dr Klein replied with an anecdotal story concerning the group of patients they have been tracking. It appears that one patient has not progressed to AIDS in the five years since the initial discovery of oral candidiasis, and that he is surface-antigen–positive for hepatitis B and a chronic active hepatitis carrier. There may be a correlation here, but there is no hard data.

Dr John Greenspan closed the session by thanking the panel for sharing their comments and unpublished work with everyone, and by thanking the audience for their participation.

6

Dental Management of HIV-Associated Oral Mucosal Lesions: Current and Experimental Techniques

Charles E. Barr

Reports indicate that oral manifestations of HIV-positive associated diseases occur in over 70% of those infected with the virus. The dentist has become not only a diagnostician of oral diseases associated with HIV infectivity but frequently assumes primary responsibility for prescribing treatment for the oral diseases. Bacterial, fungal, viral, neoplastic and certain nonspecific lesions are documented as occurring in the mouth. Various treatment modalities are available to the dentist, frequently in conjunction with the physician, to eliminate oral diseases completely or reduce them significantly. In this section major emphasis has been placed on current treatment of the most commonly encountered oral mucosal lesions such as candidiasis, herpes, oral hairy leukoplakia, human papilloma virus and Kaposi's sarcoma. The currently accepted treatment for important systemic opportunistic infections which are reported as presenting with oral lesions, are also mentioned, although the dentist will not be the primary therapist. In addition, some investigational treatment modalities are provided as an update.

The dentist has an important role in the management of oral mucosal lesions in HIV-positive patients. It has been reported that as many as 70% of all AIDS and ARC patients display some form of oral manifestations.[1-3] Therefore, therapeutic intervention in numerous instances is required. While emphasis will be placed on the oral aspects of management of these lesions, there are many instances where the treatment must be broader in scope and the dentist's role may be tangential because the disease is manifested both orally and systemically. In time, as the disease continues its inexorable path, reports of new manifestations will likely be forthcoming so that the dentist not only must be able to diagnose them, but should be updated continuously to the best therapeutic regimen to employ for each condition.

An appropriate practice to follow in treating a known HIV-positive patient who is on the spectrum from clinically asymptomatic to having extensive manifestations of AIDS is to consult with the patient's physician. In the best interest of good patient care, as well as to insure that no harm is done, the dentist should be fully aware of the patient's overall health status.

Clearly, an accurate diagnosis is critical to appropriate patient care. The determination of the cause of oral mucosal lesions in the HIV-positive or, for that matter, any patient depends on gathering of information, its synthesis, and the knowledge of what drugs or procedures are available to treat the disease properly. It is important that once a diagnosis is made and therapy for the lesion determined by the dentist, the course of treatment ought to be carried out with the full knowledge of the physician who is responsible for the patient's overall medical care.

ORAL FUNGAL INFECTIONS

The predominant oral manifestation of mycoses is due to the fungus *Candida albicans*. Though an opportunistic infection, its presence has been shown to bear no relationship to the appearance of other opportunistic diseases such as *Pneumocystis carinii* pneumonia and Kaposi's sarcoma, nor does its presence appear to be related to the degree of immunosuppression of the host. Some individuals with high levels of immunosuppression do not exhibit oral lesions while others with less immunosuppression may exhibit persistent, recurrent oral *C albicans*. There are generally two forms of the disease manifested orally: curdlike or pseudomembranous; and smooth-surfaced and erythematous or atrophic.[4] Irrespective of the type, the treatment is essentially the same, although there are several choices (Table 6-1). Nystatin, a frequently used antifungal agent, has the chemical structure of a large lactone ring, double bonds and amino sugars. It binds to sterols in the fungus membrane and

Table 6-1
Oral Fungal Infections

Fungus/Disease	Current Therapy	Experimental Therapy
Candida albicans	Nystatin, clotrimazole, ketoconazole, amphotericin B	Chlorhexidine
Cryptococcosis*	Amphotericin B with ketoconazole	
Geotrichosis*	Amphotericin B with flucytosine, ketoconazole	
Histoplasmosis*	Amphotericin B with flucytosine, ketoconazole	

*Disseminated disease with oral manifestations

causes changes in cell wall permeability. Nystatin usually requires several weeks for satisfactory results. It is usually prescribed as an oral rinse or as troches (pastilles). Clotrimazole is a synthetic substance that also acts on the fungus to increase cell membrane permeability.[5] It is of the imidazole group. Prescribed as troches, it may be more effective than nystatin rinses because there is longer contact of the medication with the mucosal lesion.

Ketoconazole is a synthetic imidazole similar to clotrimazole. It inhibits the synthesis of ergosterol and, like the other antifungal agents, alters cell membrane permeability.[6] It is frequently prescribed for highly resistant chronic mucocutaneous candidiasis; however, it may be used as well for lesions that are oral only. Ketoconazole is detoxified in the liver and prolonged use may cause liver damage as evidenced by elevated liver enzymes. Use must be carefully monitored, especially in patients with a history of hepatitis or alcoholism.[7] The use of topical antifungal agents may be beneficial along with systemic ketoconazole.

In cases of severe disseminated chronic mucocutaneous candidiasis involving the oral cavity, intravenous amphotericin B may be administered. The relapse rate is high when the drug is stopped, but prolonged administration can cause serious side effects (acute febrile reaction, anaphylaxis with symptoms of wheezing and dose-dependent azotemia and permanent renal damage, especially in patients with preexisting renal disease). These effects can also be caused by use of the drug in very high doses.[7]

In addition to *C albicans,* cases of oral histoplasmosis, geotrichosis and recently of *Cryptococcus neoformans* have been reported.[4,8,9] These diseases are treated systemically with amphotericin B in combination with oral flucytosine (5-fluorocytosine) which is incorporated into fungal RNA and inhibits protein synthesis. The second treatment of choice for these fungal diseases is oral ketoconazole.[7]

Experimental Antifungal Agents

There appears to be minimal investigational activity on a clinical level in regard to newer therapy for the treatment of *C albicans.* However, chlorhexidine 0.12% has been administered in limited clinical studies for prophylaxis against microbial infections as well as for treating mucositis in bone marrow transplant immunocompromised patients. The drug was effective in controlling *C albicans* in these patients as well as preventing rebound.[10,11] Additionally, in vitro studies have shown low-dosage chlorhexidine to reduce, and in some cases completely inhibit, fungal growth.[11] Although chlorhexidine has not yet been appropriately investigated for efficacy against candidiasis in HIV-positive patients, clinical trials to test its merit appear worth conducting.

ORAL BACTERIAL INFECTIONS

Case reports of oral lesions in AIDS patients have been noted with the opportunistic infections associated with *Enterobacter,*[4] *Klebsiella,*[4] and *Mycobacterium avium intracellulare.*[4,12] The treatment of these diseases is systemic rather than local so the management of related oral lesions will not be addressed separately. *Enterobacter* is treated systemically with an aminoglycoside; usually gentamycin is the drug of first choice (Table 6-2). *Klebsiella* is also treated with an aminoglycoside, frequently in combination with a tetracycline. *M avium intracellulare* is a very difficult infection to treat and no therapy is highly effective. It requires multiple drugs that are difficult to administer in order to achieve even a 60% success rate. An aminoglycoside (streptomycin) plus isoniazide, ethambutol, ethionamide, pyrazinamide and cycloserine with refampin is a typical combination.[12] Aminoglycosides can cause eighth nerve damage, both vestibular and cochlear. Occasionally, they exhibit

Table 6-2
Oral Bacterial Infections

Bacterium/Disease	Current Therapy	Experimental Therapy
*Enterobacter**	Aminoglycosides	Quinolone derivatives
*Klebsiella**	Aminoglycosides and tetracycline	Quinolone derivatives
*Mycobacterium avium intra- cellulare**	Aminoglycosides combined with several other drugs	Quinolone derivatives
Periodontitis†		

* Disseminated disease with oral manifestations
† Addressed in chapter 9

nephrotoxicity as well, which is usually dose related and more common in the elderly with previous renal impairment. They are poorly absorbed from the gastrointestinal tract and thus are not given by mouth.[13]

Experimental Antibacterial Agents

The use of synthetic quinolone derivatives, such as ciprofloxacin and norfloxacin, bacterial DNA gyrase inhibitors, are being investigated for use in serious bacterial infections. When bacteria divide, their DNA is normally uncoiled and copied. Gyrase is necessary for proper coiling of the newly made DNA and quinolones prevent gyrase activity, thus killing the bacteria.[14]

ORAL VIRAL INFECTIONS

Cytomegalovirus (CMV)

Kanas and coworkers have reported a case of oral mucosal cytomegalovirus.[15] Also Barr has observed one unreported case of a CMV tongue lesion. Treatment involved use of acyclovir (Table 6-3), and its mechanism of action will be noted later in this section.

Herpes Simplex Virus (HSV)

Standard therapies for HSV oral and labial lesions have been vidarabine and acyclovir.[16] However, the effect of acyclovir

82

Table 6-3
Oral Viral Infections

Virus/Disease	Current Therapy	Experimental Therapy
Cytomegalovirus	Acyclovir	DHPG
Herpes simplex virus	Acyclovir, vidarabine	BVDU, FIAC, PFA, ribavirin
Herpes zoster virus	Acyclovir	BVDU, FIAC, PFA, ribavirin
Human papilloma virus	Cryotherapy, electro-coagulation, surgery	Interferons
Oral hairy leukoplakia	Acyclovir, antifungal agents	DHPG, A515U
Varicella zoster virus	Acyclovir	BVDU, FIAC, PFA

is much greater than that of vidarabine, and it is the drug of choice in AIDS-associated oral and labial herpes simplex. Depending on the extent of the disease and location, one may use systemic acyclovir or locally applied acyclovir ointment. The drug has the effect of reducing viral shedding, crusting time and pain. Drug activity occurs when virus-coded thymidine kinase converts the monophosphated acyclovir to triphosphate which then inhibits DNA replication within the fungus.[16] Acyclovir when used for mucosal herpes infection may be prescribed as either tablets by mouth or a locally applied ointment — or both.

Herpes Zoster Virus

This frequently painful lesion is generally treated with acyclovir in high doses, requiring from 2400 mg to 3200 mg or more per day to effect a cure.[4] There are reports of varicella zostervirus causing oral manifestations of chicken pox, as well as the classic herpes zoster that affects the trigeminal nerve, noted in HIV-infected patients. These lesions may be treated with a regimen of oral acyclovir. However, parentral acyclovir has been used successfully where indicated and is effective in reducing the period of viral shedding, new lesion formation, pain, pustulation, crusting, and incidence of fever.[17] The systemic application may be coupled with topical acyclovir ointment.

Human Papillomavirus (HPV)

The presence of oral human papillomavirus has been frequently reported in HIV-positive patients.[4] HPV virions are non-enveloped particles with a molecular genome of double-stranded circular DNA. Of the many human types at least five have been identified as isolated in oral mucosal lesions: 2, 6, 11, 13, and 16.[18] Greenspan recently reported the presence of genotypes 7 and 32 in the mouth.[19]

Several treatment modalities have been used with HPV infection: caustic agents (podophyllin), antimetabolites (5-FU), cryotherapy, laser, surgical excision, immunotherapy and antiviral therapy.[20] Application of all of these to intraoral lesions is neither practical nor desirable. Specific current therapy for oral warts includes surgical excision either with conventional surgical procedures or by the use of cryotherapy (liquid nitrogen, solid carbon dioxide). Laser therapy has been used; however, it is presently being discouraged because in the process of removal, virions have been shown to be disseminated in aerosol and possibly cause new viral seeding. Electrocoagulation alone or the combination of weak caustics followed by curettage and fulguration of the base of the lesion is also an accepted therapeutic regimen.

Oral Hairy Leukoplakia

The lesion of oral hairy leukoplakia presents an important and sometimes difficult challenge to the dentist even after an accurate diagnosis has been confirmed. With the understanding that the lesion involves several infectious agents (Epstein Barr virus [EBV], HPV, fungi) either with primary or secondary involvements, it also follows that treatment should be directed toward multiple agents.

First, a confirming diagnosis of oral hairy leukoplakia should be made with a biopsy of the lesion for routine staining, followed if possible by staining for HPV antigen in the koilocytes.[21] Also the use of DNA in situ hybridization for EBV is a significant procedure to confirm the diagnosis of oral hairy leukoplakia. The HPV may be a facilitator for the EBV to enter the tissue as well as for the viability and growth of the virus once it is in place.[22] It is subsequent to the viral infection that the *Candida* probably manifests its presence in the lesion, yet

84

clinically oral hairy leukoplakia remains after the fungal infection has been resolved. It is also noteworthy that the lesion of oral hairy leukoplakia has been reported to exhibit signs of remission and exacerbation, though it is not clear if appropriate procedures had been performed to determine the actual immunochemical presence of HPV antigen and of EBV in these changing lesions.[23]

Treatment of oral hairy leukoplakia includes the use of antifungal agents such as nystatin and clotrimazole, but the major thrust of therapy should be directed in particular to the EBV. Therefore, primary therapy for oral hairy leukoplakia should include the use of acyclovir. Friedman-Kien has used 800 mg daily for up to 6 months to resolve the lesion and to prevent recurrence.[24]

The action of acyclovir against EBV as well as against CMV is different from its mechanism of action against HSV. In cells infected with EBV and CMV, acyclovir is not well phosphorylated since neither virus codes for its own thymidine kinase. However, once the acyclovir is phosphorylated to the triphosphate by cellular enzymes, the virus DNA polymerase becomes reactive to the medication.[16]

Experimental Antiviral Agents

Use of experimental drug action against CMV, a herpesvirus, will be addressed along with experimental drugs used in oral hairy leukoplakia since that oral mucosal disease involves EBV, also a herpesvirus.

There have been several clinical trials of newer compounds used against HSV, the herpes zoster virus and the varicella zoster virus.

BVDU, bromovinyldeoxyuridine, is an acyclovir analogue potent against HSV-1 and varicella zoster virus. In vitro it is more powerful than acyclovir against HSV-1 and 1000 times more against varicella zoster virus. In uncontrolled clinical trials oral BVDU was effective against mucocutaneous herpes simplex as well as herpes zoster in immunocompromised patients.[25,26] However, further controlled trials are necessary. FIAC, fluoriodoaracytosine, is a pyrimidine analogue that has been shown in vitro to have greater efficacy than acyclovir against HSV-1 and varicella zoster virus, but clinically controlled studies remain to be conducted.[27]

Trisodium phosphonoformate, foscarnet or PFA, has been shown to have in vitro and in vivo efficacy against the herpesviruses by inhibiting DNA polymerases. A preliminary clinical trial of the application of a 3% cream was effective against recurrent herpes labialis by shortening the vesicular period and decreasing formation of new vesicles. The drug is presently undergoing trials in AIDS patients.[28]

Ribavirin is a drug that exhibits broad antiviral activity against RNA and DNA viruses. It is a synthetic nucleoside applied locally, orally or by aerosol. It has been shown in one study that oral administration (800 mg/day) will reduce pain and accelerate healing in oral herpes. It may cause decreases in hemoglobin and hematocrit but the changes are reversible.[29]

An area of investigative activities related to the treatment of HPV involves the use of interferons. Interferon (INF), a glycoprotein, is a natural substance produced by many animal cells, including human, when stimulated by viral infection. It is essentially nontoxic to cells at low concentrations and nonspecifically inhibits intracellular replication of viruses after binding to the cell membrane and synthesizing new cellular RNA and proteins which mediate the antiviral effect. There are three principal INF's, IFN α (leukocyte), IFN β (fibroblast), and IFN γ (immune), plus subgroups.[30]

Several small studies and uncontrolled trials have been conducted using IFN to treat HPV. Intralesional injection of IFN has caused regression of HPV lesions and intramuscular IFN has also been reported in some cases to eliminate or at least reduce HPV lesions of the skin.[20,31] Studies with IFN α and IFN β used topically, intramuscularly and/or intralesionally are ongoing and provide conflicting results. While most lesions treated with IFNs regress or even disappear, they tend to recur. Recurrences appear more common in lesions that were not fully eliminated.[31]

The use of nonconventional treatments for oral hairy leukoplakia has been reported. Newman and Polk noted a serendipitous resolution of oral hairy leukoplakia with the use of DHPG (9-[1,3-dihydroxy-2-propoxymethyl]guanine) when treating CMV retinitis.[32] DHPG has been known to be effective not only against CMV but also against EBV although the exact mode of action is not clear. It has also inhibited replication of HSV-1 and -2 in vitro.[33] In this case, the oral hairy leukoplakia cleared in one week and the patient was placed on maintenance DHPG for the CMV retinitis. The oral hairy leukoplakia had not recurred. However DHPG is investigational so that careful monitoring is necessary. Also, in other clinical trials, when the drug was discontinued CMV infection returned in AIDS patients by 30 days after cessation of therapy.[34] The second report involves the use of A515U (6-deoxyacyclovir). It is well absorbed through oral administration. The advantage it has over acyclovir is that a high plasma concentration can be achieved by the oral route equal to that of intravenous acyclovir.[35] Greenspan reported that on a 250-mg dose of A515U three times daily for 14 days, all of seven patients exhibited either complete or almost complete resolution of oral hairy leukoplakia as confirmed by clinical photos and by biopsy. The investigator concluded that on a short term basis A515U was effective in curing oral hairy leukoplakia.[36] Studies to determine the degree of recurrence, if any, following discontinuation of A515U are clearly in order.

ORAL NEOPLASMS

Kaposi's sarcoma (KS), a form of angiosarcoma which has been reported to occur in a very large number of AIDS patients, appears to have an approximately four times higher prevalence in homosexual/bisexual HIV-positive individuals than in intravenous drug abusers also infected by the virus. Studies of various investigators in oral medicine have reported oral mucosal manifestations of KS in over 54% of those patients with a diagnosis of KS.[1-3] Usually the oral lesion is not treated as a separate entity unless it is of such proportions as to interfere with routine functions associated with eating and speaking (Table 6-4). The lesion may also be located in an area of the mouth where its overgrown nature causes an unpleasant cosmetic appearance. In these cases it is not unusual for the lesion to be treated separately. The dentist has a responsibility to insure that if chemotherapy and/or radiation therapy are to be used to treat the oral lesion, potential problems of infection are resolved prior to those definitive modes of therapy. Therapy for epidemic KS (AIDS) does not seem to have the same effective results as is the case in classic KS although it includes the same modalities.[37]

Conventional chemotherapy for KS, actinomycin D and vinblastine, as well as combination therapy with decarbazine, have

Table 6-4
Oral Neoplasms

Neoplastic Disease	Therapy
Kaposi's sarcoma	Chemotherapy, interferons, radiation, surgery
Lymphoma	Chemotherapy, radiation
Squamous cell carcinoma	Chemotherapy, radiation, surgery

not produced very successful results, and even experimental trials with combination chemotherapy have been less effective than desired. Therefore, it is generally accepted that definitive and predictable therapy for KS is not yet available, but radiation therapy and lasers for individual or multiple oral lesions have been applied successfully as palliation. IFNs may hold the greatest promise for a cure for KS and will be discussed with experimental therapy.[38]

Non-Hodgkin's lymphomas are the lymphomas most commonly associated with AIDS. Reports of the presence of this type of malignancy have been provided in several publications.[1-4] The dentist functions as a diagnostician rather than as a therapist for this malignancy. However, the dentist should also perform those procedures necessary to insure that treatment for the lymphoma will not cause oral problems that are generally associated with radiation therapy to the oral cavity and salivary glands or with systemic chemotherapy (eg, exacerbation of oral bacterial and viral infections, radiation caries, mucositis, and the sequelae that may occur as a result of these phenomena).

It is interesting to note that as early as 1982 oral squamous carcinomas were identified in several of the original nine men whom Lozada et al described in the first report in the dental literature of oral manifestations of AIDS.[39] This report is quite remarkable for the high prevalence of oral squamous carcinomas in such a young population and in fact one may question whether the presence of oral squamous carcinoma and AIDS has a direct association. Additionally, there is need to assess the possibility of EBV involvement since this herpesvirus is known to be closely identified with nasopharyngeal carcinoma and is usually at a higher level in male homosexuals than in the rest of the male population in the same age range.

Current treatment modalities for oral squamous carcinomas in AIDS patients are the same as for treatment of this malignancy in non-AIDS patients: surgery, radiation, and chemotherapy. The dentist is important to treatment in the pretherapeutic conditioning of the mouth by eliminating infection insofar as possible; during treatment, to resolve intraoral mucositis if it develops as well as to maintain a controlled oral microbiota to prevent sepsis and potential septicemia; and post-treatment, to restore function with prosthetic devices if required and/or to maintain the hard and soft oral tissues through regular recall visits for prevention of further oral disease. Chlorhexidine rinses are helpful in controlling the oral microbiota.[10,11]

IFNs have been used to improve natural killer cell activity and they appear less immunosuppressive than other cytotoxic agents. Recombinant leukocyte IFN A and IFN α2a have both been tried as cures for KS. Especially, IFN α2a has induced long-lasting tumor regression in patients with AIDS-associated KS.[38] Recently comparative trials have been conducted to evaluate therapeutic activity, toxicity, and development of opportunistic infections using IFN α2a alone and in combination with vinblastine. To date there are no differences in response, duration, and survival rate, but the "combination patients" exhibited more dose-limiting toxicity, neutropenia, and other constitutional symptoms.[40] Other approaches, such as the use of IFN α2a and interleukin 2, T-cell growth factor to restore lymphocyte ratios, have been introduced.[38] However, as long as immunoincompetence exists, no treatment to date appears to yield successful, long-term predictable results for KS.

MISCELLANEOUS ORAL MANIFESTATIONS

The presence of nonspecific oral mucosal lesions in HIV-positive patients has been reported.[1-4] Often they have been one-time observations or at best cross-sectional studies rather than longitudinal. The problems that appear to have a substantial effect on the oral tissues and that are still amenable to treatment by the dentist will be covered (Table 6-5).

Aphthouslike Ulcerations

It is difficult to confirm a direct relationship between the development of aphthouslike ulcerations of the mucosa and HIV positivity. An unpublished observation by Barr provides an

Table 6-5
Miscellaneous Oral Manifestations

Disease	Therapy
Aphthouslike ulcerations	Antibiotics (systemic, oral rinse), chlorhexidine, steroid rinse, topical steroid ointments
Mucositis	Antibiotics, antihistamines, chlorhexidine, steroid rinse, topical steroid ointments
Xerostomia	Fluoride gel, pilocarpine, saliva substitutes, sodium carboxymethylcellulose

interesting facet to the appearance of aphthouslike ulcerations (Dr C. E. Barr, unpublished data). He examined a 19-year-old homosexual male with a diagnosis of AIDS. The patient was hospitalized for *Pneumocystis carinii* pneumonia (PCP) and also presented with multiple oral ulcerations that appeared to be aphthae. The lesions were positive for *P carinii*. The patient was treated for the protozoal lung infection with trimethoprim-sulfamethoxazole and as the lung *P carinii* pneumonia improved, the oral aphthae also began to resolve. Shortly thereafter the patient developed a toxic reaction to the medication; it was discontinued and the oral lesions immediately returned. The patient was switched to pentamidine and the oral lesions began to resolve once more. Do some of the aphthouslike ulcerations represent autoinfection within the oral mucosa linked with decreased presence of Langerhans cells, as has been reported in oral mucosal tissues in AIDS?[41] Perhaps the protective capacity of secretory IgA in saliva is reduced, thus making the mucosal tissue more susceptible to disease. Also Reiter's syndrome and psoriasis have both been reported with some frequency in AIDS patients.[42] Both of these autoimmune diseases may manifest oral ulcerations which have been described as necrotic and/or aphthouslike. Clearly there is much to be assessed to determine the relationship, if any, between aphthouslike ulcerations and the immunoincompetent HIV-positive individual.

Treatment for "aphthous lesions" may involve two different approaches; there is the one conventional approach which includes the use of tetracyclines in oral suspension and the other conventional approach which is to use topical steroids. In the case of multiple disseminated oral lesions one may have the patient use dexamethasone elixir as a mouth rinse. A prudent approach to therapy is to establish a dialogue with the patient's physician and coordinate treatment since the lesion, as noted previously, may have a relationship to a general pathologic process in which the resolution of the oral problem is part of the resolution of a more generalized phenomenon.

Xerostomia

There may not be specific oral mucosal lesions associated with xerostomia but the effect of reduced saliva may produce oral problems that require dental resolution. Xerostomia has been reported by Silverman in 13% of 375 homosexual males either with or at high risk for AIDS. Sjögren's syndrome has been noted in HIV-positive patients and recently a report on sicca complex and infection with HIV was reported.[43] It appears that a relationship between HIV and dry mouth exists in some HIV-positive patients. In another study of AIDS patients with CMV infection of the parotid glands, results did not show any statistically significant decrease in parotid saliva flow rate.[44] However, some HIV-positive patients do have dry mouth. Therefore, if the dentist is faced with the problem of xerostomia, that practitioner should pursue further the cause as well as assume responsibility for treating the problem.

The current preventive and/or therapeutic regimes have included artificial saliva substitutes, sodium carboxymethylcellulose aqueous solution, and the use of various types of fluoride applications in custom-made trays to reduce coronal, cervical and root caries.[45-47]

Studies have been conducted at the National Institute for Dental Research involving the use of pilocarpine as a stimulant for saliva production.[48] The results have been promising and the method is probably no longer considered investigational. However, caution should be taken to be sure that the gland is not fibrosed to the point where there is little or no exocrine function available and also that it is used with caution in patients with bronchial asthma, bradycardia or hypertension.

Mucositis

Treatment depends on the causative agent, although recently the use of chlorhexidine rinses has been extremely beneficial in controlling this problem. Broad spectrum antibiotics such as tetracycline or penicillin have been used to prevent oral sepsis. The combination of Benadryl and Kaopectate is used as a coating in cases of mucositis, though its efficacy varies. Steroids in both the rinse and the ointment have also been applied to the oral mucosal surfaces to reduce pain and inflammation.

GENERAL DENTAL TREATMENT

The provision of routine dental care for the known HIV-positive individual is an important issue. Generally, there is no reason why an HIV-positive person who is essentially stable should not receive general dental services. As in any immuno-compromised person, the elimination of dental and oral infections as well as the use of prophylactic measures may be an important adjunct to the maintenance of oral health over an extended time period. Unless the person is extremely leukopenic, thrombocytopenic or in medical distress, usually he/she is able to sustain routine dental care including, if necessary, oral surgery. A regularly scheduled periodontal prophylaxis to eliminate plaque and calculus is a highly desirable service for the HIV-positive patient. In addition, the routine use of a daily antibacterial rinse such as chlorhexidine may be a valuable adjunct.

Clearly, the extent of restorative, periodontal, and surgical services depends on several factors related to the patient's disease state. Good judgment and prudent application of techniques are important in treating the HIV-positive patient just as they are in treating any other patient. There are no prescribed rules as to when or when not to treat. Each case must be assessed individually, but certainly there is an appropriate level of care for every patient.

CONCLUDING REMARKS

The determination of appropriate drug therapy for oral lesions demands an accurate diagnosis. This requires careful history taking, a thorough clinical examination, and often, laboratory analysis. Very frequently, a consultation with the physician managing the patient's general medical care, if there is a physician of record, is also appropriate. As more individuals become HIV positive, the likelihood of the dentist encountering oral mucosal lesions that are HIV related will become greater. However, not only will the dentist encounter and be required to treat the more common currently documented oral manifestations, but surely oral lesions from previously unreported origins will develop and the dentist will have to assume responsibility for diagnosing and often treating these lesions as well.

It is critical that the dentist develop understanding of the pharmacologic action of various groups of drugs. This is important not only to select the correct drugs for the specific lesions but also to understand the risks in their use, especially in the immunocompromised HIV-positive patient.

REFERENCES

1. Silverman S Jr, Migliorati CA, Lozada-Nur F, et al: Oral findings in people with or at high risk for AIDS: A study of 375 homosexual males. *J Am Dent Assoc* 1986;112:187-192.
2. Barr CE, Torosian JP: Oral manifestations in patients with AIDS or AIDS-related complex. *Lancet* 1986;2:288.
3. Barr CE, Torosian JP, Quinones-Whitmore GD: Oral manifestations of AIDS: The dentist's responsibility in diagnosis and treatment. *Quintess Int* 1986;17:711-717.
4. Schiødt M, Pindborg JJ: AIDS and the oral cavity. Epidemiology and clinical oral manifestations of human immune deficiency virus infection: A review. *Int J Oral Maxillofac Surg* 1987;16:1-14.
5. Beggs WH, Andrews FA, Sarosi GA: Action of imidazole-containing antifungal drugs. *Life Sci* 1981;28:111-118.
6. Montgomery EH: Antifungal and antiviral agents, in Neidle EA, Schroeder DC, Yagiela JA (eds): *Pharmacology and Therapeutics for Dentistry,* ed 2. St Louis, CV Mosby, 1985, pp 586-592.
7. Antifungal agents for systemic mycoses, in Lampe KF: *Drug Evaluations,* ed 6. Chicago, American Medical Association, 1986, pp 1553-1563.
8. Glick M, Cohen SG, Cheney RT, et al: Oral manifestations of disseminated *Cryptococcus neoformans* in a patient with acquired immunodeficiency syndrome. *Oral Surg* 1987;64:454-459.
9. Lynch DP, Naftolin LZ: Oral *Cryptococcus neoformans* infection in AIDS. *Oral Surg* 1987;64:449-453.
10. Ferretti GA, Hansen IA, Whittenburg K, et al: Therapeutic use of chlorhexidine in bone marrow transplant patients: Case studies. *Oral Surg* 1987;63:683-687.

11. Ferretti GA, Ash RC, Brown AT, et al: Chlorhexidine for prophylaxis against oral infections and associated complications in patients receiving bone marrow transplants. *J Am Dent Assoc* 1987;114:461-467.

12. Volpe F, Schwimmer AM, Barr CE: Oral manifestations of disseminated *Mycobacterium avium intracellulare* in a patient with AIDS. *Oral Surg* 1985;60:567-570.

13. Aminoglycosides, in Lampe KF: *Drug Evaluations,* ed 6. Chicago, American Medical Association, 1986, pp 1425-1449.

14. Wolfson JS, Hooper DC: Fluoroquinolones: Structures, mechanisms of action and resistance, and spectra of activity in vitro. *Antimicrob Agents Chemother* 1985;28:581-586.

15. Kanas RJ, Jensen JL, Abrams AM: Oral mucosal cytomegalovirus as a manifestation of the acquired immune deficiency syndrome. *Oral Surg* 1987;64:183-189.

16. Antiviral Agents, in Lampe KF: *Drug Evaluations,* ed 6. Chicago, American Medical Association, 1986, pp 1615-1631.

17. Shepp DH, Dandliker PS, Meyers JD: Treatment of varicella-zoster virus infection in severely immunocompromised patients: Randomized comparison of acyclovir and vidarabine. *N Engl J Med* 1986;314:208-212.

18. Kutcher M, Naghashfar Z, Sawada E, et al: Papilloma virus lesions of the mouth: Genotypes and malignant potential. *J Dent Res* 1987;66:183 (abstr #615).

19. Greenspan D: Unpublished data presented at Perspectives on Oral Manifestations of AIDS: Diagnosis and Management of HIV-Associated Infections, San Diego, January 16-17, 1988.

20. Quinn TC, Horn JE: Viral STDs: Herpes simplex and human papillomavirus. *Md State Med J* 1987;36:64-72.

21. Schiødt M, Greenspan D, Daniels TE, et al: Clinical and histologic spectrum of oral hairy leukoplakia. *Oral Surg* 1987;64:716-720.

22. Greenspan JS, Greenspan D, Lennette ET, et al: Replication of Epstein-Barr virus within the epithelial cells of oral "hairy" leukoplakia: An AIDS associated lesion. *N Engl J Med* 1985;313:1564-1571.

23. Lupton GP, James WD, Redfield RR, et al: Oral hairy leukoplakia: A distinctive marker of human T-cell lymphotropic virus type III (HTLV-III) infection. *Arch Dermatol* 1987;123:624-628.

24. Friedman-Kien AE: Viral origin of hairy leukoplakia. *Lancet* 1986;2:694-695.

25. DeClercq E, Descampo J, Verhelst G, et al: Comparative efficacy of antiherpes drugs against different strains of herpes simplex virus. *J Infect Dis* 1980;141:563-574.

26. Mayo ER: Differentiation of herpes simplex virus types 1 and 2 by sensitivity to (E)-5-(2-bromovinyl)-2-deoxyuridine. *J Clin Microbiol* 1982;15:733-736.

27. Young CW, Schneider R, Leyland-Jones B, et al: Phase 1 evaluation of 2'-fluoro-5-iodo-1-ß-D arabinofuranosylcytosine in immunosuppressed patients with herpesvirus infection. *Cancer Res* 1983;43:5006-5009.

28. Helgstrand E, Eriksson B, Johansson NG: Trisodium phosphono-formate, a new antiviral compound. *Science* 1978;201:819-821.
29. Bierman SM, Kirkpatrick W, Fernandez H: Clinical efficacy of rib-avirin in the treatment of genital herpes simplex virus infection. *Chemotherapy* 1981;27:139-145.
30. Preble OT, Friedman RM: Interferon induced alterations in cells: Relevance to viral and nonviral diseases. *Lab Invest* 1983; 49:4-18.
31. Weck PK, Brandsma JL, Whisnant JK: Interferons in the treat-ment of human papillomavirus diseases. *Cancer Metastasis Rev* 1986;5:139-165.
32. Newman C, Polk BF: Resolution of oral hairy leukoplakia during therapy with 9-(1,3-dihydroxy-2-propoxymethyl)guanine (DHPG). *Ann Intern Med* 1987;107:348-350.
33. Smee DF, Martin JC, Verheyden JP, et al: Antiherpesvirus activity of the acyclic nucleoside 9-(1,3-dihydroxy-2-propoxymethyl)gua-nine. *Antimicrob Agents Chemother* 1983;23:676-682.
34. Masur H, Lane HC, Palestine A, et al: Effect of 9-(1,3-dihydroxy-2-propoxymethyl)guanine on serious cytomegalovirus disease in eight immunosuppressed homosexual men. *Ann Intern Med* 1986;104:41-44.
35. Selby PJ, Blake S, Mbidde EK, et al: Amino(hydroxyethoxy-methyl)purine: New well absorbed prodrug of acyclovir. *Lancet* 1984;2:1428-1430.
36. Greenspan D, Greenspan JS, DeSouza Y, et al: Efficacy of BWA 515U in treatment of EBV infection in hairy leukoplakia, abstract. *J Dent Res* 1987;66:184.
37. Safai B, Johnson KG, Myskowski PL: The natural history of Kaposi's sarcoma in the acquired immunodeficiency syndrome. *Ann Intern Med* 1985;103:744-750.
38. Krown SE, Real FX, Cunningham-Rundles S, et al: Preliminary observation on the effect of recombinant leukocyte a interferon in homosexual men with Kaposi sarcoma. *N Engl J Med* 1983;308:1071-1076.
39. Lozada F, Silverman S Jr, Conant MA: New outbreak of oral tumors, malignancies, and infectious diseases strikes young male homosexuals. *J Calif Dent Assoc* 1982;10:39-42.
40. Redd E: Interferon alpha-2a used to induce tumor regression in Kaposi's sarcoma. *Oncology Times* 1987;165:1.
41. Daniels TE, Greenspan D, Greenspan JS, et al: Absence of Langerhans cells in oral hairy leukoplakia, an AIDS associated lesion. *J Invest Dermatol* 1987;89:178-182.
42. Johnson TM, Duvig M, Rapini RP: AIDS exacerbates psoriasis, let-ter. *N Engl J Med* 1986;313:1415.
43. Couderc LJ, D'Agay MF, Danon F, et al: Sicca complex and infec-tion with human immunodeficiency virus. *Arch Intern Med* 1987;147:898-901.
44. Marder MZ, Barr CE, Mandel ID: Cytomegalovirus presence and salivary composition in acquired immunodeficiency syndrome. *Oral Surg* 1985;60:372-376.

45. Wright WE, Haller JM, Harlow SA, et al: An oral disease prevention program for patients receiving radiation and chemotherapy. *J Am Dent Assoc* 1985;110:43-47.
46. Shannon JL, McCrary BR, Starke EN: A saliva substitute for use by xerostomic patients undergoing radiotherapy to the head and neck. *Oral Surg* 1977;44:656-661.
47. Swango PA: The use of topical fluorides to prevent dental caries in adults: A review of the literature. *J Am Dent Assoc* 1983;107:447-450.
48. Fox PC, Van der Ven PF, Baum BJ, et al: Philcarpine for treatment of xerostomia associated with salivary gland dysfunction. *Oral Surg* 1986;61:243-248.

7

Overview of the Microbiology of Periodontal Disease

Joseph J. Zambon

Several important concepts have emerged as a result of periodontal research performed over the past decade. First among these is the infectious nature of periodontal disease, that is, the idea that periodontal diseases are caused by the microorganisms in dental plaque. A second related concept is the specific plaque hypothesis which proposes that only a small number of bacterial species in dental plaque are responsible for the different forms of periodontal disease. Among these periodontal pathogens are *Actinobacillus actinomycetemcomitans, Bacteroides gingivalis, Bacteroides intermedius,* and *Wolinella recta.* Initial studies of the subgingival microflora in patients with AIDS suggest the importance of these same periodontal pathogens as well as several microorganisms not usually associated with human periodontal disease.

THE SUBGINGIVAL MICROFLORA IN HEALTH AND DISEASE

Early studies of the periodontal microflora utilized light microscopy to compare those microorganisms found in periodontal health with those found in periodontal disease. Periodontal health is clinically characterized by coral-pink, firm gingival tissue with knife-edged margins, the absence of both gingival bleeding and periodontal pockets, and radiographic alveolar crestal bone height which approximates the cementoenamel junction. If one examines the bacteria which are present in the healthy gingival crevice, one finds relatively few bacteria, mainly Gram-positive cocci. By contrast, chronic adult periodontitis is clinically characterized by large accumulations of plaque and calculus, reddened, edematous gingiva which may bleed when the patient brushes or when the dentist probes, the presence of periodontal pockets and radiographic evidence of alveolar bone loss. If one examines the subgingival microflora in the periodontal pockets of chronic adult periodontitis patients, one finds large numbers of bacteria of a variety of species. In chronic adult periodontitis, there are reduced proportions of the Gram-positive species associated with periodontal health and a corresponding increase in the proportions of Gram-negative microorganisms.

Thus, even by light microscopy, there are clear differences in the subgingival microflora found in periodontal health as compared to that found in periodontal disease.[1,2] A key question then arises, "Is the shift in the subgingival microflora toward higher proportions of Gram-negative species a cause or an effect of periodontal disease?" Over the past decade, a great deal of evidence has accumulated which supports the former hypothesis, that is, that periodontal diseases are caused by the bacteria in dental plaque. This evidence follows certain lines. First, there are cross-sectional and longitudinal oral hygiene studies in which the increased severity of periodontal disease can be correlated with increased accumulations of dental plaque. Second, periodontal treatment studies demonstrate clinical improvement following mechanical or chemotherapeutic reduction in the total numbers of plaque microorganisms. Third, the pathogenicity of plaque bacteria has been demonstrated both in vivo and in vitro. Together, the data is consistent with the idea that periodontal diseases are the result of bacterial plaque infections.

THE SPECIFIC PLAQUE HYPOTHESIS

A further refinement of the infectious nature of periodontal disease is the concept of a specific plaque. This hypothesis proposes that not all dental plaques are the same. It holds that dental plaques from different sites in the same patient and from different sites in different patients are qualitatively and quantitatively distinct. For example, the periodontal pocket mesial to the mandibular right first molar in a localized juvenile periodontitis patient may harbor large numbers of *Actinobacillus actinomycetemcomitans* while this species may be absent from the gingival sulcus mesial to the adjacent mandibular right second bicuspid tooth. As a corollary, this hypothesis proposes that only certain microorganisms in dental plaque are responsible for the different forms of periodontal disease. Thus, the microbial concept of the etiology of periodontal disease has been refined from one affirming the infectious nature of periodontal diseases to one which associates specific forms of periodontal disease with certain bacterial species in dental plaques.

Accordingly, the most exciting advance in periodontology in the past decade has been the identification of the periodontal pathogens — research which is comparable in importance to the discovery of *Streptococcus mutans* as the cause of dental caries. Out of the two to three hundred different bacterial species which can inhabit the human oral cavity,[3] there are less than a dozen which have been associated with periodontal infections (Table 7-1). Among these bacterial species are *A actinomycetemcomitans, Bacteroides gingivalis, Bacteroides intermedius, Capnocytophaga* spp, *Eikenella corrodens, Eubacterium* spp, *Fusobacterium nucleatum, Treponema* spp and *Wolinella recta.* These putative periodontal pathogens have been identified by criteria proposed originally by Dr S. S. Socransky. A microorganism can be implicated in the etiology of a particular form of periodontal disease if it is found in high numbers in proximity to the periodontal lesion. By contrast, this microorganism will either be absent or present in much smaller numbers in periodontally healthy subjects or in subjects with other forms of periodontal disease. A microorganism can also be implicated if it is found that those periodontally diseased patients who are infected with these periodontal pathogens develop high levels of serum, salivary, and gingival crevicular fluid antibody against the microorganisms. Third, these microorganisms can often be found to produce virulence factors in vitro which can be correlated with clinical histopathology. Fourth, experimental implantation of the microorganism into the gingival crevice of an appropriate animal model may lead to development of at least some of the characteristics of naturally occurring periodontal disease. Fifth, a microorganism can be implicated in the etiology of a specific form of periodontal disease if there is clinical improvement following treatment which eliminates the putative pathogen from periodontal lesions.

Table 7-1
Subgingival Microorganisms Associated with
Periodontal Diseases

Acute necrotizing ulcerative gingivitis	*Bacteroides intermedius,* intermediate-sized spirochetes
Adult periodontitis	*Actinobacillus actinomycetem-comitans, B intermedius, B forsythus, B gingivalis, Capnocytophaga gingivalis, Eikenella corrodens, Eubacterium* spp, *Fusobacterium nucleatum, Propionibacterium acnes, Streptococcus intermedius, Wolinella recta*
Localized juvenile periodontitis	*A actinomycetemcomitans, Bacteroides* spp
Generalized juvenile periodontitis	*B gingivalis, B intermedius, Capnocytophaga* spp, *E corrodens, Neisseria*
Periodontal abscesses	Gram-negative anaerobic rods, *B gingivalis, Fusobacterium* spp, *Capnocytophaga* spp, *Vibrio* spp
Peridontitis associated with diabetes mellitus	Anaerobic vibrios, *Campylobacter* spp, *Capnocytophaga* spp, *B gingivalis, B intermedius, Fusobacterium* spp, *W recta*
Pregnancy gingivitis	*B intermedius*
Prepubertal periodontitis	*Bacteroides* spp, *Capnocytophaga* spp, *Fusobacterium* spp, *Selenomonas* spp, *Wolinella* spp
Rapidly progressing periodontitis	*A actinomycetemcomitans, B gingivalis, B intermedius,* small-sized spirochetes
Refractory periodontitis	*B forsythus, B gingivalis, B intermedius, W recta*

PUTATIVE PERIODONTAL PATHOGENS

Among the species implicated in the etiology of the different forms of periodontal disease are:

Actinobacillus actinomycetemcomitans

This is a Gram-negative, capnophilic, nonmotile coccobacillus associated with localized juvenile periodontitis, generalized juvenile periodontitis, and rapidly progressing periodontitis in

adults. To briefly summarize the data incriminating *A actinomycetemcomitans,*[4] patients with these types of periodontal
disease often harbor large numbers of *A actinomycetemcomitans* in periodontal pockets.[5-9] The microorganism is, however,
not seen in adjacent periodontally healthy sites in the same
patient nor in periodontal pockets in other types of periodontitis. These patients develop high levels of serum, salivary, and
gingival crevicular fluid antibodies against *A actinomycetemcomitans* compared to the very low levels of antibodies seen in
patients with other types of periodontal disease.[10-12] *A actinomycetemcomitans* produces a number of virulence factors
which may be involved in the pathogenesis of periodontitis,
including tissue-destructive factors such as a lipopolysaccha-
ride endotoxin, collagenase,[13] and fibroblast inhibiting factor.
Finally, periodontal treatment which results in elimination of
A actinomycetemcomitans from subgingival sites can be correlated with clinical improvement.

Black-Pigmented *Bacteroides*

These are Gram-negative, anaerobic, nonmotile bacilli that
produce brown to black-pigmented colonies when grown on
medium containing blood. They are divided into strongly sugar-
fermenting, weakly sugar-fermenting and sugar nonfermenting
groups including *B melaninogenicus, B intermedius,* and *B gingivalis* as well as several other species.[14] *B gingivalis* has been
associated with certain cases of rapidly progressing adult periodontitis, adult periodontitis, and juvenile periodontitis.[15,16] *B
intermedius* is associated with adult periodontitis, acute necrotizing ulcerative gingivitis,[17,18] and pregnancy gingivitis.[16,19]
These microorganisms are also found in endodontic lesions and
odontogenic abscesses.

Wolinella

Wolinella are Gram-negative, motile anaerobes which can be
found as helical, curved, or straight bacterial cells 0.5 to 1.0 μm
by 2 to 6 μm with tapered or round ends. These microorganisms
can be found in large numbers in the subgingival dental plaque
of adult periodontitis patients, including adult periodontitis
patients with non-insulin-dependent diabetes mellitus, and may

be involved in the pathogenesis of this form of periodontal disease.[20]

Oral Spirochetes

Human oral spirochetes are Gram-negative, strict anaerobes, 5 to 20 µm long and 0.1 to 0.5 µm wide, with a cell morphology consisting of very flexible cytoplasmic cylinders surrounded by an outer sheath or envelope. Between the outer sheath and the cytoplasmic cylinder is a third cell structure unique to these microorganisms known as the axial filament. The light microscopic appearance of spirochetes can also be used to classify them as small, intermediate, or large.

THE ORAL MICROFLORA IN HIV INFECTION

Infection with HIV-1 can result in several clinical manifestations including AIDS and ARC. This retrovirus attacks human lymphocytes, macrophages, and monocytes, leaving infected individuals susceptible to infection by a number of microorganisms including those which are normally not pathogenic.

The oral cavity is a prime site for soft tissue lesions associated with AIDS. These lesions include hairy leukoplakia,[21] Kaposi's sarcoma,[22] and candidiasis.[23] Some patients with AIDS also develop particularly virulent forms of periodontal disease, including HIV gingivitis and HIV periodontitis. HIV gingivitis is characterized by severe gingival inflammation which extends beyond the mucogingival junction and which is disproportionate to the local factors. HIV periodontitis is also characterized by severe gingival inflammation as well as extremely rapid alveolar bone loss. The clinical presentation of the gingival tissues is similar to that seen in acute necrotizing ulcerative gingivitis, which is another form of periodontal disease associated with depressed host immune responses.

The development of these new clinical entities, HIV gingivitis and HIV periodontitis, affords us the opportunity to ask several questions which may shed light on the etiology of periodontal disease in otherwise healthy individuals. For example, what are the microorganisms associated with periodontal disease in HIV-infected patients? Do these patients develop periodontal disease from infection with the same microorganisms which cause periodontal disease in non-AIDS patients, or do they develop periodontal disease due to other, possibly as yet undefined, microorganisms?

Initial studies from our laboratory suggest that both possibilities may be correct. Anaerobic culture of subgingival plaque from AIDS patients reveals many of the same bacterial species as are found in subgingival plaque from otherwise healthy periodontitis patients (Table 7-2). Among these species are putative periodontal pathogens such as the black-pigmented *Bacteroides* species. On the other hand, we find relatively high numbers of as yet unspeciated microorganisms not normally associated with periodontal disease. These species include a Gram-negative microorganism similar to *Wolinella* as well as a *Clostridia* species.

Immunofluorescence examination of subgingival dental plaque from AIDS patients also reveals the importance of the black-pigmented species (Table 7-3). In 32 patients and 100 sites examined, *B gingivalis* was found in 10 subjects and in 29 sites in proportions as high as 13% of the total cell count. *B intermedius* was found in 21 subjects in 44 sites in proportions as high as 14% of the total cell count. In 29 patients and 87 sites examined for *W recta,* 21 of the subjects and 45 of the sites demonstrated this microorganism in proportions up to 16% of the total cell count. *A actinomycetemcomitans* was not prominent in the subgingival plaque from this population. While 14 of the subjects demonstrated this species in 23 sites, it was generally found only as a small proportion of the subgingival microflora, ranging up to 4% of the total cell count in one site.

Clearly, such studies of the subgingival flora in AIDS patients with periodontitis may yield significant information which can be used to prevent this very painful and destructive sequela of HIV infection and which may be applicable to the general population.

Table 7-2
Predominant Cultivable Microflora
in Subgingival Plaque from AIDS Patients

Bacteroides gingivalis	*Fusobacterium* spp
B intermedius	*Peptococcus* spp
Wolinella-like microorganism	*Campylobacter* spp
Unidentified Gram-positive, spore-forming, anaerobic rods	*Capnocytophaga* spp
	Streptococcus spp

Table 7-3
Immunofluorescence Assays for Periodontal Pathogens in AIDS Patients

	Number (%) Positive Patients	Number (%) Positive Sites
Actinobacillus actinomycetemcomitans	14 (44)	23 (23)
Bacteroides gingivalis (32 patients, 100 sites)	10 (31)	29 (29)
Bacteroides intermedius (32 patients, 100 sites)	21 (66)	44 (44)
Wolinella recta (29 patients, 87 sites)	21 (73)	45 (52)

REFERENCES

1. Löe H, Theilade E, Jensen SB: Experimental gingivitis in man. *J Periodontol* 1965;36:177-187.
2. Theilade E, Wright WH, Jensen SB, et al: Experimental gingivitis in man. II. A longitudinal clinical and bacteriological investigation. *J Periodont Res* 1966;1:1-13.
3. Moore WE, Holdeman LV, Smibert RM, et al: Bacteriology of severe periodontitir in young adult humans. *Infect Immun* 1982;38:1137-1148.
4. Zambon JJ: *Actinobacillus actinomycetemcomitans* in human periodontal disease. *J Clin Periodontol* 1985;12:1-20.
5. Christersson LA, Slots J, Zambon JJ, et al: Transmission and colonization of *Actinobacillus actinomycetemcomitans* in localized juvenile periodontitis patients. *J Periodontol* 1985;56:127-131.
6. Mandell RL, Socransky SS: A selective medium for *Actinobacillus actinomycetemcomitans* and the incidence of the organism in juvenile periodontitis. *J Periodontol* 1981;52:593-598.
7. Newman MG, Socransky SS, Savitt ED, et al: Studies of the microbiology of periodontosis. *J Periodontol* 1976;47:373-379.
8. Slots J, Reynolds HS, Genco RJ: *Actinobacillus actinomycetemcomitans* in human periodontal disease: A cross-sectional microbiological investigation. *Infect Immun* 1980;29:1013-1020.
9. Zambon JJ, Christersson LA, Slots J: *Actinobacillus actinomycetemcomitans* in human periodontal disease: Prevalence in patient groups and distribution of biotypes and serotypes within families. *J Periodontol* 1983;54:707-711.
10. Ebersole JL, Taubman MA, Smith DJ, et al: Human immune responses to oral microorganisms. II. Serum antibody responses to antigens from *Actinobacillus actinomycetemcomitans* and the correlation with localized juvenile periodontitis. *J Clin Immunol* 1983;3:321-331.

11. Genco RJ, Zambon JJ, Murray PA: Serum and gingival fluid antibodies as adjuncts in the diagnosis of *Actinobacillus actinomycetemcomitans*–associated periodontal disease. *J Periodontol* 1985;56:41-50.

12. Ranney RR, Yanni NR, Burmeister JA, et al: Relationship between attachment loss and precipitating serum antibody to *Actinobacillus actinomycetemcomitans* in adolescents and young adults having severe periodontal destruction. *J Periodontol* 1982;53:1-7.

13. Robertson PB, Lantz M, Marucha PT, et al: Collagenolytic activity associated with *Bacteroides* species and *Actinobacillus actinomycetemcomitans*. *J Periodont Res* 1982;17:275-283.

14. Slots J: Importance of black-pigmented *Bacteroides* in human periodontal disease, in Genco RJ, Mergenhagen SE (eds): *Host-Parasite Interactions in Periodontal Diseases*. Washington, DC, American Society for Microbiology, 1982.

15. Slots J, Genco RJ: Black-pigmented *Bacteroides* species, *Capnocytophaga* species, and *Actinobacillus actinomycetemcomitans* in human periodontal disease: Virulence factors in colonization, survival, and tissue destruction. *J Dent Res* 1984;63:412-421.

16. Zambon JJ, Reynolds HS, Slots J: Black-pigmented *Bacteroides* spp in the human oral cavity. *Infect Immun* 1981;32:198-203.

17. Listgarten MA: Electron microscopic observations on the bacterial flora of acute necrotizing ulcerative gingivitis. *J Periodontol* 1965;36:328-339.

18. Loesche WJ, Syed SA, Laughon BE, et al: The bacteriology of acute necrotizing ulcerative gingivitis. *J Periodontol* 1965;53:223-230.

19. Kornmann KS, Loesche WJ: The subgingival microbial flora during pregnancy. *J Periodont Res* 1980;15:111-122.

20. Zambon JJ, Reynolds H, Fisher JG, et al: Microbiological and immunological studies of adult periodontitis in patients with non-insulin-dependent diabetes mellitus. *J Periodontol* 1987;59:23-31.

21. Greenspan D, Greenspan JS, Conant M, et al: Oral "hairy" leukoplakia in male homosexuals: Evidence of association with both papillomavirus and a herpes-group virus. *Lancet* 1984;2:831-834.

22. Eversole LR, Leider AS, Jacobsen PL, et al: Oral Kaposi's sarcoma associated with acquired immunodeficiency syndrome among homosexual males. *J Am Dent Assoc* 1983;107:248-253.

23. Lozada F, Silverman S Jr, Migliorati CA, et al: Oral manifestations of tumor and opportunistic infections in the acquired immunodeficiency syndrome (AIDS): Findings in 53 homosexual men with Kaposi's sarcoma. *Oral Surg Oral Med Oral Pathol* 1983;56:491-494.

8

Microbiology of HIV-Associated Gingivitis and Periodontitis

*Patricia A. Murray, James R. Winkler,
Lee Sadkowski, Kenneth S. Kornman,
Bjorn Steffensen, Paul B. Robertson,
and Stanley C. Holt*

Two intraoral lesions associated with HIV infection have recently been described: an atypical gingivitis and a rapidly progressive periodontitis. We investigated the microbiota associated with these lesions. Subgingival plaque samples from HIV-seropositive men and from HIV-seronegative control subjects were examined by indirect immunofluorescence and microbiological culturing. Each sampled site was clinically classified as HIV-associated gingivitis, HIV-associated periodontitis, disease-free in an HIV-seropositive subject, or disease-free or conventional gingivitis in a control subject. Microbiological analysis revealed that HIV-gingivitis and HIV-periodontitis sites harbored significantly more *Candida albicans* when compared to the control sites. In addition, *Bacteroides gingivalis, B intermedius, Fusobacterium nucleatum, Actinobacillus actinomycetemcomitans, Eikenella corrodens,* and *Wolinella* spp were more prevalent in HIV-periodontitis sites and HIV-gingivitis sites than in HIV-seropositive healthy and control sites. On a comparative basis, the distribution of the microbiota in HIV-periodontitis and HIV-gingivitis sites appeared similar to that typically found in classic periodontitis sites, while the microbiota from HIV-seropositive healthy and HIV-seronegative control sites was characteristic of a healthy periodontium. Of particular interest was the unusually high prevalence of these bacteria in the HIV-gingivitis lesion. These findings suggest that HIV-gingivitis may be a precursor to the HIV-periodontitis, and that early detection and treatment of the HIV-gingivitis lesion may prevent the rapid and extensive breakdown of periodontal tissues.

Immunocompromised individuals, especially those with AIDS, are predisposed to a variety of opportunistic infections.[1-3] In addition, many of those infected with HIV suffer from a variety of oral lesions,[4-7] one of which is a very rapid and painful progressive periodontal disease (HIV-P).[8] A more subtle HIV-associated lesion of the oral tissues is an atypical gingivitis (HIV-G).[9] Although the etiology of HIV-P remains unclear, preliminary observations (see chapter 5) seem to indicate that HIV-G may progress to HIV-P if left untreated.

Although the literature is clear that periodontal diseases are microbially mediated,[10-14] there are essentially no data available on the nature of the microbial load or distribution of selected periodontopathogens in HIV-G and HIV-P, nor on the role of the host's resident microbiota in the progression of HIV-G to HIV-P. To lay the groundwork for more in depth studies of the progression of HIV-G to HIV-P, it was first essential to investigate the subgingival microbiota of both HIV-seropositive and HIV-seronegative individuals. Our aim was to compare the microbiota in the HIV-associated lesions with that seen in the gingivitis and periodontitis in nonimmunocompromised individuals. These studies will provide a better understanding of the role of the resident, commensal microbiota in the oral disease process not only of the HIV-compromised individual, but also of immunocompromised individuals in general. These studies also establish the basis for future studies on the mechanism by which the oral microbiota of the HIV-G and HIV-P lesions contributes to the periodontal disease process and on the role of immunoregulation in the emergence of pathogenic bacteria in the subgingival microbiota.

MATERIALS AND METHODS

Patient Population

The subject population was recruited from patients at the Periodontal Research Clinic of the University of California, San Francisco. For ease of data presentation, we have divided these individuals into two groups: a San Francisco group and a San Antonio group, based on the location where samples were processed. The San Francisco subjects consisted of 45 homosexual men who were seropositive for antibody to HIV and a control group of 39 heterosexual men and 40 homosexual men, all of whom were seronegative for HIV antibody. The San Antonio group consisted of 40 subjects, 25 of whom were seropositive homosexual men, and 15 seronegative heterosexual or homosexual men. None of the HIV-seronegative subjects converted to seropositive during any of the follow-up evaluations.

Oral Examination

All of the subjects in the study received a complete oral examination, including scoring of plaque index[15] and gingival index[16] and measurement of pocket depth from the gingival margin and attachment loss from the cementoenamel junction. In addition, the gingiva and alveolar mucosa adjacent to the facial surface of each tooth was examined for the presence or absence of erythema of the free gingival margin, punctate erythema of the attached gingiva or mucosa, and diffuse erythema of the gingiva or mucosa. HIV-G is described as a bandlike marginal erythema usually accompanied by petechial or diffuse redness which extends into the vestibular mucosa. HIV-P, in contrast, is defined as HIV-G associated with blunted or cratered papillae, loss of attachment, soft tissue ulceration and necrosis, as well as the classical clinical indicators of periodontitis — radiographic evidence of bone loss, bleeding on probing, and a distinct tendency toward spontaneous bleeding (see chapter 5). In HIV-seropositive subjects, gingival sites that were clinically disease free were classified as HIV-healthy (HIV-H).

Microbiological Sampling

Subgingival plaque was collected by the paper-point procedure as described previously.[17] Samples were taken from at least three sites in each subject; two sites were periodontally diseased, and the other site was clinically healthy. Paper points were placed into reduced transport fluid[17] and either processed immediately or placed into Brewer jars under an atmosphere of $N_2 + CO_2 + H_2$ and transported to the research laboratory. In all cases, specimens were plated or processed for indirect immunofluorescence (IDIF) within 15 hours of collection. The plaque samples for microbiological culture analysis were dispersed and then plated to selective and nonselective growth media.

Statistical Analysis

The data in Table 8-1 and Figures 8-1 through 8-4 were analyzed by one-way analysis of variance to test the null hypothesis that the percentage of specific microbiota (*Candida albicans, Bacteroides gingivalis, Bacteroides intermedius, Fusobacterium nucleatum,* and *Actinobacillus actinomycetemcomitans*) was indistinguishable between patient groups or sites. Specific microbial differences were then evaluated by disease severity employing the two-sample *t*-test. Correlations between microbial parameters and disease were determined by linear regression analysis.

RESULTS

Indirect Immunofluorescence Analysis

The prevalence of selected periodontopathogens as determined by IDIF analysis is seen in Table 8-1 for subjects whose samples were analyzed in San Francisco. The HIV-negative and HIV-healthy (HIV-H) sites did not differ significantly with respect to percentages of sites that harbored *B gingivalis, B intermedius, F nucleatum,* or *A actinomycetemcomitans.* However, a significantly greater percentage of HIV-G and HIV-P sites harbored these organisms than did either the HIV-H or HIV-negative. There was no significant difference between the percentages of HIV-G and HIV-P sites harboring these organisms.

Table 8-1
Percentage of Sites Harboring Putative Periodontopathogens, as Determined by Indirect Immunofluorescence (San Francisco Group)

Diagnosis	N	B inter-medius	B gingi-valis	F nucle-atum	A actino-mycetem-comitans
HIV-neg	2	15.0	20.0	20.0	0.0
HIV-H	16	6.3	0.0	0.0	0.0
HIV-G	23	60.9	69.6	52.2	52.2
HIV-P	49	79.6	65.3	59.2	61.2

N = number of sites; HIV-neg = a clinically healthy or gingivitis site from an HIV-seronegative subject; HIV-H = a clinically healthy site from an HIV-seropositive subject; HIV-G = a gingivitis site from an HIV-seropositive subject; HIV-P = a periodontitis site from an HIV-seropositive subject.

Table 8-2
Percentage of Sites Harboring Putative Periodontopathogens, as Determined by Indirect Immunofluorescence in HIV-Seronegative Men (San Antonio Group)

Organism	Gingivitis (N = 3)	Periodontitis (N = 6)
Actinomyces viscosus	0	83
Actinobacillus actinomycetemcomitans	33	17
Eikenella corrodens	33	17
Capnocytophaga spp	0	17
Bacteroides intermedius	100	66
Bacteroides gingivalis	100	66
Fusobacterium nucleatum	33	50
Wolinella recta	66	33

N = number of sites.

Results of the IDIF microbiological analysis by the San Antonio group are shown in Tables 8-2 and 8-3. In the HIV-negative subjects, all of the gingivitis and most of the periodontitis sites of the HIV-negative subjects contained *B intermedius* and *B gingivalis*. *A actinomycetemcomitans*, *Eikenella corrodens*, *F nucleatum* and *Wolinella recta* were also found in both lesions. In

Table 8-3
Percentage of Sites Harboring Putative Periodontopathogens, as Determined by Indirect Immunofluorescence in HIV-Seropositive men (San Antonio group)

Organism	HIV-G (N = 7)	HIV-P (N = 20)
Actinomyces viscosus	86	70
Actinobacillus actinomycetemcomitans	43	20
Eikenella corrodens	43	30
Capnocytophaga spp	29	30
Bacteroides intermedius	100	90
Bacteroides gingivalis	86	100
Fusobacterium nucleatum	86	45
Wolinella recta	43	60

N = number of sites.

contrast, 83% of the periodontitis sites harbored *Actinomyces viscosus,* whereas none of the gingivitis sites contained this organism. In the HIV-positive subjects, both the HIV-G and the HIV-P sites had a high prevalence of *A viscosus. B intermedius, B gingivalis, F nucleatum* and *W recta* were also found in a significant number of both HIV-G and HIV-P sites. The other selected periodontopathogens were found in fewer numbers in these HIV-positive patients.

Cultural Analysis

The prevalence of the opportunistic fungus *C albicans* as determined by cultural analysis of the San Francisco group is shown in Figures 8-1 and 8-2. The percentage of subjects in the HIV-seropositive group who harbored *C albicans* was significantly greater than in either HIV-seronegative group (Figure 8-1). When analyzed by sites, a significantly greater percentage of HIV-G and HIV-P sites harbored *C albicans* than did either

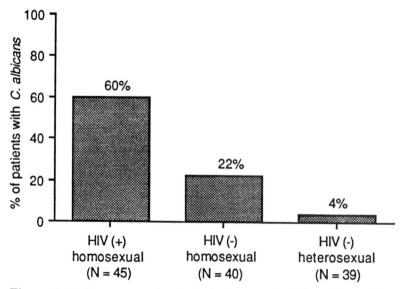

Figure 8-1 Percentage of patients harboring *Candida albicans* (San Francisco group). HIV+ = patients seropositive for HIV antibody; HIV– = patients seronegative for HIV antibody; N = number of subjects.

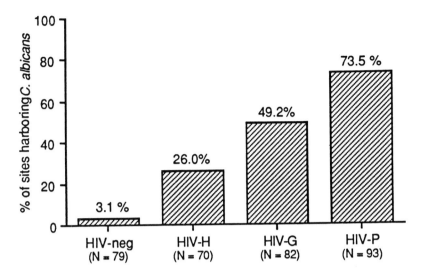

Figure 8-2 Percentage of sites harboring *C albicans* (San Francisco group). HIV-neg = seronegative for HIV antibody; HIV-H = healthy and conventional gingivitis sites in seropositive subjects; HIV-G = HIV-associated gingivitis. HIV-P = HIV-associated periodontitis; N = number of sites.

HIV-negative sites or HIV-H sites (Figure 8-2). However, while *C albicans* was recovered from fewer HIV-G sites than HIV-P sites, the difference was not statistically significant. Also, whereas *C albicans* was recovered from the majority of the sites in the HIV-positive study population, the HIV-negative subjects had very few sites harboring *C albicans*.

The prevalence of the selected microorganisms in the HIV-seronegative and HIV-seropositive subjects in the San Francisco group as determined by culture is shown in Figure 8-3. Between 64% and 86% of the HIV-seropositive subjects in the San Francisco group harbored black-pigmented *Bacteroides* (BPB), *Fusobacterium* spp, or *A actinomycetemcomitans*, while few of the HIV-seronegative individuals had detectable levels of these organisms. When these data were analyzed by sites (Figure 8-4), significantly more of the HIV-G and HIV-P sites contained these particular periodontopathogens than did the HIV-seronegative or HIV-H sites. However, there was no significant difference in the prevalence of organisms in the HIV-G and HIV-P lesions.

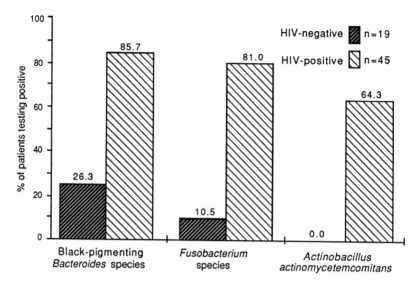

Figure 8-3 Percentage of patients testing positive for selected periodontopathogens (San Francisco group). N = number of subjects.

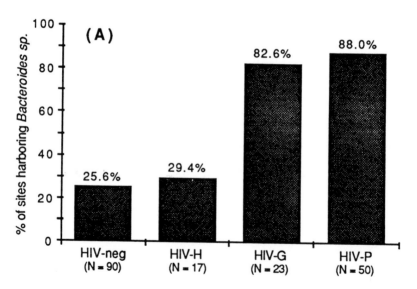

Figure 8-4a-c Percentage of sites harboring selected periodontopathogens (San Francisco group). Abbreviations as in Figure 8-2. N = number of sites.

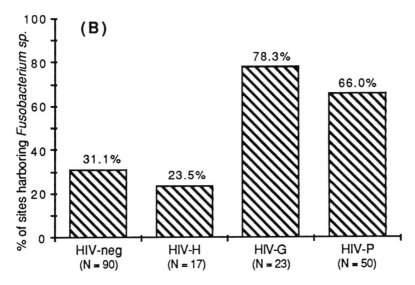

Figure 8-4b

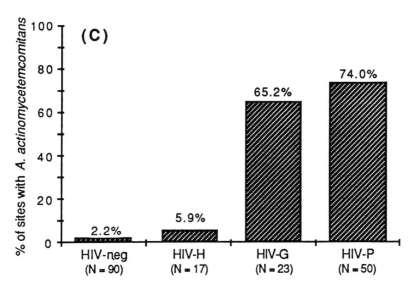

Figure 8-4c

The prevalence of selected organisms in the San Antonio group as determined by culture is shown in Tables 8-4 and 8-5. In the HIV-seronegative subjects, the BPBs were recovered from 37% of the sites. *B intermedius* occupied 31% of these sites, *B gingivalis* occupied 2% of these sites, and the remainder of the BPB population (classified as "other" *Bacteroides* spp) occupied 4% of the sites. This latter group was very similar to the *B melaninogenicus/denticola* group. *W recta* and *Capnocytophaga* spp were the next most predominant groups, with recoveries of 15% and 6%, respectively. *E corrodens* was recovered from 4% of the sites, and the "unidentified surface translocating bacteria," morphologically and biochemically similar to members of the genus *Wolinella,* were recovered from 2% of sites.

The HIV-seropositive subjects presenting with HIV-P (Table 8-5) displayed a distribution of these selected bacteria reminiscent of that reported previously for adult periodontitis.[18] For example, elevated levels of *B intermedius* and *B gingivalis* were observed in our study population, with 2.8% of the cultivable microbiota consisting of "other BPBs." In addition, *Wolinella* spp composed 3.5% of the flora, while unidentified species similar to *Wolinella* composed less than 1% of the flora. The Gram-positive cocci, which were predominantly α-hemolytic, were similar to *Streptococcus sanguis* or *S mitis*. Note in Table 8-5 that streptococci accounted for 56.7% of the cultivable microbiota in these subjects, while the Gram-positive rods (eg, *Eubacterium* spp, and *Actinomyces* spp) constituted only 10.9% of the cultivable microbiota. Gram-negative rods (eg, *Bacteroides, Fusobacterium,* and *Wolinella*) made up the remainder of the cultivable microbiota.

DISCUSSION

Under ordinary conditions, the oral cavity is fairly resistant to infection by opportunistic microorganisms. However, with impairment of the immune system, there is an increased susceptibility of the host to the many commensal or opportunistic microbiota usually resident in the oral cavity. This alteration or shift in the microbial balance, in conjunction with a compromise of the host's immune system, results in a variety of oral lesions.[1-7,19,20] This is especially true for AIDS, in which the extent of immunocompromise is severe. Most acute periodontal lesions in immunocompetent subjects are self-limiting and respond to conventional therapy. However, when associated

Table 8-4
Percentage of Sites Harboring Periodontal
Microorganisms, as Determined by Culture in
HIV-Seronegative Men (San Antonio Group)

Organism	Health & Gingivitis (N = 48)
Actinobacillus actinomycetemcomitans	0
Bacteroides gingivalis	2
Bacteroides intermedius	31
Other BPBs	4
Capnocytophaga spp	6
Eikenella corrodens	4
Wolinella recta	15
Surface translocator (unidentified)	2

N = number of sites.

with HIV infection, acute periodontal lesions often fail to respond and can progress rapidly into extensive disease, culminating in potentially life-threatening lesions.[8,9] There are essentially no data regarding whether these HIV-associated periodontal lesions are in fact the result of a "new" or unique microbiota capable of invading the immunocompromised host, or the result of a newly acquired ability of this large commensal microbiota to become opportunistic and pathogenic. In this study, we began preliminary characterizations of the microbiota associated with these lesions in order to determine the presence of a "unique" HIV-seropositive microbiota.

It is apparent from our results that there were significantly greater numbers of the opportunistic fungus *C albicans* in the HIV-seropositive subjects than in the seronegative group. In addition, we noted an increase in the prevalence of *A actinomycetemcomitans, B intermedius, B gingivalis, F nucleatum* and *Wolinella* spp with HIV-seropositive subjects. In general these flora are consistent with the major bacterial genera thought to be associated with adult periodontitis.[18]

Several investigators have suggested that the destructive periodontal lesions observed in HIV-seropositive subjects represent an especially aggressive form of acute necrotizing ulcerative gingivitis, or ANUG.[21,22] However, we have provided evidence that substantial differences existed between ANUG

Table 8-5
Predominant Cultivable Microbiota in HIV-P Sites
in Seropositive Men (San Antonio Group)

Organism	% of Total Cultivable Flora (N = 17)
Total Gram (+) Cocci	**63.5 ±17.0***
Unidentified anaerobes	4.9 ± 7.9
Facultatives	58.5 ±18.1
Streptococci	56.7 ±19.1
Unidentified	0.7 ± 3.0
Total Gram (+) Rods	**10.9 ± 8.4**
Anaerobes	5.5 ± 5.8
Eubacterium spp	0.8 ± 2.3
Unidentified	4.8 ± 5.8
Facultatives	5.4 ± 6.3
Actinomyces spp	3.4 ± 5.4
Unidentified	1.9 ± 4.5
Total Gram (–) Rods	**24.0 ±12.0**
Anaerobes	24.0 ±12.0
B gingivalis spp	0.8 ± 2.8
B intermedius spp	8.7 ± 9.7
Other BPBs	2.8 ± 5.3
Fusobacterium spp	3.0 ± 3.6
Selenomonas spp	1.4 ± 3.0
Wolinella spp	3.5 ± 5.5
Unidentified	0.3 ± 1.0
Facultatives	0.0 ± 0.0

*Means ± standard deviation.
N = number of sites.

and HIV-P.[8,9] For example, the levels of black-pigmented *Bacteroides* (including *B intermedius* and *B gingivalis*), *Fusobacterium* spp, *Wolinella* spp, and *Actinobacillus* spp were significantly greater in the HIV-P than in the HIV-H or HIV-negative sites. In contrast, the levels of spirochetes (ie, *Treponema* spp) were variable, and inconsistent with the microbiota typically associated with ANUG (data not shown).

These results indicate that the microbiota of the HIV-seropositive subject with periodontal lesions is very similar to that reported for classic periodontitis.[18] The distribution of these microbiota in the HIV-G and HIV-P sites is important for a better understanding of the progression of HIV-G to HIV-P. Of particular interest was the similarity in the type and distribution of the microbiota associated with HIV-G and HIV-P. However, these lesions are clinically very different; HIV-G is characterized by a very subtle red band of inflammation around a tooth, whereas HIV-P typically presents as a severely destructive painful lesion often resulting in significant tissue and bone loss. Therefore, despite an apparent similarity in the composition of the two microbial populations, significant differences in the virulence of the microorganisms may exist between the two groups. Alternatively, the respective immune status of the host may play a central role in the progression of HIV-G to HIV-P. For example, Winkler and Murray[8] and Winkler at al[9] have proposed that the levels of T4 lymphocytes may be an important factor in this progression. The degree of virulence of the oral microbiota in these conditions, in conjunction with the study of host immune competence in the progression of periodontal disease, is under active investigation.

REFERENCES

1. Gottlieb MS, Schroff R, Sehanker HM, et al: *Pneumocystis carinii* pneumonia and mucosal candidiasis in previously healthy homosexual men. *N Engl J Med* 1983;305:1425-1431.
2. Masur H, Michelis MA, Greene JB, et al: An outbreak of community-acquired *Pneumocystis carinii* pneumonia: Initial manifestation of cellular immune dysfunction. *N Engl J Med* 1981;305:1431-1438.
3. Mildvan D, Mathur U, Enlwo RW, et al: Opportunistic infections and immune deficiency in homosexual men. *Ann Intern Med* 1982;96:700-704.
4. Klein RS, Harris CA, Small CB, et al: Oral candidiasis in high-risk patients as the initial manifestation of the acquired immunodeficiency syndrome. *N Engl J Med* 1984;311:354-358.
5. Greenspan D, Greenspan JS, Hearst N, et al: Oral hairy leukoplakia—AIDS retrovirus status and risk for development of AIDS. *J Infect Dis* 1987;155:457-481.
6. Rindum JL, Sommer M, Pindborg J, et al: Acquired immunodeficiency syndrome (AIDS) — Literature reviewed and report on 13 cases. *Danish Dent J* 1987;89:131-141.
7. Silverman S Jr, Migliorati CA, Lozada-Nur F, et al: Oral findings in people with or at high risk for AIDS: A study of 375 homosexual males. *J Am Dent Assoc* 1986;112:187-192.
8. Winkler JR, Murray PA: Periodontal disease — A potential intra-oral expression of AIDS may be a rapidly progressive periodontitis. *Calif Dent Assoc J* 1987;15:20-24.
9. Winkler JR, Grassi M, Murray PA: Periodontal manifestations of HIV infection, abstract. *Third International Conference on AIDS*, Washington, DC, 1987.

10. Socransky SS: Microbiology of periodontal disease — Present status and future considerations. *J Periodontol* 1977;48:497-504.
11. Tanner ACR, Haffer C, Bratthall GT, et al: A study of the bacteria associated with advanced periodontitis in man. *J Clin Periodontol* 1979;6:1-30.
12. Slots J, Genco RJ: Black pigmented *Bacteroides* species, *Capnocytophaga* species, and *Actinobacillus actinomycetemcomitans* in human periodontal disease: Virulence factors in colonization, survival, and tissue destruction. *J Dent Res* 1984;63:412-421.
13. Slots J: Subgingival microflora and periodontal disease. *J Clin Periodontol* 1979;6:351-382.
14. Newman MG: Current concepts of the pathogenesis of periodontal disease: Microbiology emphasis. *J Periodontol* 1985;56:734-739.
15. Silness J, Löe H: Periodontal disease in pregnancy. II. Correlation between oral hygiene and periodontal conditions. *Acta Odontol Scand* 1964;22:112-135.
16. Löe H, Silness J: Periodontal disease in pregnancy. I. Prevalence and severity. *Acta Odontol Scand* 1963;21:533-551.
17. Kornman KS, Holt SC, Robertson PB: The microbiology of ligature-induced periodontitis in the cynomolgus monkey. *J Periodont Res* 1981;16:251-258.
18. Slots J: Subgingival microflora and periodontal disease. *J Clin Periodontol* 1979;6:351-382.
19. Reichart PH, Pohle HD, Gelderblom H: Oral manifestations of AIDS. *Deutsch Z Mund Kiefer Gesichts Chir* 1985;9:167-176.
20. Schøidt M, Pindborg J: AIDS and the oral cavity — Epidemiology and clinical oral manifestations of human immune deficiency virus infection: A review. *Int J Oral Maxillofac Surg* 1987;16:1-14.
21. Pindborg JJ, Holmstrup P: Necrotizing gingivitis related to human immunodeficiency virus (HIV) infection. *Afr Dent J* 1987;1:5-8.
22. Johnson BD, Engel D: Acute necrotizing ulcerative gingivitis: A review of diagnosis, etiology and treatment. *J Periodontol* 1986;57:141-150.

9

Management of HIV-Associated Periodontal Diseases

Markus Grassi, Cynthia A. Williams
James R. Winkler, Patricia A. Murray

Thirty patients seropositive for antibody to the human immunodeficiency virus were referred for treatment of gingivitis and periodontitis. In many cases, rapidly progressing gingival necrosis with exposure of alveolar bone, severe pain, and spontaneous or nocturnal gingival bleeding were present. All patients received a complete baseline oral examination that included assessments of plaque index, gingival index, pocket depth, attachment loss, and presence or absence of erythema at the free gingival margin and punctate or diffuse erythema of the gingival and alveolar mucosa. Fourteen of the 30 patients were treated with conventional therapy (individualized oral hygiene instructions, scaling and root planing). Six patients were treated by conventional therapy supplemented with 10% povidone-iodine (Betadine) irrigation, and 10 patients by conventional therapy plus 0.12% chlorhexidine gluconate (Peridex) rinses. The oral examination was repeated at 1 and 3 months after scaling and root planing was completed.

Patients treated by conventional therapy alone showed no improvement in any clinical assessments, and mean attachment loss increased 0.5 mm during the 3-month period. Patients treated by conventional therapy supplemented with povidone-iodine irrigation showed similar results, but benefited from povidone-iodine's topical anesthetic and hemostatic effects during scaling and root planing as well as in personal oral hygiene procedures. Patients treated by conventional therapy and chlorhexidine rinses showed significant improvement in all clinical measures, including complete resolution of spontaneous bleeding, and experienced no further loss of attachment during the treatment period.

Several intraoral changes secondary to infection with HIV have been described,[1,2] including forms of periodontal disease.[3] These HIV-associated periodontal changes may be divided into two clinical categories: lesions characterized by inflammation of the gingiva and alveolar mucosa that do not respond to personal and professional oral hygiene (HIV-associated gingivitis), and lesions resulting in extensive periodontal soft tissue necrosis and severe loss of periodontal attachment (HIV-associated periodontitis). Progression of the disease from HIV-associated gingivitis to periodontitis may be rapid, often occurring in a period of a few days to several weeks. Clinical signs of HIV-associated gingivitis include erythema and edema of the free gingiva, often presenting as a distinct linear red band, and punctate or "petechialike" red lesions of the attached gingiva and adjacent vestibular mucosa. These punctate areas become masked by diffuse erythema of the gingiva and alveolar mucosa as the disease advances. Bleeding upon probing is prevalent, and pain is not usually associated with mild to moderate cases. In HIV-associated periodontitis, an acute necrotizing ulcerative gingival lesion is superimposed upon a rapidly progressive severe loss of attachment. There is pain, and spontaneous or nocturnal bleeding. Severe lesions are intensely painful and exhibit extensive necrosis that often involves alveolar bone and produces osseous sequestration.

During the past two years, we have used three treatment approaches to manage these HIV-associated lesions in patients referred to the Periodontology Research Center at the University of California, San Francisco. Initially, patients were given oral hygiene instructions and treated by scaling and root planing. Clinical improvement after this conventional therapy was minimal, and pain and bleeding associated with the lesions did not resolve. Therefore we began to supplement conventional treatment with 10% povidone-iodine (Betadine) irrigation. Iodine solutions have long been recommended for treatment of acute necrotizing ulcerative gingivitis.[4] Povidone-iodine has antimicrobial activity against some oral bacteria and fungi,[5] appears to improve early periodontal wound healing,[6] and provides some topical anesthesia. When 0.12% chlorhexidine gluconate (Peridex) was approved recently for human use, we instituted a third form of treatment, consisting of conventional therapy plus twice daily rinsing with chlorhexidine after personal oral hygiene. Chlorhexidine gluconate exhibits potent antimicrobial activity against a wide variety of oral microorganisms,[7,8] and has been recommended for the oral management of immunocompromised patients.[9]

We report here the clinical results of local treatment of HIV-associated periodontal lesions by conventional therapy consisting of scaling, root planing and oral hygiene instructions; conventional therapy supplemented by povidone-iodine irrigation; and conventional therapy combined with chlorhexidine rinsing.

MATERIAL AND METHODS

This report describes treatment results in 30 male homosexual patients, age 23 to 49 years, who were referred for management of HIV-associated periodontal lesions. Many had clinical symptoms of severe periodontal pain, spontaneous or nocturnal bleeding and, in many cases, rapidly progressing gingival necrosis with exposure of alveolar bone. All patients tested seropositive for antibody to HIV by ELISA (enzyme-linked immunosorbent assay) and Western blot test, and many patients showed other clinical signs of the acquired immunodeficiency syndrome.[10] None of the patients used a systemic antibiotic during the 3- to 4-month period of localized treatments described in this report.

All patients received a complete oral examination that included the plaque index (PI),[11] gingival index (GI),[12] and measurement of pocket depth from the gingival margin and attachment loss from the cementoenamel junction. A score of 3 for the GI was recorded if a site showed the presence of a blood clot or bled in response to light external pressure with a probe. These assessments were obtained on the facial, lingual, mesial and distal surfaces of all teeth. In addition, the gingiva and alveolar mucosa adjacent to the facial surface of each tooth was assessed for the presence or absence of erythema of the free gingival margin; punctate or petechialike erythema of the attached gingiva or mucosa; and diffuse erythema of gingiva or mucosa. Intraoral photographs were taken.

After the baseline examination, all patients received individualized oral hygiene instructions that stressed the modified Bass technique of toothbrushing with a soft brush, and interproximal cleaning with floss or an interproximal brush. The teeth were scaled and root planed during a period of 1 to 3 appointments, using local anesthetic if needed. The baseline examination was repeated at 1 month and 3 months after scaling and root planing was completed.

Fourteen patients received conventional therapy alone. In six patients, conventional therapy was supplemented with home use of povidone-iodine irrigation throughout the 3-month period; these patients used a LeurLok irrigation syringe to apply 5 mL of povidone-iodine into interproximal craters and gingivally 3 to 5 times daily after personal oral hygiene measures. Povidone-iodine was applied professionally as required during scaling and root planing to control pain and bleeding. In ten patients, conventional therapy was supplemented with home use of chlorhexidine mouthrinse. These patients rinsed twice daily with 15 mL of chlorhexidine throughout the 3-month period.

Clinical measurements were expressed as means with standard deviations in each patient for PI, GI, pocket depth, and attachment loss. We calculated the mean percentage of sites in each patient that showed visible plaque (PI > 1), spontaneous bleeding (GI > 2), bleeding on probing (GI > 1), the presence of erythema of the free gingival margin, punctate gingival or mucosal erythema, or diffuse gingival or mucosal erythema. Differences in each measure for examinations at baseline and at 1 month and 3 months after the completion of scaling and root planing were assessed with repeated measures analysis of variance.

RESULTS

Conventional Therapy

Patients treated for HIV-associated periodontal lesions by conventional treatment showed little clinical improvement at the 1- and 3-month examinations. Means (and standard deviations) at the baseline and 3-month examinations for pocket depth were 3.3 (±1.2) mm and 3.2 (±0.9) mm, and for attachment loss were 3.4 (±1.0) mm and 3.9 (±0.9) mm, respectively. The initial mean PI, 1.3 (±0.8), and frequency of sites with visible plaque, 42%, remained essentially unchanged throughout treatment. Gingival and mucosal assessments are shown in Figure 9-1. Baseline values for mean percentage of sites with erythema of the free gingival margin (97%), punctate gingival (53%) and mucosal (26%) erythema, and diffuse gingival (23%)

and mucosal (67%) erythema were not affected by conventional treatment. Initial GI scores showed 68% of sites bled on probing (GI = 2 or 3), and of those sites, 5% bled spontaneously (GI = 3). These scores showed no improvement by the end of the treatment period.

Conventional Therapy with Povidone-Iodine Irrigation

In patients treated by conventional therapy and the adjunctive use of povidone-iodine, mean baseline and 3-month measurements for pocket depth were 3.5 (±1.1) mm and 3.4 (±1.0) mm, and for attachment loss were 4.0 (±1.5) mm and 4.7 (±1.5) mm, respectively. Mean scores for the PI were 1.6 (±0.7), 1.4 (±0.6), and 1.4 (±0.7) at the initial, 1-month and 3-month examinations, respectively. A slight decrease in percentage of sites with visible plaque from the baseline (48%) to the 3-month examination (41%) was not statistically significant ($P > .05$).

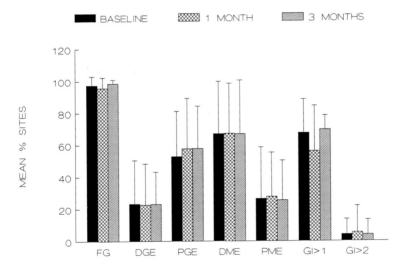

Figure 9-1 Mean percentage of sites that were positive for erythema of the free gingival margin (FGE), diffuse gingival erythema (DGE), punctate gingival erythema (PGE), diffuse mucosal erythema (DME), punctate mucosal erythema (PME), spontaneous bleeding or bleeding on probing (GI > 1) and spontaneous bleeding (GI > 2) at a baseline examination and examinations 1 and 3 months after conventional therapy, consisting of oral hygiene instructions and scaling/root planing.

124

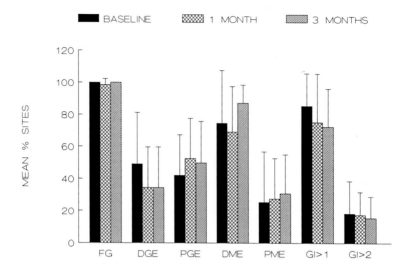

Figure 9-2 Mean percentage of sites that were positive for clinical signs defined in Figure 9-1 at a baseline examination and 1 and 3 months after conventional therapy supplemented with 10% povidone-iodine irrigation.

Gingival and mucosal assessments are shown in Figure 9-2. There were slight improvements from baseline to the 3-month examination in the percentage of sites with diffuse gingival erythema (49%, 34%) and percentage of sites with a GI score of 2 or 3 (86%, 73%), but there were no statistically significant differences in any of the soft tissue assessments during the treatment period. At the baseline examination, 18% of sites showed spontaneous bleeding. After conventional therapy plus povidone-iodine, 16% of sites continued to bleed spontaneously. However, the topical hemostatic and anesthetic effects produced by povidone-iodine irrigation aided professional debridement of ulcerated lesions and those with exposed alveolar bone. All patients reported that home use of povidone-iodine irrigation substantially reduced the pain associated with the lesions.

Conventional Therapy with Chlorhexidine Rinsing

In patients treated by conventional therapy and chlorhexidine rinses, the mean baseline and 3-month examination measurements for pocket depth were 3.5 (±1.2) mm and 3.0 (±1.0) mm, and for attachment loss were 4.0 (±1.6) mm and 4.0 (±1.5) mm, respectively.

Mean PI scores and percentage of sites with visible plaque decreased significantly ($P < 0.05$), from 1.4 (±0.6) and 47% at baseline to 0.9 (±0.6) and 29% at the 1-month and 0.7 (±0.6) and 6% at the 3-month examinations. Soft tissue assessments (Figure 9-3) also showed marked improvement during the 3-month treatment period. Before treatment, erythema at the free gingival margin was found in 97% of sites. The percentage was reduced to 83% after 1 month of therapy and to less than 5% after 3 months. The number of sites positive for punctate gingival or mucosal erythema was increased at the 1-month examination, then declined by the 3-month examination. The percentages of sites with diffuse gingival or mucosal erythema were significantly reduced ($P < .01$) by this treatment regimen. At baseline, 90% of sites showed gingival bleeding, and 24% of sites bled spontaneously. Conventional therapy with chlorhexidine rinses resulted in a significant

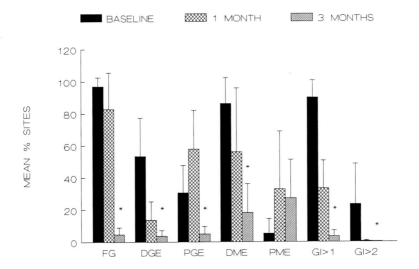

Figure 9-3 Mean percentage of sites that were positive for clinical signs defined in Figure 9-1 at a baseline examination and 1 and 3 months after conventional therapy plus twice daily rinsing with 0.12% chlorhexidine gluconate.
* Significant decrease from baseline to 3-month examinations ($P < .05$).

decrease in bleeding sites ($P < .001$), to less than 4%. Moreover, no spontaneous bleeding was observed at the 3-month examination.

Many patients with areas of gingival ulceration and severe periodontal involvement reported that chlorhexidine rinses initially caused discomfort, but this abated within a few days. Areas of severe necrosis involving exposed alveolar bone resolved within several days, and most patients reported essentially complete relief from chronic pain and bleeding. Examples of HIV-associated periodontal lesions in two patients at the baseline examination and at one month after scaling and root planing plus chlorhexidine rinsing are shown in Figures 9-4 through 9-7.

DISCUSSION

In this series of patients, conventional therapy, consisting of oral hygiene instructions, scaling and root planing, was not effective in resolving HIV-associated periodontal disease. Gingival bleeding, pain, and erythema of the gingiva and alveolar mucosa showed little improvement during the 3-month period of therapy. Moreover, attachment loss increased an average of 0.5 mm from the baseline to the 3-month examination. The clinical response to povidone-iodine irrigation combined with conventional therapy was similar to the response to conventional therapy alone. There were slight but statistically insignificant improvements in plaque and gingivitis scores and in the percentage of gingival and mucosal sites with diffuse erythema. Most soft tissue changes were unaffected, and attachment loss increased an average of 0.7 mm during the 3-month treatment period. The ability of povidone-iodine irrigation to reduce pain, however, greatly assisted thorough scaling and root planing by the therapist, as well as personal oral hygiene by the patient.

In contrast to these results, patients treated with chlorhexidine rinses combined with conventional therapy showed major improvements in all clinical measures during the 3-month treatment period. The percentages of sites with visible plaque, erythema at the free gingival margin, punctate and diffuse gingival and mucosal erythema, and gingival bleeding all decreased sig-

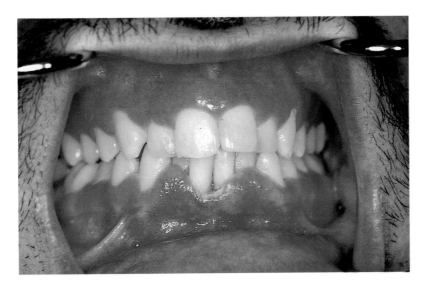

Figure 9-4 Baseline examination.

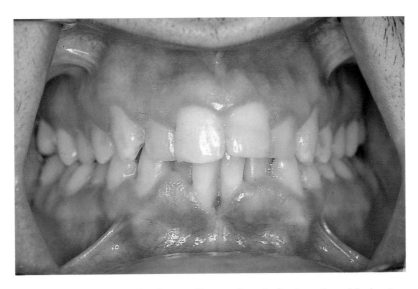

Figure 9-5 One month after scaling and root planing plus chlorhexidine rinsing in the patient shown in Figure 9-4.

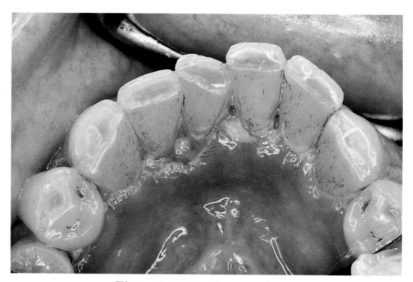

Figure 9-6 Baseline examination.

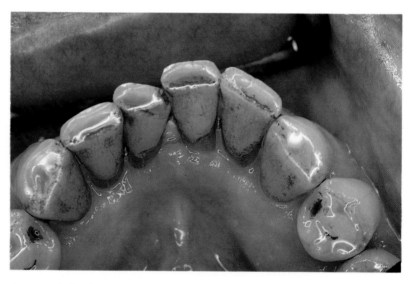

Figure 9-7 One month after scaling and root planing plus chlorhexidine rinsing in the patient shown in Figure 9-6.

nificantly. No sites bled spontaneously at the 3-month examination. Mean pocket depths were reduced, and no further loss of attachment occurred when this treatment regimen was used.

It is not clear whether chlorhexidine acted directly on the causative microflora, prevented recolonization of these pathogens after scaling/root planing, or both. In most forms of periodontitis, the efficacy of an antimicrobial is limited by the agent's inability to reach the bottom of periodontal pockets. Formation of deep pockets is not a major clinical feature of HIV-associated periodontal disease. Indeed, the mean pocket depth of all patients at the initial examination was 3.3 mm. In HIV-associated lesions, necrosis of the gingival margin appears to parallel loss of alveolar bone, resulting in progressive recession rather than increased pocket depth.

Based on results presented here, local treatment of patients with HIV-associated gingivitis and periodontitis is effective, and should include intensive oral hygiene instructions, scaling and root planing with povidone-iodine irrigation as required for access and patients' comfort, and twice daily rinsing with chlorhexidine after personal oral hygiene.

REFERENCES

1. Greenspan JS, Greenspan D, Schiødt M, Pindborg JJ: *AIDS and the Dental Team.* Kopenhagen, Munksgaard, 1986, p 96.
2. Silverman S Jr, Migliorati CA, Lozada-Nur F, et al: Oral findings in people with or at risk for AIDS: A study of 375 homosexual males. *J Am Dent Assoc* 1986;112:187-192.
3. Winkler JR, Murray PA: Periodontal disease — Potential intraoral expression of AIDS may be a rapidly progressive periodontitis. *Calif Dent Assoc J* 1987;15:20-24.
4. Beust TB, Albray RA, Hirschfeld I: Microbial phase of the oral manifestations of Vincent's infection. *J Dent Res* 1930;10:97-106.
5. Molinari JA: Sterilization and disinfection, in Schuster GS (ed): *Oral Microbiology and Infectious Disease*, ed 2. Baltimore, Williams & Wilkins, 1983, p 77.
6. Rosling GB, Slots J, Webber RL, et al: Microbiological and clinical effects of topical subgingival antimicrobial treatment on human periodontal disease. *J Clin Periodontol* 1983;10:487-514.
7. Loë H, Schiødt CR: The effect of chlorhexidine mouthrinses and topical application of chlorhexidine on the development of dental plaque and gingivitis in man *J Periodont Res* 1970;5:79-83.
8. Schiødt CR, Löe H, Jensen SB, et al: The effect of chlorhexidine mouthrinses on the human flora. *J Periodont Res* 1970;5:84-89.

9. Lang NP, Brecx MC: Chlorhexidine digluconate — An agent for chemical plaque control and prevention of gingival inflammation. *J Periodont Res* 1986;16(Suppl):74-89.

10. Centers for Disease Control: Revision of the CDC surveillance case definition for acquired immunodeficiency syndrome. *MMWR* 1987;36:3-15.

11. Silness J, Löe H: Periodontal disease in pregnancy. II. Correlation between oral hygiene and periodontal conditions. *Acta Odontol Scand* 1964;22:112-135.

12. Löe H, Silness J: Periodontal disease in pregnancy. I. Prevalence and severity. *Acta Odontol Scand* 1963;21:533-551.

Panel Discussion: Session II

Dr Pindborg introduced the Session II speakers and welcomed additional members to the panel:

Dr David Dennison, Department of Periodontics, University of Texas at Houston

Dr Morton Schiødt, Royal Dental College, Copenhagen and University of California, San Francisco

Dr James Winkler, Department of Stomatology, University of California, San Francisco

Dr Dennison described studies of HIV-infected patients with acute necrotizing ulcerative gingivitis (ANUG), including characterization of their immune status. He noted that results were similar to those reported by Dr Winkler. The T4/T8 ratio in homosexual men with ANUG was approximately 1.66. Absolute T4 values were reduced about 50% in these patients compared to heterosexual males with ANUG. Polymorphonuclear leukocyte function in HIV-infected patients was increased, though not as markedly as reported by Dr Winkler. All homosexual males seen thus far with ANUG have been HIV-seropositive. Unlike the lesions Dr Winkler described, the ANUG lesions are typical, and resolve with conventional treatment. He suggested that differences observed in the behavior of the lesions may be due to patient selection or, less likely, to geographical differences in virulence, and stressed the need for well-designed studies to yield cross-sectional and longitudinal data.

Dr Barr agreed that there were differences in the periodontal lesions among HIV-infected individuals. In intravenous drug abusing HIV-positive patients, he had observed relatively little ANUG or rapidly destructive periodontal disease.

Dr Pindborg said that in Copenhagen, 25 cases of necrotizing gingivitis had been seen, mostly in HIV-seropositive individuals. Denmark has 220 documented cases of AIDS and approximately 1500 HIV-seropositive individuals. In the last few years, ANUG has been virtually nonexistent in Denmark, Sweden and many industrial countries. In contrast, 210 cases of ANUG were described among 10,000 people presenting to the admissions clinic of the Dental College of Bangalore in 1964, and Emslie

131

and Sheiham reported many cases of ANUG among immuno-compromised Nigerian children suffering from malaria. Paradoxically, ANUG is not seen in transplantation patients, who are also immunocompromised. Dr Pindborg noted that ANUG in Copenhagen is treated with careful dental prophylaxis followed by rinsing with chlorhexidine, a procedure much like that of Drs Winkler, Murray and Grassi.

Dr Holt raised the question of how the oral status of HIV-positive homosexuals compared with that of intravenous drug abusers, who may tend to be less fastidious in their personal habits. Dr Phelan noted that in her study of 103 patients with AIDS, 75% were intravenous drug abusers and none showed the characteristic gingivitis or periodontal disease. Dr Murray said that because the HIV-positive population in San Francisco is now more educated and is seeking treatment earlier, fewer severe cases of HIV-associated periodontitis are seen.

Dr Robertson observed that one of the striking features of HIV-associated periodontal disease was rapid loss of attach-ment. Data shown by Drs Winkler and Grassi did not suggest increased pocket depth in these patients. In fact, gingival necro-sis paralleled bone loss so pocket depths were never very great, but attachment loss averaged between 0.5 and 0.7 mm during a 3-month period in two of the groups described by Dr Grassi. Thus, the observation of no additional attachment loss in the chlorhexidine-treated group is very important.

Dr Robertson expressed surprise at the amount of agree-ment among the oral microbiologists. He asked whether the unusual organisms isolated by Drs Holt and Zambon might also be similar. Dr Zambon replied that it was remarkable that samples from patients in geographically disparate areas were so alike and that the unusual organisms might well be the same.

In response to a question from Dr D. Greenspan about the presence of the periodontal disease in Africa, Dr Schiødt responded that among 50 AIDS patients he examined in Tanzania, he saw none with necrotizing gingivitis. In contrast, there were a number of candidiasis and hairy leukoplakia cases. He noted that there may be not only geographical differ-ences but also differences with regard to the various groups being investigated. These 50 patients, for example, had acquired AIDS predominantly through heterosexual transmis-sion. Dr Pindborg concurred, noting that in Kenya fewer AIDS patients have *Pneumocystis carinii* pneumonia but more have tuberculosis.

Dr Sciubba noted that AIDS progresses differently in the hemophilia population and said he had not seen ANUG or destructive oral lesions in the hemophilia subset of AIDS patients. Dr Schiødt described having examined 77 hemophiliacs in Denmark (half the hemophiliac population) without knowing their HIV status. It was later disclosed that 42 of these were HIV positive; six of these were identified in the oral examination by the presence of hairy leukoplakia. There were very few cases of candidiasis and none of necrotizing gingivitis. Dr Pindborg added that while there was a trend toward a greater incidence of hairy leukoplakia in the Danish homosexuals with AIDS than in the hemophiliacs, the difference was not statistically significant.

Dr Winkler observed that there seemed to be almost a cyclic pattern to the appearance of cases of HIV-associated periodontal disease in the San Francisco patient population: one month there will be lots of cases, then very few for several months. He agreed that differences in reports of periodontal manifestations of HIV infection might be related to whether a particular study population was intravenous drug abusing, homosexual, or hemophiliac. In addition, such lesions may be influenced by patient age, indigenous microflora and length of time since HIV infection.

Dr Redding noted that of 40 AIDS patients he had seen in San Antonio in the last two years, there were only two cases of HIV periodontitis, both in teenage hemophiliacs.

Dr Holt asked whether there was any relationship between the periodontal lesion and the stage of the disease. Dr Winkler replied that the gingivitis lesion seems to be associated with people who have few other intraoral or extraoral HIV-associated lesions, whereas the periodontitis cases, particularly the more aggressive ones, typically were associated with candidiasis or hairy leukoplakia or, in one case, *P carinii* pneumonia. He suggested there might be a connection with the T4/T8 ratio.

Dr Abel reported observing a site specificity in his patients with HIV periodontitis, almost predictably the mesial surface of first mandibular molars and the molar maxillary anteriors. He asked about the criteria for the San Francisco cases, which seemed to show a general distribution, and about open flap debridement as treatment.

Dr Winkler answered that at first he and his colleagues thought the disease was only located in the lower anteriors in the molar region, perhaps because these are regions of high accumulations of plaque and calculus. However, as more data were gathered, they found that the distribution was fairly even. He added that at first they had done many flap surgeries in these patients and had not specifically noticed any difference in healing, but found that they had difficulty keeping these patients from continuing to break down.

Dr Murray added that HIV-positive subjects treated with surgery have healed well but very slowly, excessively slowly in some cases. These patients are followed very closely through recalls. In the ten cases she has done, she found no recurrence of disease.

Dr Grassi added that since, as Dr Robertson had pointed out, these patients showed no deep pockets, the accessibility for debridement is sufficient without flap surgery.

Dr Pindborg asked Dr Grassi to explain the difference between the "erythema" and the "petechiae" he had pointed out as characteristic clinical features. From a pathological point of view, a petechia is a submucosal bleeding, whereas erythema is just an overlying atrophic epithelium. Dr Grassi responded that he and his colleagues had decided to use the term "punctate lesions," but agreed that the pathology of these lesions was not known

Dr Ayer raised the question of whether patients on azidothymidine (AZT) may have better periodontal health than other AIDS patients. Dr Reichart spoke of observing two patients on AZT who had lesions very comparable to what is seen in leukemia patients. During AZT treatment patients sometimes develop agranulocytosis and then slough off huge areas of periodontal tissue.

Dr D. Greenspan reported that during the early months of their course with AZT, patients complain less of candidiasis, bouts of oral ulceration, and subjective xerostomia. There have been some instances in which hairy leukoplakia has disappeared in patients on AZT. This may be because of AZT's effects on the immune system or its activity against Epstein Barr virus.

Dr Phelan reported seeing one patient in whom hairy leukoplakia completely disappeared 6 weeks after initiation of AZT.

Dr Pindborg raised Dr Scully's question, with reference to the EEC classification, whether hyperpigmentation may also be an oral feature. Dr Reichart responded that he and his colleagues had observed hyperpigmentation of skin, oral mucosa, tongue and fingernails in six or seven patients, which they thought might be due to several causes. One is medication. These patients were treated with clofazimine (Lamprene), well known in the treatment of leprosy, or with ketoconazole, which has side effects in the adrenal cortex resulting in a clinical picture comparable to Addison's disease. Dr Barr pointed out that analyzing electrolytes in patients receiving ketoconazole would confirm whether an Addison's-like process was going on that could cause pigmentation.

Dr Scully recalled a paper where a drug addict had oral pigmentation that was unrelated to HIV infection. And Dr Pindborg noted work done in Sweden on smoker's melanosis, adding that one should exclude in advance patients who are smokers.

Dr Fox pointed out that these patients have many, many different characteristics — they are on different medications, some use recreational drugs, some smoke, some abuse alcohol. It is essential that these patients not be grouped simply on the basis that they are either HIV positive or HIV negative. Some of the other factors involved make big differences.

Dr Scully asked what the rationale was for treating hairy leukoplakia. Dr Pindborg added that most of the hairy leukoplakias detected in Denmark were absolutely asymptomatic. Dr J. Greenspan replied that that is not always the case. There are complaints of occasional discomfort, of feeling something that should not be there, of unsightly appearance; there is also the possibility of candidal superinfection. Clinicians have to base the judgment on whether to treat on the needs of individual patients. Patients who agree that it is appropriate, on an experimental basis, to attempt therapy, or who urgently want therapy, can be treated, if other indications are in favor, with fairly high doses of acyclovir.

Dr Schiødt added that a number of hairy leukoplakia cases he has seen in San Francisco have bothersome symptoms, some of which may be due to the superimposed *Candida*. Treatment should be to remove the superimposed *Candida* infection first, and then to give acyclovir, at least on an experimental basis. The important question is whether removal of Epstein Barr virus in the hairy leukoplakia, as well as removal or possible removal of Epstein Barr virus in the body of the patient, will affect the long term prognosis of these patients.

Dr Pindborg reported observing two patients in Copenhagen in whom hairy leukoplakia disappeared during treatment with AZT. However, he did not know what other drugs they may have been treated with. When examining patients that have been treated for several different opportunistic infections, we do not know exactly how these drugs act upon candidiasis or hairy leukoplakia.

Dr J. Greenspan asked what the tissue pathogenesis is in HIV-associated periodontitis, aphthous ulceration, and salivary gland lesions. Dr Winkler responded with a working hypothesis of why in their patient population the damage is occurring so quickly. He and his colleagues see high levels of peripheral antibodies to basically any bacteria they are looking for, periodontopathic or not. There seems to be a hyperreactive polymorphonuclear cell population. These patients have a high antigen load that may be reacting with the locally high levels of antibody. The combination of antigen-antibody response with the hyperreactive polymorphonuclear leukocytes may be leading to the rapid destruction seen in these patients. By removing the bacteria, with chlorhexidine for example, and thus reducing the antigen load, they may be allowing what is left of the immune system to respond in a more normal fashion.

Dr Greenspan asked whether, since there is a very heavy antigen load in other places in the body of HIV-infected individuals, this kind of immune-complex-mediated damage could be postulated to occur elsewhere. Dr Winkler thought probably not; the mouth contains a flora that has a capacity for damage.

Dr Robertson pointed out that the high numbers of *Wolinella, Bacteroides,* and *Actinobacillus* species probably provide considerable machinery needed to do damage. Direct effects of these microorganisms could partially explain the tremendous necrosis that occurs.

Dr Holt agreed, adding that this is a mixed infection in which 12 or 15 microorganisms may be involved. Under ordinary conditions, the virulence factors which are held in check by the host are now out of control and microorganisms such as *Wolinella* or *Capnocytophaga,* an organism which causes large numbers of brain abscesses in immunocompromised patients, have the ability now to activate a variety of cytokines, interleukin-1 and a whole variety of other etiologic factors at very high levels. These microorganisms are probably spewing out large amounts of collagenase, elastase, and other proteolytic enzymes. These are very virulent invasive organisms. While not ruling out immune complexes, he felt that the host was no longer in a situation where it could defend itself against the tremendous overload of potentially very harmful virulence factors which could now further compromise the host.

Before closing the session, Dr Pindborg reported the successful use of miconazole, in the gel form, for treatment of the erythematous type of candidiasis, and success in using colostrum from cows immunized with *Candida albicans* for treating a seropositive man with a heavy pseudomembraneous type of candidiasis.

In summarizing the session, Dr Pindborg said that while there had been progress in the area of microbiology related to HIV infection, there had not been a breakthrough in regard to the microbiology of HIV-associated ANUG. However, it appears that severe periodontal lesions can be successfully treated with chlorhexidine. Follow-up studies of these patients are very much needed, and the differences observed between the patient populations in Copenhagen, New York and San Francisco point up the need also to study geographic differences.

10

Ethical Considerations for Providing Health Care to HIV-Infected Individuals

Laurence B. McCullough

This paper examines some of the central ethical issues confronting dental professionals in response to HIV contagion. The author argues that on the basis of the two defining virtues of the moral life of professionalism, self-effacement and self-sacrifice, dental professionals are ethically obligated to accept the very low risks of infection and fulfill their beneficence-based ethical obligation to provide oral health care for HIV-infected individuals. The author also argues that, in doing so, dental professionals will provide lay persons with powerful role models of a calm, rational, morally committed response to the needs of vulnerable fellow citizens. Failure to meet these ethical obligations will contribute significantly, perhaps finally, to the erosion of professionalism in dentistry in the United States.

Any discussion of the ethical considerations of providing health care to HIV-infected individuals must begin with an acknowledgement and consideration of the concerns of health care professionals about their exposure to this virus, the diseases that it causes, and to the medical, social, and economic sequelae of those diseases. Obviously, the main concern is with infection — of oneself and, if one becomes infected, through oneself the infection of one's sexual partner or spouse, as well as future children. In addition, health care professionals who become infected or who take care of infected individuals are at risk for loss of employment, eg, when an associate is informed by the owner of a dental practice to accept no known HIV-infected patients, and for threats to quit by auxiliaries who refuse to be exposed to patients with known HIV infection. Finally, health care professionals in private practice — the vast majority of dentists in the United States — are concerned about the loss of income that they might incur if patients in their practice leave out of fear that HIV-infected patients are being cared for and about the loss of income that would follow inability to practice if one became infected with HIV oneself. There are surely other concerns, but these seem to be the chief ones and, as we shall see shortly, these concerns raise fundamental ethical considerations for dental professionals and for society, as well.

These concerns are compounded by the apparent perception among many dentists that, if they conscientiously do their part and take care of a fair share of HIV-infected patients (or those at risk for infection) in the community, they will be among a small minority or even alone in doing so. This perception, if it takes widespread hold, will only increase the gravity of the concerns just listed. It should come as no surprise, therefore, that such a perception would contribute to a strong unwillingness to care for HIV-infected patients.

The impact of these concerns on dental professionals and on our society is compounded by the erosion of professionalism in dentistry, an erosion the causes of which — I submit — are chiefly *internal* and not external to the profession. External sources, to be sure, are frequently blamed for this erosion, chief among them the decisions of the Federal Trade Commission and federal courts to forbid the prohibition of advertising in the *Principles of Ethics* of the American Dental Association (ADA).[1] Such external forces, however, at most *permit* behavior that is thought to be destructive to professionalism; they do not *require* such behavior. Advertising is undertaken as the result of free choice and the perception of competitive behavior by other dentists, not under court order. Similarly, the behaviors of dental professionals in response to HIV contagion are free behaviors — in the legal sense. When such behaviors undermine the ethics of professionalism, they pose a considerable internal threat to the moral integrity of professionalism in dentistry and may well succeed in making final the erosion of the ideals and reality of professionalism in dentistry.

It goes without saying at this point that an indispensable

response in the dental office to HIV infection is the prevention of infection through rigorous infection control in the provision of dental care and services.[2,3] Only the most invincibly ignorant believe anything to the contrary. However, calls for rigorous infection control will not work in the absence of a commitment by dental professionals to care for patients — all patients — in the face of a very low risk of infection that will remain when rigorous infection control is employed, because the latter is not foolproof, eg, it cannot prevent all accidents that can cause infection. In short, more than information is involved — namely how dental professionals will understand and live out the commitments of the moral lives of professionals. *The core of the moral life in the professions is accepting the daily, routine obligation to blunt or even to sacrifice self-interest in meeting the needs of those who present themselves for care and, in so doing, expect to become patients.* Dentistry is not alone in being bound by this fundamental ethical obligation. It also should characterize medicine and has long been a staple of professionalism in the military. Indeed, the military is an important role model of the willingness to live with the threat of death for the health care professions, an ethical consideration regarding HIV infection that has been altogether overlooked to date.

There is also a larger issue at stake in how dental and other health care professionals respond to HIV contagion. We "lay people" require for our guidance as citizens role models of rational, calm, morally committed response to contagion so that we can respond in the same way as the contagion touches our lives — as it must and already has, eg, in how our schools will respond to the enrollment of HIV-infected children and in how we will respond to infected coworkers or coworkers with infected family members. That is, *citizens need to cultivate and live by the core of the moral life of citizenship: the daily, routine obligation to blunt or even sacrifice self-interest so that the needs of fellow citizens, especially those made vulnerable by serious infection or lethal disease, can be met.*

The balance of this paper is devoted to an ethical analysis of these two fundamental ethical considerations for providing health care to HIV-infected individuals. After a consideration of HIV infection and the ethics of professionalism and the ethics of citizenship, this paper will close with a brief reflection on a number of related ethical considerations.

HIV INFECTION AND THE ETHICS
OF PROFESSIONALISM

In this section of the paper I want to examine more closely the claim that moral life in professionalism involves the willing assumption of the obligation to be self-sacrificing. David Ozar has recently provided a very useful analysis of three models of dentistry: the guild, the commercial, and the interactive models.[4] The guild model accents the self-interest of the profession as an organized, mercantile group, in the manner of the great merchant guilds of the past. The autonomy of the professional group, the freedom of its members from external — mainly legal — control in the conduct of their professional transactions is a defining feature of this model. The commercial model accents the economic interests of individual dentists. The freedom of the individual dentist to contract for services with whom he or she chooses is a central feature of this model. Both the guild model and the commercial model assume, in my own view, that the dental professional group or the individual dentist has unabridged property rights to the services that they provide to those to whom they choose to provide those services. As we shall see shortly, this assumption cannot be sustained. The interactive model accents the dentist's response to the needs of patients. The *ethical* obligations of the dentist — as distinct from his or her *legal* freedom from outside interference — constitute a central feature of this model.

Ozar's interactive model can be more fully interpreted in the following terms. An individual becomes a patient for dental care when three conditions are met. The first two are factual in nature, the third ethical: (1) the individual presents with a need that the dental professional is capable of identifying; (2) the dental professional is in a position to meet that need by virtue of his or her training and experience; and (3) the dental professional, as such, has a beneficence-based obligation to meet that need.

The third condition requires some explanation of the technical term from ethical theory, "beneficence." Beauchamp and Childress provide a pertinent ethical analysis of general beneficence-based obligations.[5] An individual, X, is bound by such obligations to another individual, Y, when the following conditions obtain:

1. Y is at risk of significant loss or damage;
2. X's action is directly relevant to the prevention of this loss or damage;
3. X's action would probably prevent it; and
4. the benefit that Y will gain outweighs any harms that X is likely to suffer and does not present more than minimal risk to X.[5]

All of these conditions clearly apply to the ethical obligations of dental professionals to HIV-infected individuals who present themselves for care. They can be summarized in the following terms: the dental professional is obligated to respond to such individuals by accepting them as patients.

In light of this analysis, it is very important to distinguish the legal guidance recently provided by the ADA on the care of HIV-infected individuals from the ethical obligations of professionals. According to the ADA, "A dentist in most situations historically has had the right to decline treatment to new prospective patients."[6] There are special circumstances in which the dentist needs to consider legal problems that can arise from refusing to treat HIV-infected individuals, eg, in emergencies, to patients of record, and in communities with statutes forbidding discrimination against handicapped individuals.[6] This analysis seems consistent with the provisions of the ADA *Principles of Ethics,* which sanctions "reasonable discretion" in the selection of patients.[7] This legal, code-based approach to the limits of providing dental care to HIV-infected individuals is grounded in the guild model, which is at a very far remove from the model that is consistent with professionalism in its core ethical sense, the interactive model. An ethically sound approach does not emphasize the legal and contractual autonomy of the dental professional, but rather his or her ethical obligations to those in need of care that the dental professional is trained to provide.

Those ethical obligations have their foundation in two fundamental virtues that, together, define the core of the moral life of the professional. These two virtues form that core because by forming his or her character in response to them the professional becomes the sort of person who focuses *primarily* on the interests of those in need and only secondarily on his or her own self-interest.[8] The first virtue is self-effacement, the willing putting aside of the sociocultural differences that can blunt the turning of the dental professional's attention to the needs of others. This virtue is especially relevant to the care of HIV-infected individuals because many of them are members of vulnerable, stigmatized social groups. As such, they pose a personal challenge to the dental professional to put aside and thus never act on such emotions as revulsion or disgust toward the life and behaviors of another person.

The second virtue is self-sacrifice. In general terms, this virtue requires the dental professional to place systematic priority on the protection and promotion of the best interests of those in need of dental care and systematic secondary status on her or his own self-interest. The clear implication here is that the latter should be willingly sacrificed to the former.

The central ethical challenge to dental professionals of caring for HIV-infected individuals can now be stated. It is not a question about whether the dental professional is obligated to lose his or her life as the price of caring for patients; given the analysis above of the nature of beneficence-based ethical obligations, this is an imprecise and thus irrelevant attempt to dismiss the ethical demands of the virtue of self-sacrifice. The precise question regarding the care of HIV-infected individuals is the following: *is the dental professional under an ethical obligation to take health risks that can be managed effectively, in such a way as to reduce the incidence of risks to health, including the risk of lethal infection, to a minimum?* We know, as a matter of scientific finding, that rigorous infection control decreases the incidence of such risk to a minimum. Thus, the question must be answered in the affirmative, if professionalism is to mean anything in dentistry.

This conclusion is reinforced by the recent analysis of Edmund Pellegrino, one of the most distinguished scholars in the field of bioethics, to the effect that the services of health care professionals are not proprietary:

> The [dental professional's] knowledge, therefore, is not individually owned and ought not to be used primarily for personal gain, prestige, or power. Rather, the profession holds this knowledge in trust for the good of the sick. Those who enter the profession are automatically parties to a collective covenant — one that cannot be interpreted unilaterally.[9]

What are the dental professional's ethical obligations regarding the demands of self-sacrifice when it comes to economic self-interest of the sort that were noted at the beginning of this paper? On the basis of the ethical analysis developed so far, it seems clear that economic self-interest is mere self-interest when economic loss, as a potential risk to the dental professional, is compared to the potential benefit to be gained by the HIV-infected individual from receiving care. This aspect of the moral life in dentistry is completely ignored by the guild and commercial models and thus renders them, finally, irrelevant to the topic under present consideration.

Given this ethical analysis, we are now in a position to understand the full significance for dental professionalism of threats by the owner of a practice to dismiss an associate if she or he cares for HIV-infected patients, or threats of dental auxiliaries to quit if such patients are admitted to or continued in the practice. We can also now appreciate the significance of the circumstances that would cause a professionally conscientious dentist to worry that others are not picking up their share of the burdens of self-sacrifice. These phenomena — if they persist as responses to HIV contagion — may well be diagnostic of the triumph of the guild and commercial models and thus of the collapse of professionalism in dental practice in the United States. In short, whether the process of erosion of professionalism in dentistry may finally run its course is at stake in how dentists respond to the ethical challenges of caring for HIV-infected individuals.[10,11]

When the dental professional weighs his or her professional obligations as just analyzed against obligations to prevent infection of sexual partners or future children, she or he must recognize that there are ways to meet the latter obligation that do not require failure to provide care for HIV-infected individuals. Sexual abstinence or "safer sex" practices may impose psychological burdens on the dental professional and his or her sexual partner, but these are not so overwhelming as to justify failing to meet one's ethical obligations to the sick.

One possible preventive measure here is the regulatory response available to lay persons. After all, Pellegrino's analysis is correct and should be extended to its underlying implication: we lay people own the professions; they do not own themselves. We are therefore justified in acting through the regulatory mechanism of licensure — as New Jersey has announced it will — to restrain the guild and commercial models in the attempt to protect sick people from dentists who act on models that, in ethical terms, are systematically predatory on, even destructive of, the best interests of individuals already unfortunate enough to suffer from HIV infection.

HIV INFECTION AND THE ETHICS OF CITIZENSHIP

HIV contagion is in the process of destroying an illusion in the developed countries of the world, including the United States, about our invulnerability, an illusion that the biomedical sciences and health care professions taught us, viz, that the microbe was in retreat and that the age of lethal communicable diseases was a thing of the past.[12] We thought — wrongly — that we had tamed at least this one part of the natural order to our will, thus hiding from ourselves the fact that we live in an environment on this planet that is at once accommodating and unremittingly hostile to the presence of our species. Fifteen years ago Joshua Lederberg stated succinctly a lesson that HIV contagion requires us to relearn:

> The natural evolutionary process has placed no special premium on *human* life. It might be perfectly "natural" for a new virus to emerge that would eliminate our own species as others have been eliminated.[13]

We live, in my view, in a time when we increasingly fail to exhibit the capacity to live comfortably with persistent uncertainty in our lives, perhaps because such uncertainty, and the confusion and stress it inevitably engenders, infect so many dimensions of our lives, regarding, eg, the goals or purposes of economic, political, social, educational, and health care institutions upon which we depend for order and meaning. HIV contagion has increased our uncertainty about our relationships not only to our health care professionals, but to the very world in which we make our daily routine. Are coworkers, neighbors, strangers on a train, or children in school with my children threats to my existence or to that of those whom I love? If we come to think so, then the moral traditions of citizenship that have sustained and enriched our lives in the United States will be lethally imperiled.

By citizenship here I mean simply the willingness to care for those in need and, when necessary, to sacrifice for the sake of those in need, especially those whose need is compounded by sickness, disease, and social stigmatization or even ostracization. Citizenship, thus understood, requires lay persons, as citizens, to cultivate the virtues of self-effacement and self-sacrifice, although not always to the degree required of professional people. Thus, professional people are important role models to citizens of the moral life of service to the needs of others.

If this vision of the human good is to animate the moral lives of citizens as we grope to find the right responses to HIV contagion, there must be powerful role models of calm, rational, morally committed responses to that contagion. I do believe that, in an inchoate way, we citizens are looking to our health care professionals to provide such role models. The ethical — as well as the social and political — issue at stake here is the extent to which we should think of others as threats to our own well being, because any such response to others is corrosive of citizenship. As health care professionals — and anyone who reads a newspaper or gets news from the electronic media — know, there is a great deal of fear about what is not known about HIV infection. Should that fear run out of control, we place ourselves at risk for the Hobbesian world of all against all,[14] a risk already increased by the myriad forces — internal and external alike — promoting mere self-interest in our daily lives.

Scientific evidence indicates that the routes of infection are blood products and body fluids such as semen. Casual contact cannot be included as a vector for infection, because there is no evidence that it is a vector. That is, scientific thinking — which should be role modeled for us by all health care professionals, because such thinking is one of the foundations of being a health care professional — imposes a discipline on what health care professionals are free to believe, say, and act on when it comes to HIV infection. Citizenship imposes a similar discipline, but we citizens depend on health care professionals to know what that discipline should be. Any dental — or other health care — professional who refuses to care for HIV-infected individuals out of fear of risk to him or herself provides citizens with a role model of *unreasoning fear,* not the discipline of scientific thinking and the calm, rational, morally committed response that should characterize the scientifically trained health care professional. Any dental professional who expresses (already bad enough) or, worse, acts on unreasoning fear explicitly promotes the unjustified pursuit of mere self-interest and thus has an ethical impact far beyond the confines of the dental office. She or he contributes to the erosion not only of the moral life of professionalism but, in a parallel way, to the erosion of the moral life of citizenship, because the latter depends vitally on the former in the face of HIV or any other lethal infection, ie, those that are bound to follow in the near as well as distant

148

future. "Professional" persons who are caught up only in themselves are miserable role models for citizens, not to mention for young people contemplating a life in service to others as a health care professional.

CONCLUSION

I want in closing to draw out three general lessons from the preceding ethical analysis, because their urgency requires that we attend to them.

First, I want to underscore that the moral integrity and vitality of our professions, already imperiled social institutions, are placed at further risk by health care professionals who fail to acknowledge and act on their beneficence-based obligations to the sick as these are grounded in and expressed by the virtues of self-effacement and self-sacrifice. This is a matter of vital importance to all of us, not just to the professions themselves.

Second, the very fabric of our society and the trust that we place in the social institutions of self-government, education, health care, and commerce depend on a vital moral tradition of citizenship. Thus, the ethical dimensions of HIV infection reach far beyond health care. Recognition of this on the part of health care professionals would also probably serve to reduce some of the pressure that any group experiences when it believes that it is "going it alone."

Finally, attending to the ethical dimensions of citizenship and professionalism in response to HIV contagion might help us in the United States to break out of the chauvinism that has characterized much of the discussion to date of the ethical dimensions of HIV contagion and infection. To be sure, these are serious, urgent matters in our country. But in other countries these are matters of emergency, even (irreversible) calamity. In this light, the ethical obligations of a rich nation like the United States to share its bounty with those in dire need should be a matter of vivid concern for the health care professions, who can provide key leadership in animating the international ethical dimensions that ought to characterize the moral traditions of citizenship in a nation that is still a world power and, certainly when it comes to health care, an economic giant.

REFERENCES

1. American Dental Association 1963-1986. *J Am Dent Assoc* 1984;108:561-571, 574-579.
2. Jakush J, et al: AIDS: The disease and its implications for dentistry. *J Am Dent Assoc* 1987;115:394-403.
3. Silverman S: AIDS update: Oral findings, diagnosis, and precautions. *J Am Dent Assoc* 1987;115:559-563.
4. Ozar DT: Three models of professionalism and professional obligation in dentistry. *J Am Dent Assoc* 1985;110:173-177.
5. Beauchamp TL, Childress JF: *Principles of Biomedical Ethics*, ed 2. New York, Oxford University Press, 1983.
6. Logan MK: Legal, ethical issues for dentists. *J Am Dent Assoc* 1987;115:402.
7. American Dental Association: *ADA Principles of Ethics and Code of Professional Conduct*. Chicago, American Dental Association, 1983.
8. McCullough LB: Ethics in dental medicine. *J Dent Ed* 1985;49:219-224.
9. Pellegrino ED: Altruism, self-interest, and medical ethics. *JAMA* 1987;258:1939-1940.
10. When doctors refuse to treat AIDS, editorial. *NY Times,* August 3, 1987.
11. Zuger A, Miles SH: Physicians, AIDS, and occupational risk. *JAMA* 1987;258:1924-1928.
12. Taylor RB, Denham JW, Ureda JR: Health promotion: A perspective, in Taylor RB (ed): *Health Promotion: Principles and Clinical Application*. New York, Appleton-Century-Crofts, 1982, pp 1-18.
13. Lederberg J: The genetics of human nature. *Soc Res* 1973;40:375-406.
14. Hobbes T: *Leviathan*, Oakeshott M (ed). Oxford, Oxford University Press, 1947.

11

Legal Implications of Infectious Disease in the Dental Office

Mary K. Logan

Alarming statistics, plus new regulations, make use of barrier techniques essential in today's dental practice. With the readily available precautions for minimizing the risk of infectious disease, dentists have the unique opportunity of improving their profession and practices before legal precedents are established.

From a legal perspective, the results of a recent survey of Midwest dentists are alarming: only 52% of the surveyed dentists have been inoculated against hepatitis B, and only 20% of their office staff members have been vaccinated.[1] Another nationwide survey of dentists found that only 13.6% of dentists wear gloves routinely.[2] With all due respect to the profession, these figures indicate a certain blindness to infectious disease in the dental office.

Another alarming set of statistics points out the fallacy that infection control is not necessary: approximately 1 million people are carriers of hepatitis B, and more than 42,182 people to date in the United States have contracted AIDS.[3] Sixty of these people with AIDS are dental personnel,[3] and the disease presently doubles in its number of victims every 15 months.[3]

In the United States, 1.5 to 2 million people have evidence of carrying the HIV, and these people are all infectious.[3] The

Centers for Disease Control (CDC) estimates there will be 270,000 AIDS cases and 129,000 deaths by the end of 1991.[3]

All patients who are disease carriers certainly do not seek regular professional dental care. However, we can only assume that hundreds of thousands do seek care from thousands of dentists who may not be adequately protecting themselves, their staff members, and other patients from the risk of contracting disease. Everyone associated with dental and other health care professions should be concerned with the potential legal implications of these facts. This paper explores several of the most critical of these legal questions.

What is my potential liability to others if I (or my staff members) contract AIDS, hepatitis B, or some other serious communicable disease?

Liability to staff members is clear. If an employee contracts an infectious disease and can trace its cause to the work environment, the dentist employer is responsible under the worker's compensation laws.[4] These laws, unlike civil tort remedies, do not require the injured person to prove negligence, or fault, of the dentist employer. If the person can prove employment status (which should be relatively easy) and that the cause of the disease was work related, he or she will be entitled to recover under the worker's compensation laws.[5] Liability to patients is less clear and more complex because of the element of fault. The usual tort, or malpractice, standards apply. If there was a duty, then simply stated, the issues are whether the duty was breached, and whether the breach of duty resulted in injury to the patient.

The most important of these issues in a case involving infectious disease, such as AIDS or hepatitis B, would be breach of duty, also known as negligence. The question is whether a dentist who is a carrier of AIDS or hepatitis B is negligent if he continues to treat patients. The obvious, if not blatant, case of liability should be examined first. The dentist has contracted AIDS and has been diagnosed. He fails to inform his patients or staff, or take any particular precautions for infection control (such as wearing gloves, protective eyewear, and mask, or using sterilization techniques). If a patient not otherwise in a high-risk group contracts AIDS and sues the dentist (assuming the patient can establish causation), this case likely will result in liability to the dentist, for a number of reasons.

The most obvious problem is the dentist's failure to take appropriate precautions for infection control. According to the guidelines issued by the CDC, the dentist could have fully protected his patients (and staff members) from the disease simply by wearing gloves, protective eyewear, and mask, and using proper sterilization techniques.[6] These guidelines are well published, if not common knowledge, and it is likely that a court or jury would find that a reasonably prudent dentist under the circumstances would or should have taken these precautions. In fact, it is possible that a dentist in this situation could be charged with punitive damages for "blatant disregard" of the patient's safety.[7]

In a modification of the case scenario to make the liability issue less clear, we can consider a case in which the dentist has contracted hepatitis B but is unaware of it. The dentist does not use infection control precautions, and a patient contracts hepatitis B and sues the dentist. The dentist in this case may not receive a ruling any more favorable than that in the foregoing example, although punitive damages would not be an issue. This dentist, although seemingly innocent of any wrongdoing, faces a potential liability problem in that arguably he has failed to follow the standard of care for infection control — using gloves, mask, protective eyewear, and sterilization techniques in all cases, at all times.

No reported cases to date have issued definitive rulings that the standard of care requires a dentist to use these barrier techniques at all times. However, if such a case arises, and it will, a definitive precedent likely will be established to that effect. Barrier techniques have been recommended in the literature by the CDC and by the American Dental Association (ADA) for some time. These precautions are easy and relatively inexpensive to adopt. Most importantly, barrier techniques are effective. In addition, the recent decision of the Occupational Safety and Health Administration (OSHA) to make barrier techniques mandatory would be damaging evidence against a dentist regarding the standard of care. The dentist in this example would be destroyed on cross-examination by a well-prepared plaintiff's attorney.

In the next example, we assume the dentist has hepatitis B, but is not aware of it. The dentist has not been vaccinated. He wears gloves in most instances and sterilizes the office equipment, but occasionally removes the gloves to expand dexterity on difficult procedures. The dentist probably would be held liable to the patient who contracts hepatitis B, if the patient is able to trace the disease to the dentist's office.

This is a troublesome case because the dentist arguably is using reasonable care by wearing gloves most of the time. The two issues are whether the dentist used reasonable care in his barrier procedures, and whether a reasonably prudent dentist would or should have been vaccinated.

The first issue (reasonable care in wearing gloves and sterilizing the equipment) is a close one. It would require the dentist's testimony as to the procedures and a credible expert's testimony that the dentist's procedures were reasonable, particularly the procedure of occasional glove removal. The second issue is more difficult for the dentist, an easier case for the plaintiff patient. The hepatitis B vaccine is widely available; its use by dentists is urged by the ADA, the CDC, OSHA, and other public groups, and it entails few risks. The vaccine also is relatively inexpensive and highly effective. Few valid reasons (pregnancy, age, medical problems, religion, or the presence of antibodies) exist that a dentist may offer for failing to be vaccinated. In all likelihood, a jury would conclude that the dentist failed to use reasonable care because he should have been vaccinated and but for this failure to act, he would not have contracted and spread hepatitis B.

A final point is critical on this issue of infection control. OSHA recently announced it is using existing safety regulations to declare that the use of barrier techniques is not mandatory.[8] From a regulatory standpoint, OSHA's authority is to regulate the conduct of employers in the workplace to ensure the workplace is safe for employees. As a practical matter, OSHA will now require all dentist employers to provide appropriate infection control barriers (following the most recent CDC and National Institute of Occupational Safety and Health [NIOSH] guidelines) to all employees. OSHA also has authority under this regulation to require employees to use the infection control barriers provided.[9]

The ultimate impact of this new interpretation of existing OSHA regulations is yet to be seen.[10] However, OSHA will make inspections of dental offices as necessary, and will impose fines against those dentist employers who violate the rules.[11] The OSHA regulation also could have a subtle influence in the area of professional liability. Any lingering doubt about the standard of care has now disappeared entirely. Any judge or jury, with the facts properly brought before them, would find that barrier techniques are the standard of care.[12]

Do state dental practice acts restrict my ability to practice dentistry if I have or carry an infectious disease?

The dental practice acts in six states — Alabama, Illinois, Louisiana, North Carolina, Oklahoma, and Washington — expressly limit or prohibit the practice of dentistry by those with infectious diseases (Category I).[13] Seventeen other practice acts limit the practice of dentistry by dentists with physical illnesses that threaten the patient or public health and safety. These states are Arizona, California, Colorado, Connecticut, Georgia, Kentucky, Maine, Michigan, Missouri, New Hampshire, New Jersey, Ohio, Pennsylvania, Tennessee, Texas, Virginia, and Wisconsin (Category II). Twelve practice acts broadly restrict or prohibit the practice of dentistry by a dentist with a "physical disability or illness" (Category III). These states are Alaska, Maryland, Minnesota, Montana, Nebraska, New Mexico, New York, Oregon, South Dakota, Utah, Vermont, and the District of Columbia. Finally, the remaining 13 state practice acts contain no restrictions in this area. These states are Arkansas, Delaware, Hawaii, Idaho, Iowa, Kansas, Massachusetts, Mississippi, Nevada, North Dakota, Rhode Island, West Virginia, and Wyoming.

The five states in Category I clearly are the most specific in their ability to restrict the practice of a dentist who has or carries an infectious disease. However, if a Category II or III state elected to restrict the hypothetical dentist's ability to practice, the statutory language exists that would allow the state to do so.

To date, there have been no challenges to the constitutionality of these restrictions, and no reported cases involving the use of these provisions of the dental practice acts. A case could be made, however, challenging the constitutionality, or at least challenging the applicability of these restrictions to a dentist who has or carries an infectious disease but who is physically capable of handling the work and who poses no material risk of harm to others (that is, the dentist follows a strict infection control regimen).

By way of example, a Chicago physician with AIDS has filed a civil rights lawsuit against a hospital that restricted his staff privileges. He was not permitted to perform any invasive procedure, nor was he even allowed to place a thermometer into a patient's mouth. As of October 1987, the hospital has consented to restore the physician to full staff privileges. The physician will be required to wear double gloves when treating patients, and to adhere to an infection control regimen. The court retained jurisdiction so that the ultimate outcome of the case is not yet known.[14]

The point of this entire discussion regarding barrier techniques should be painfully obvious. A great number of dentists may be placing themselves in a legally precarious position, unnecessarily so, by failing or refusing to be vaccinated for hepatitis B, to wear gloves, and to take other precautions for control of serious infectious disease in the dental office. The dentist who fails to take these precautions risks not only potential liability to others but also problems with OSHA and state dental boards. He also places his own health in jeopardy.

Do I have a responsibility to my staff and patients to inform them that I or a staff member has AIDS or hepatitis B?

This is perhaps the most dubious professional, ethical, and legal question facing dentists who are disease carriers (or who have a disease carrier working in their offices). If the dentist informs patient and staff, hysteria will close the doors of his office. If the dentist fails to advise, however, he undoubtedly will be accused of failure to follow informed consent standards. The choice is not an easy one.

A dentist in this situation would be well advised to seek expert legal and medical advice immediately, from an attorney familiar with local case law and local juries, as well as from a physician knowledgeable about the disease. The answer to this troubling question from a legal perspective will depend on the specific facts of the dentist's situation. The underlying principle is that of informed consent. A patient must be advised of significant risks inherent in a procedure, and in some instances, the risk of contracting AIDS or hepatitis B in the dental office might be construed by a judge or jury as the type of risk of which a patient should be informed.

However, infection control experts contend that a carrier of AIDS or hepatitis B may fully protect himself and others even in an invasive health care setting, as long as the individual strictly conforms to the recommended barrier techniques. Again, the legal question is whether the individual who complies with this regimen poses any material risk or harm to patients, colleagues, and staff members. This is the underlying basis of informed consent.

Experts on infection control have reported there is no material risk of harm to others in this situation. Therefore, a dentist (or staff person) carrier should be safe legally in continuing to work without disclosure to others. Without a material risk of harm, there is no need to inform.

However, if a patient contracts hepatitis B and is not otherwise in a high-risk category for contracting the disease, he may point to the dental office as the source of infection. Technically, the patient as a plaintiff would have the burden in a professional liability lawsuit of proving that the dental office was the source or cause of the disease, a difficult task. As a practical matter, however, the dentist also may be placed in the equally difficult position of disproving that the plaintiff patient contracted the disease through the dental office.

In short, this is a complex area with no easy solutions. However, with the advice of legal and medical counsel, together with sound professional judgment, an answer should become apparent on an individual basis.

Do I have a duty to inform my staff of the risks of contracting serious infectious diseases in the dental office?

An employer has a legal duty to inform employees of any hazards accompanying the job.[15] An employer also has a related duty to maintain a safe workplace.[16] With respect to hepatitis B, these basic rules suggest that a dentist may be obligated to inform his staff of the risk of contracting hepatitis B in the dental office.[17] However, this duty may even include the obligation to advise staff of the hepatitis B vaccine and to make the vaccine readily available to them. One author has suggested that the dentist may even have a legal duty to pay for the vaccine for the staff members, and that the dentist should obtain signed informed consent forms from employees who elect not to be vaccinated.[18]

AIDS is a more difficult issue. There is no vaccination and no cure if a staff member contracts the disease. However, the risk of contracting AIDS in a health care setting is, according to experts, minimal. For this reason, if a dentist properly educates staff members about appropriate barrier techniques, and also ensures that his staff generally understands the basic risks of transmission of the disease, any problem should be negligible.

If a dentist elects to take a chance and not provide or use appropriate barrier techniques in the dental office, then, at the least, he has a duty to inform staff members that the CDC and other guidelines urge, and that OSHA mandates, the use of infection control precautions and of the potential risks of not using these techniques. In addition, using the analogy of the hepatitis B vaccine, the dentist perhaps should provide and pay for gloves, masks, and protective eyewear for the office staff. He may have no choice under the new OSHA rules.

What are my legal rights if my staff refuses to assist in the treatment of a patient who has AIDS?

A number of dentists already have been in the unfortunate situation of dealing with a staff plagued with fear that they will contract AIDS if they treat a patient with AIDS or an individual in a high-risk group. Many dentists share this fear and believe they can transmit the disease to other patients. One of the most perceptive comments about the fear of AIDS is worth noting: "There are two epidemics sweeping the country today; the first is AIDS. The second, and I believe the more pervasive epidemic, is AIDS anxiety. . . . The reason this anxiety is so widespread is that this disease touches upon three widely held taboos in our society — sex, death, and homosexuality. AIDS, unlike any other disease, brings together these three taboos in a unique and unprecedented way, causing heightened anxiety."[19]

It is particularly difficult to provide reliable legal information to alleviate these fears because of the current state of medical and legal knowledge about AIDS.[20] Until it is proved that a health care worker cannot contract AIDS from needlesticks, for example, and that AIDS definitely is or is not a "handicap" under state and federal discrimination laws, then accurate, timely information relating to a health care employer's legal rights and responsibilities in treating AIDS patients will not be available.

A dentist traditionally has had the right not to accept a prospective new patient for treatment. As long as the individual was not already a patient of record, and no immediate emergency existed, the dentist did not have to consider the problem of possible abandonment, among others.[21]

The courts have yet to address a case involving a dentist's right to refer or refuse treatment of a prospective new patient who has AIDS. However, the issue has arisen informally in a number of instances because a staff member believes a new patient is a member of a high-risk group and thus refuses to assist in the treatment, or the dentist is fearful that the individual may have AIDS.

A number of administrative human rights commissions are bringing discrimination charges against dentists on behalf of AIDS patients. The basic claim in these administrative actions is that a refusal to treat violates handicap discrimination laws. Los Angeles, for example, has an ordinance specifically prohibiting AIDS discrimination in housing, employment, and medical and dental care.[22] This and similar ordinances arguably could require a dentist to treat a new patient for whom treatment under any other circumstance would be the dentist's free choice.[23]

Moreover, many states have made an official declaration that AIDS is a handicapping condition and, therefore, that AIDS discrimination is prohibited under the state's handicap discrimination laws.[24] The federal handicap discrimination law also is being interpreted in this manner.[25] The federal statute applies only to recipients of federal funding.[26] Arguably, however, a dentist who accepts Medicaid or Medicare funding is a recipient of federal monies within the meaning of the statute.[27] One state, Oregon, has gone so far as to rule administratively that a dentist cannot charge more for treatment of an AIDS patient, citing the Oregon handicap laws.[28] The extra fee is not allowed, although the dentist might incur additional costs associated with special infection control precautions.[29]

Many dentists understandably struggle with the notion that a government agency is interfering with their right to refuse treatment or refer patients for treatment elsewhere. It is helpful to understand the basic underlying contention in these AIDS discrimination claims.

First, the human rights commissions, particularly in New York, contend that AIDS is a handicap within the meaning of the particular handicap discrimination law. The basis for this argument is a 1987 decision from the US Supreme Court, in which the Court ruled that tuberculosis, another infectious disease, is a handicap within the meaning of the federal handicap discrimination laws.[30] That case involved a teacher who was terminated from her position because she had tuberculosis.

The second step in the discrimination analysis involves the contention that a dental office is a place of "public accommodation" subject to the jurisdiction of the handicap discrimination laws.[31] To be reached by these laws, a dental office must be one of the types of businesses the laws were intended to cover. Most laws of this type include places of "public accommodation" and, therefore, the human rights commissions argue that a dental office is included within the meaning of that term.[32]

The third step in the discrimination analysis is what is a "reasonable accommodation" of an AIDS patient by a dental office, assuming, of course, that a dental office is a place of public accommodation. The human rights advocates argue vehemently that the only reasonable accommodation is treatment in the office during regular business hours. They do not care that dentists have staff members who refuse to assist, that healthy but uninformed patients threaten to go elsewhere for treatment if an AIDS patient is treated in their dentist's office or that a dentist's family is concerned for his well-being. These human rights advocates base their position on the argument that there is no health risk to the dentist or the staff in providing treatment to AIDS patients in the dental office (assuming a dentist follows the infection control guidelines). They contend that without any health risk, there is no legitimate reason for refusal to treat or referral.

It is critical to note that these arguments have not yet been tested in the courts. The answers, therefore, unfortunately will not be forthcoming for months or years. In the meantime, however, dentists who receive federal funding, or who reside in jurisdictions with handicap discrimination laws that arguably protect people with AIDS, must come to terms with the fact that they may become embroiled in a discrimination claim if they refuse to treat or refer an AIDS patient for treatment elsewhere. It is impossible to predict the outcome of these issues in the courts because of the current state of medical and legal knowledge about AIDS. The results of the administrative discrimination cases, in particular, will be critical to an accurate

160

legal interpretation of a dentist's right to refuse treatment, refer for treatment elsewhere, require testing of, or charge more for services provided to AIDS patients.

For those dentists who have a problem with staff (such as staff members refusing to work with AIDS patients or another staff person who has AIDS), the recommendation from all fronts is education. The CDC guidelines indicate it is safe for health care workers to work around, and even perform invasive treatment procedures on, AIDS patients, provided the CDC barrier techniques are followed.[33]

On the basis of these guidelines, authorities in employment law suggest that staff problems should be handled by educating staff about AIDS in an effort to alleviate irrational and unfounded fears.[34] There are no easy answers to the troubling legal questions surrounding infection control issues (such as, can an employer fire an employee who has AIDS), and thus the suggestion of education is offered to resolve problems without running into legal difficulties. A dentist employer, however, should seek legal counsel if a staff problem arises which the dentist cannot resolve.

CONCLUSION

Currently, only one dentist not otherwise in a known high-risk group has contracted AIDS and no known cases of dentist-to-patient transmission have occurred. Moreover, a relatively small number of hepatitis cases have shown transmission from dentist (or staff members) to patient. Given the number of dentists who apparently have not been vaccinated against hepatitis B and who do not use the CDC recommended barrier techniques, it is fortunate that not more patients, staff members, and dentists have contracted infectious diseases through the dental office. The potential for an AIDS problem in the dental office still is unknown, although currently there is no evidence of occupational transmission. Dentists have the unique opportunity today to improve the profession and their practices before, instead of after, lawyers and juries set legal precedents. Given the relatively easy and cost-effective precautions for minimizing the risk of infectious disease, many dentists seem content to take a legal gamble by failing to adhere strictly to infection control precautions. Is the gamble worth it?

The opinions in this paper are those of the author and should not be construed as policy or opinion of the American Dental Association.

The paper is not intended to provide legal advice. It attempts to summarize general principles and emerging trends in the law, but it should not be substituted for consultation with one's own attorney.

References to gender are for convenience only.

The author thanks the background research assistance of Ms Beth Jacobson, Ms Tina Petrica, and Ms Lori Loeb.

Ms Logan is associate general counsel, American Dental Association. Address requests for reprints to the author.

REFERENCES

1. Dilemma: Treating the AIDS patient. *Dentistry Today* 1986;5:1.
2. Echavez MI, and others: Hepatitis B vaccine usage among dental practitioners in the United States: An epidemiologic survey, 1986.
3. These figures are from CDC statistics, which change frequently as more AIDS cases are reported.
4. See, eg, *Sacred Heart Med Ctr vs Department of Labor, Etc,* 92 Wash 2d 631, 1979. (Employer hospital held responsible under workers' compensation laws when nurse's hepatitis B more probably than not arose from work in hospital's intensive care unit). See generally, Larson A, *Workmen's Compensation Law* 1985;§6,14.
5. See note 4.
6. Some fear there is a problem with gloves if they are punctured. However, CDC and other reports indicate, to the contrary, that gloving is adequate protection, because the hands can be washed after treatment, as an added protection. In any event, however, even if puncturing of gloves does present a risk of transmission, does that justify not wearing them at all?
7. For a variation on this situation, see a discussion of punitive damages in the context of a worker's compensation case. In Baker C and Brennan J: Special report: Keeping health care workers healthy. *New Engl J Med* 1984;311:684,687.
8. The regulations on which OSHA relies are contained in 29 CRF §§1910.132, et seq, entitled "Personal Protective Equipment." The basic requirement is that, "[p]rotective equipment, including personal protective equipment for eyes, face, head and extremities, . . . should be provided, used and maintained in a sanitary and reliable condition whenever it is necessary by reason of hazards of processes or environment . . . encountered in a manner capable of causing injury or impairment." 29 CFR §1910.132.
9. For a history of OSHA's action see *ADA News* 1987;18(3):1, and *ADA News* 1987;18(16):1.
10. OSHA may be considering a more stringent set of regulations within the next year. Union groups have requested that OSHA consider requiring health care employers to provide the hepatitis B vaccine and a staff educational program on the transmission of infection.
11. See note 9, supra.

12. It should also be noted that one state dental board, Ohio, has taken a very assertive position in this area by recently adopting its own regulations for infection control under the authority of the state dental practice act. See OSDB Proposed Infection Control Rules (July 16, 1987). As long as these rules do not conflict with OSHA regulations, they will not be preempted by OSHA's actions in this area. The most significant distinction between the federally mandated OSHA rules and the state-mandated board rules is in the area of enforcement. Only the dental board has control regarding a dentist's license to practice. OSHA's authority basically is restricted to inspections and the imposition of substantial fines. In addition, the Washington Dental Disciplinary Board has adopted infection control guidelines. Those guidelines, however, are not mandatory and, therefore, are not as restrictive as the Ohio rules. See WSDB Infection Control Guidelines (October 1986) clarifying Wash Rev Code §18.32.330).
13. Ala Code 1986;§34-9-18; Ill Rev Stat ch III 1985;§2323; La Rev Stat Ann 1985;§777; NC Gen Stat 1986;§90-41; Okla Stat tit 1985;59,§32; Wash Rev Code 1986;§18.130.180.
14. *Dr John Doe vs County of Cook, Illinois, et al*, 1987;no. 87-6888.
15. Baker and Brennan, supra, note 7, at 685-686.
16. See note 15.
17. See generally, Baker CH and Hawkins VL: Law in the dental workplace: Legal implications of hepatitis B for the dental profession, *J Am Dent Assoc* 1985;110(4):637-642.
18. See note 17, at 639.
19. Kadzielski M, Siegel M, and Wolfe P: Legal aspects of AIDS, 8 Whittier L Rev 1986;503.
20. See discussion in Wing D: AIDS in the workplace: The emerging legal issues. 1986;163.
21. For discussion of the doctrine of abandonment, see Hirsh H: Abandonment: Actual or constructive premature termination of the physician-patient relationship. Transactions & Studies of the College of Physicians of Philadelphia 1984;207:6; Gerber P: How to move a problem patient out of your practice. *Dent Mgmt* 1983;12(11):23. See also ADA principles of ethics and code of professional conduct, §1-A (refusal on the basis of race, creed, color, sex, or national origin).
22. Los Angeles Municipal Code, Ch IV, Art 5.8, §45.84 (1985).
23. West Hollywood, Hayward, and San Francisco have similar ordinances. Austin, TX, also has a similar ordinance, adopted in December 1986. New York City has a handicap discrimination ordinance, also. The human rights commission there is arguing that a dental office is a place of "public accommodation" subject to the ordinance's jurisdiction. These ordinances have subtle variations and may not be applicable in all instances.
24. As of September 1986, those states were: California, Colorado, Connecticut, Florida, Illinois, Maine, Massachusetts, Michigan, Minnesota, Missouri, New Jersey, New Mexico, New York, Oregon, Pennsylvania, Rhode Island, Texas, Washington, West Virginia,

and Wisconsin, as well as the District of Columbia. Thus far, only Kentucky and Georgia have specifically ruled that AIDS is not a handicap under the state's handicap discrimination law. Other states (Louisiana, Montana, New Hampshire, and North Carolina) have determined informally that AIDS-based discrimination is improper. See National Gay Rights Advocates, Aids and handicap discrimination: A survey of the 50 states and the District of Columbia, 1986. Some states, such as Idaho, do not have handicap discrimination laws.

25. See *School Board of Nassau County, Florida vs Arline,* 107 SCt 1123 (1987), a tuberculosis case in which the court expressly declined to comment as to whether a carrier of AIDS is a handicapped person, but which is being cited by civil rights advocates and human rights commissions as authority on this point.
26. Rehabilitation Act of 1973, §504, 29, USC §794.
27. *US vs Baylor University Medical Center* 736 F2d 1039 (5th Cir, 1984).
28. See Infection control costs questioned. *ADA News* 1986;17(24):1.
29. See note 28. Presumably, therefore, a dentist under the Oregon ruling would need to spread these extra costs among all patients.
30. *School Board of Nassau County, Florida vs Arline,* 107 SCt 1123 (1987).
31. For a detailed analysis of the scope of the "public accommodation" provisions in various state discrimination laws, see Corboy: AIDS: Dental implications, presented at 1987 American Dental Association Management Conference, pages 5-13.
32. There is very little case law on the public accommodation issue involving health care offices. In addition, the definitions of public accommodation in the statutes are not uniform. A timely state by state analysis is therefore critical. See Corboy, supra, at 5-13.
33. This is particularly true because of the minimal risk of transmission of AIDS in the workplace. See, eg, Curiale R, and others: Communicable diseases in the work place: Legal, medical, economic, and human resource issues (PLI 1986); see also discussion, supra note 14, regarding the "Dr John Doe" case.
34. See note 33, at 361. See also Wing, supra note 20.

12

Rationale and Goals for Infection Control

John A. Molinari

Procedures aimed at preventing the spread of communicable disease during dental treatment are constantly being evaluated by the profession and an increasingly inquisitive public. The areas discussed in the present manuscript are representative of topics of concern within the profession. The rationale for prescribed modes of sterilization and chemical disinfection has been developed by the Centers for Disease Control and health professional organizations. While some practitioners may view published recommendations as an infringement upon their professional choice, one must keep in mind that the adage "What you cannot see will not hurt you" is unrealistic. The development of a reasonable series of aseptic procedures requires a joint effort by the practitioner and auxiliary staff. The risks associated with disease transmission can thus be minimized only when effective logical practices have been routinely implemented.

The routine exposure of practitioners and auxiliaries to a multitude of bacterial, viral and other microbial pathogens led to development of recommended infection control precautions initially directed at preventing hepatitis B virus (HBV) transmission.[1,2] The same basic protocol was later recommended for situations where diagnosed AIDS patients are provided treatment in dental clinics and offices.[3,4] Statements included within subsequent published guidelines reinforced the Centers for Disease Control (CDC) and the American Dental Association

(ADA) position that infection control procedures be used to routinely minimize the transmission of all infectious diseases.[5-7]

Similar guidelines were adopted by the federal government's Occupational Safety and Health Administration (OSHA) in 1987.[8] These recommendations are directed at the protection of all health care workers from HBV, HIV and other bloodborne infections by having employers initially evaluate working conditions and provide appropriate training and employee safeguards. Also included in the OSHA document is a request calling for evaluation of specific work-related tasks. These would then be subsequently classified into one of three categories (Table 12-1).

Microbial transmission by dental-related secretions and exudates occurs by three general routes: (1) direct contact with a lesion, organisms, or debris when performing intraoral

Table 12-1
Health-Care Workers' Exposure Categories

Category I: Tasks that involve exposure to blood, body fluids, or tissues.

All procedures or other job-related tasks that involve an inherent potential for mucous membrane or skin contact with blood, body fluids, or tissues, or a potential for spills or splashes of them, are Category I tasks. Use of appropriate protective measures should be required for every employee engaged in Category I tasks.

Category II: Tasks that involve no exposure to blood, body fluids, or tissues, but employment may require performing unplanned Category I tasks.

The normal work routine involves no exposure to blood, body fluids, or tissues, but exposure or potential exposure may be required as a condition of employment. Appropriate protective measures should be readily available to every employee engaged in Category II tasks.

Category III: Tasks that involve no exposure to blood, body fluids, or tissues, and Category I tasks are not a condition of employment.

The normal work routine involves no exposure to blood, body fluids, or tissues (although situations can be imagined or hypothesized under which anyone, anywhere, might encounter potential exposure to body fluids). Persons who perform these duties are not called upon as part of their employment to perform or assist in emergency medical care or first aid or to be potentially exposed in some other way. Tasks that involve handling of implements or utensils, use of public or shared bathroom facilities or telephones, and personal contacts such as handshaking are Category III tasks.

procedures; (2) indirect contact via contaminated dental instruments, equipment, or supplies; and (3) inhalation of microorganisms aerosolized from a patient's blood or saliva while using highspeed or ultrasonic equipment. A problem which occurs in many dental practices is that treatment providers fail to comprehend or appreciate the dissemination potential of saliva and/or blood by these routes. Potential dangers are often missed since much of the spatter coming from the patient's mouth is not readily noticed. Organic debris may be transparent or translucent, drying as a clear film on skin, clothing and other surfaces.

A novel demonstration was first developed by Dr James Crawford in the 1970s using the premise "If saliva were red."[9] This was later expanded to include restorative dentistry and dental prophylaxis techniques. The resultant salivary spatter was visible as red droplets on multiple tissue, instrument, and operatory surfaces (Figures 12-1 through 12-3) during the procedures.[10,11]

Major areas which must be addressed when considering the concepts of infection control are: aseptic technique, patient screening, personal protection, instrument sterilization, surface disinfection, equipment asepsis, and laboratory asepsis. Prevention of cross-contamination via each of these should consider the use of specific objectives in the formulation of precautionary measures. Included are: (1) reducing the number of pathogens so normal resistance can prevent infection; (2) breaking the cycle of infection and eliminating cross-contamination; (3) treating every patient and instrument as capable of transmitting infection; and (4) protecting patients and personnel from infection.

Aseptic Technique

Aseptic technique refers to the use of procedures which break the cycle of infection, and ideally eliminate cross-contamination. The application of logic in developing good aseptic technique should routinely occur in all areas of dentistry. Considerations here actually provide threads that permeate each of the other aspects of infection control. These may include: integrating individual infection control areas into an organized, efficient program; minimizing surface exposure and contact during patient treatment; minimizing the number of items that are contaminated during patient care; preventing disturbances in patient treatment; and use of a pretreatment mouthrinse for the

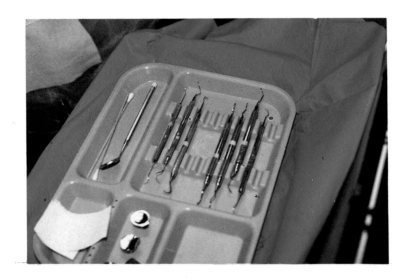

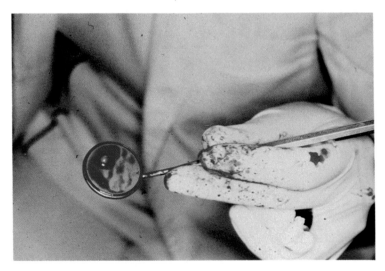

Figure 12-1 The instrument tray (top) and instruments (bottom) become contaminated with accumulated "saliva" as items are handled during treatment.

patient, using a microbicidal agent. Basically, appropriate aseptic technique depends on heightening the awareness of each dental professional as to ways in which to minimize contamination.

PATIENT SCREENING

It is important to develop an informative patient history profile prior to the provision of dental treatment. An appropriate medical history is useful in identifying factors that assist in the diagnosis of oral conditions, alter or modify the routine delivery of care, and/or alert dental professionals to prepare for medical emergencies. Unfortunately many patients capable of transmitting certain infections to dental care providers either have had an asymptomatic infection of which they were unaware, or they purposely do not relate the information, fearing loss of confidentiality or refusal of care. Since the communicable disease status cannot therefore be routinely determined from a medical history or examination, "universal precautions" should be employed for all patients.[6,7] All patients should be treated the same, as potentially capable of transmitting HBV, HIV, or other blood-borne pathogens. The use of routine blood and body fluid precautions can substantially reduce the clinical guesswork previously used to determine a patient's infection status.

The history form or other means of gathering health data in the office should also allow the practitioner or hygienist the

Figure 12-2 The frequently touched light handles should be covered or properly disinfected between patient appointments.

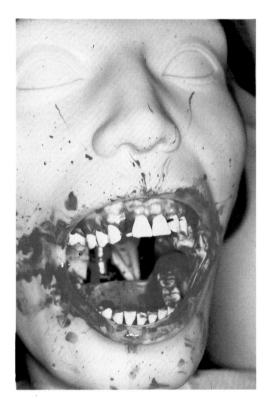

Figure 12-3 Visualized saliva is evident on the patient's face immediately following treatment.

opportunity to obtain pertinent information in a confidential manner, without embarrassing the patient. When suspicions arise about the infection potential of a nonemergency patient, the practitioner may postpone treatment until appropriate laboratory tests are performed and interpreted.

PERSONAL PROTECTION

Repeated exposure to saliva and blood during intraoral, often invasive, procedures challenges the health professional's immune defenses with a variety of microbial agents. Effective protection of treatment providers against virulent organisms involves both immunologic and barrier strategies.

Approved effective vaccines include those available for measles, rubella, influenza, hepatitis B, polio, tetanus and diphtheria, and should be utilized by individuals providing patient care. Two forms of the hepatitis B vaccine are now routinely available. Both Heptavax-B and Recombivax-HB have been shown to stimulate protective circulatory titers of anti-HBs immunoglobulins in ≥ 90% of the immunocompetent recipients.

While vaccination and the subsequent development of protective immunity are effective in minimizing the transmission of certain infections, they are not sufficient for protection against the wide range of potential pathogens encountered during patient treatment. Thus, physical barriers make up an essential component of an infection control program. The routine use of disposable gloves, face masks and protective eyewear during treatment procedures minimizes the infection exposure.

Gloves

Properly fitting gloves protect the dental care provider from exposure through cuts and abrasions often found on hands. The latter serve as routes of microbial entry into the system when ungloved hands are placed in patients' mouths. Even scrupulous handwashing cannot serve as a replacement for the use of gloves. In one study, dental personnel who practiced with bare hands retained occult blood from patients' mouths under their fingernails for several days after treatment.[12]

Since the surfaces of gloves are much smoother than those of hands, there is less chance of attachment by the microorganisms present in oral fluids. Therefore colonization by microbes is minimized. It must also be stressed that gloves should be changed after each conventional treatment procedure. Glove reuse is not recommended, since washing of gloves with handwash antiseptics increases both the size and number of pinholes in the gloves, and removes the outer coating of most commercial gloves. The latex examination gloves employed during routine nonsurgical treatment were not formulated to withstand prolonged exposure to secretions or chemical agents. Glove integrity may be compromised during extensive procedures which require long treatment periods.

The reality exists that dentists and auxiliaries who learned their professional techniques using bare hands may experience more difficulty adapting to the routine use of gloves than those recently graduated professionals who may have worn gloves throughout their training years. The hope is that as more and more practitioners provide treatment with gloved hands they will convert other colleagues by their example.

Protective Eyewear

The eyes of a dental professional are particularly susceptible to physical and microbial injury by virtue of their limited vascularity and diminished immune capacities. Aerosolized droplets containing microbial contaminants can at the least lead to development of conjunctivitis. This may keep the individual away from work for a minimum of one to two weeks. Although the incidence of such occurrences is more numerous than reported, documented cases of macroscopic- and microscopic-induced injury are appearing more frequently in the dental literature.[13,14] Appropriate eyewear should therefore be worn during treatment procedures, in the dental laboratory, and in the sterilization/disinfection area when chemicals are mixed and poured.

Masks

The use of an approved face mask or face shield will likewise protect the dentist, hygienist and assistant from microbe-laden aerosolized droplets. Entrance of these droplets into the respiratory tract or even an open mouth can lead to infection. The best masks are those which can filter at least 95% of droplet particles 3.0 to 3.2 µm in diameter. In addition, a proper fit is required for both wearer comfort and barrier efficiency. As in the case of gloves, masks should be changed for each patient, since a mask's efficiency decreases as it traps moisture during dental procedures. The wet fabric serves as a vehicle for microbial transfer through the mask.

Operatory Attire

Appropriate uniforms or gowns must be worn for all dental treatment. Debate regarding the appropriateness of either long- or short-sleeve uniforms and clinic jackets is continuing, as positive and negative features are inherent with each type. The 1987 CDC guidelines provide current guidance.[7]

Changing of the gown or uniform, or wearing a protective cover over the uniform when an aerosol spray is being generated, is recommended. All clinical attire should be of synthetic material so contaminants are not easily absorbed into the material. Seams, buttons and buckles should be kept to a minimum for the same reason.

Other Barriers to Consider

Most students in dental schools learn to use a rubber dam when performing restorative or endodontic procedures. A rubber dam is especially helpful when water-spray handpieces are used. A combination of a high-speed suction device and rubber dam can sharply reduce the microbial load in the aerosols produced. The use of disposable covers or drapes on operatory surfaces that can only be disinfected will also diminish the collection of splatter on equipment.

INSTRUMENT STERILIZATION

A basic guideline for infection control is: Do not disinfect when you can sterilize. The distinction between terms is fundamental to understanding the implementation of appropriate asepsis procedures.

Sterilization is defined as the destruction or removal of all forms of life, with particular reference to microorganisms. The limiting requirement or measure of sterilization is the destruction of bacterial and fungal spores, the most heat-resistant microbial forms.

Disinfection, on the other hand, properly refers only to the inhibition or destruction of pathogens. Spores are not destroyed during routine use of disinfectants. By custom, the term disinfectant is reserved for chemical agents applied to inanimate objects.

Heat has long been recognized as the most efficient, reliable method of achieving sterilization of dental instruments.[6,15,16] The CDC and the ADA Council on Dental Therapeutics have repeatedly stressed this. Accordingly, heat sterilization is required for all instruments and items that can withstand repeated exposure to high temperatures.

Steam under pressure, prolonged dry heat, and chemical vapor sterilization are the preferred methods for achieving heat sterilization. The penetration capabilities of these methods are superior to those noted for any chemical sterilant/disinfectant. Routine use of any of these modalities is effective, although the inherent advantages and disadvantages may cause a practitioner to select a type of sterilizer that is most compatible with the individual setting.[17] Many busy dental practices employ more than one type of unit, in order to maintain maximum efficiency for instrument sterilization and recirculation. It must also be noted that ethylene oxide gas is actually classified as a chemical capable of sterilizing instruments and other contaminated objects. It is for this reason, as well as for its excellent penetration powers, that ethylene oxide is included with procedures that achieve sterilization.

INSTRUMENT RECIRCULATION

Consideration for processing reusable items includes cleaning, packaging, sterilizing, monitoring and storage of packaged instruments. Accumulated debris such as blood and saliva can lengthen the time required for sterilization, or even prevent sterilization under certain conditions. An initial requirement for instrument recirculation, therefore is to remove collected organic matter.[18] Handscrubbing of instruments can accomplish this, although caution should be utilized. Puncture-resistant utility gloves should be worn by the individual to prevent percutaneous wounds. Utility gloves should also be used when handling any chemical preparation which is used for sterilization/disinfection. An alternative or additional means of cleaning instruments utilizes an ultrasonic bath. This apparatus is to be operated with a cover to prevent expulsion of contaminants via an aerosol. Cleaning solutions may be purchased that are suitable for use with the ultrasonic bath. The metal container within the ultrasonic unit should also be wiped with a hypochlorite solution after each use.

The packaging of items for heat sterilization will depend on the type of sterilizer used and the type of instruments. Cleaned instruments should be placed in heat-stable wraps, sealed and dated. Sterilized instruments should remain wrapped until used. Many commercial wraps and sealed plastic pouches can maintain sterility for months if unopened. Taking sterilized instruments out of a package and placing them in cabinet drawers for later use is not recommended. At best, the patients treated with these will get clean instruments. Remember, patients deserve and must be treated with sterile instruments whenever possible.

MONITORING

Dental practitioners should monitor the efficiency of office sterilization procedures. Many factors may diminish the effectiveness of an autoclave, dry heat sterilizer, or unsaturated chemical vapor apparatus. Three of the more frequent problems encountered are operator error, improper wrapping of instruments preventing adequate penetration to the instrument surface, and defective control gauges that do not reflect actual conditions inside the sterilizer.

One may employ chemically treated tapes that change color or biological controls to check for the proper functioning of an office sterilizer. Materials that change color generally inform the practitioner that sterilizing conditions have been reached, but do not necessarily indicate that sterilization of the chamber contents has been achieved. These specific chemical indicators to monitor sterilization serve as routine checks for each load of items processed through the sterilizer.

Calibrated biologic controls remain as the main guarantee of sterilization. Ampule or paper strip preparations contain bacterial spores that are more resistant to heat than are viruses and vegetative bacteria. Since the spore preparations are relatively heat resistant, the proof of their destruction after exposure to the sterilization cycle is used to infer that all microorganisms exposed to the same conditions have been destroyed. The demonstration of sporicidal activity by an office sterilizer thus represents the most sensitive check for efficiency.

Monitoring of the dialdehyde concentration level in glutaraldehyde solutions is also available. These chemical indicators are effective with any glutaraldehyde solution with an initial use concentration of 2%.

HANDPIECES, ULTRASONIC SCALERS AND DENTAL UNITS

The issue of dental handpiece asepsis was only minimally addressed until recently. Heat sterilization was not feasible in most instances, since the equipment was unable to withstand elevated temperatures. As a result, dental practitioners became used to disinfecting handpiece outer surfaces. Asepsis of internal components, which were also exposed to saliva and/or blood, was not accomplished.

Advances in technology have solved these problems, with manufacturers now marketing heat-sterilizable dental handpieces. As a result, the CDC guidelines for infection control specifically state: "Handpieces should be sterilized after use with each patient . . ."[7] At the present time, the recommended heat modalities are sterilization in an autoclave or chemiclave, although proposed dry heat units may also be feasible in the future. For those units which cannot be sterilized, the following is suggested by the CDC as a compromise for cleaning and disinfection between treatment use:

1. Scrub handpiece with either soap and water or another cleansing detergent to remove external bioburden;
2. Spray handpiece with an EPA-approved, hospital-level disinfectant;
3. Wrap treated handpiece with impervious material which has been saturated with the disinfectant;
4. Allow intermediate-level disinfection to occur for 10 minutes;
5. Remove wrap material and rinse excess disinfectant from handpiece with water before wiping dry.[7]

Handpieces should never be immersed in a disinfectant solution or treated with 2.0% to 3.2% glutaraldehyde preparations. These procedures will shorten handpiece life substantially and increase the chances of glutaraldehyde toxicity reactions during operator handling. In addition, the handpiece should be properly lubricated prior to bagging and sterilization. Failure to lubricate will also shorten handpiece life. These same procedures and precautions apply for such items as air and water syringe tips and ultrasonic scalers.

A second major concern regarding handpiece asepsis involves the role of antiretraction valves. When a handpiece is turned off, expansion of attached tubing under pressure may occur, causing water retraction (ie, draw-back, suck-back). The potential exists for drawing water or saliva into the instrument fluid line. Microorganisms entering into the water line may then be passed into the mouth of the next patient when the handpiece is activated.

Table 12-2
Properties of an Ideal Disinfectant

1. Broad spectrum: Should always have the widest possible antimicrobial spectrum.
2. Fast acting: Should always have a rapidly lethal action on all vegetative forms and spores of bacteria and fungi, protozoa and viruses.
3. Not affected by physical factors: Active in the presence of organic matter such as blood, sputum and feces; should be compatible with soaps, detergents and other chemicals encountered in use.
4. Nontoxic
5. Surface compatibility: Should not corrode instruments and other metallic surfaces; should not cause the disintegration of cloth, rubber, plastics, or other materials.
6. Residual effect on treated surfaces
7. Easy to use
8. Odorless: An inoffensive odor would facilitate its routine use.
9. Economical: Cost should not be prohibitively high.

Adapted from Molinari JA et al.[17]

Installation of antiretraction valves can prevent this occurrence, and most of the newer handpieces come with them already in place. Older units can be fitted with antiretraction valves which may be purchased separately. It is important to note that handpiece manufacturers provide detailed instructions for use and maintenance of their products. When these recommendations are followed, handpieces should continue to function at a maximal level and provide prolonged efficient use.

CHEMICAL STERILANTS AND DISINFECTANTS

The use of chemical sterilants and disinfectants in certain instances is warranted since it is not possible to heat-sterilize all items and surfaces contaminated during dental treatment. When selecting a chemical agent, its clinical applicability and limitations should be compared with those of an ideal agent. These properties are summarized in Table 12-2.

IMMERSION AGENTS

For those items that cannot withstand repeated heat sterilization and are not disposable, 2.0% to 3.2% glutaraldehydes offer the best alternative as immersion sterilants/disinfectants.[16,19] Other classes of products have received Environmental Protection Agency (EPA) approval as immersion disinfectants, but not for sterilization. The reuse life (as differentiated from the use life) of activated glutaraldehydes remains an active investigation area.

Manufacturers of chemical sterilants and disinfectants are required to submit data to the EPA substantiating claims for prolonged reuse (over one day) of prepared solutions. As of this writing, only a few of the glutaraldehydes have been approved for reuse as sterilizing solutions. All other glutaraldehydes should be disposed of daily. The reader is cautioned to read the label carefully on glutaraldehydes before purchase to review their reuse claim, if any.

SURFACE DISINFECTION

Although the use of disposable covers is increasing, dental professionals must also strive to clean and disinfect the numerous fixed operatory surfaces. Included are counters, cabinets, light handles, switches, drawer handles, faucets, x-ray cones, bracket trays, controls, and other exposed portions of the dental units. These items must be thoroughly cleaned and disinfected not only for esthetic reasons, but because effective disinfection minimizes cross-contamination from environmental surfaces.

When the large number of operatory surfaces which become coated with saliva, blood and/or exudate (bioburden) are considered, it becomes apparent that the use of surface disinfectant products constitutes a major portion of effective asepsis. Disinfection of environmental surfaces is actually a two-step procedure. Basically this involves a "spray-wipe-spray" technique.[6] An initial mechanical removal of organic debris (precleaning) is required, followed by application of an appropriate disinfectant, with time allowed for the chemical to achieve disinfection. The use of a disinfectant which provides a residual antimicrobial effect with repeated use is also desirable.[20] Since deposited bioburden renders coated microorganisms more resistant to the biocidal effects of many disinfectants, surface precleaning, the removal of accumulated bioburden, is a mandatory first step prior to disinfection with any chemical.[21] The ability of disinfectants to penetrate and preclean surfaces contaminated with blood, saliva and/or exudate is thus a fundamental consideration in the selection of an appropriate preparation.[20,22] A

178

product that is unable to penetrate and remove accumulated bioburden would fail at the first step of surface asepsis.

It is also important to note that manufacturers recommend their products for use on precleaned surfaces. While a separate surface cleaner and surface disinfectant may be employed, the use of a chemical agent which accomplishes both functions during the two-step protocol provides a more efficient approach. Water-based disinfectants achieve substantially better surface cleaning than products containing high concentrations of protein denaturants (ie, alcohols).[20] Diluted sodium hypochlorite (household bleach), iodophors and complex synthetic phenols presently provide the best precleaning/disinfection when used appropriately. Since all currently available products have drawbacks under different conditions, the "ideal agent" has not been developed. This area will therefore continue to provide new information as other strategies are investigated.

HANDWASHING

Hands must be washed thoroughly immediately prior to and after the treatment of each patient. The use of gloves does not serve as a substitute for routine handwashing with an effective liquid antiseptic. The rationale here includes the recognition that gloves may tear or perforate during patient treatment and that bacteria either remaining on the skin after washing or entering through a compromised glove can multiply rapidly under the glove.

Substituted phenol preparations, such as chlorhexidine gluconate (a bisphenol) and parachlorometaxylenol (PCMX), are the best handwashing agents currently available. While most data support the primary use of a 4% chlorhexidine gluconate antiseptic,[23] evidence has also been presented for similar efficacy with products containing 3% PCMX as the active ingredient.[24] Although a microbicidal effect occurs following a single application, both agents require repeated washings throughout the day to attain maximal effectiveness. These preparations accumulate and remain in the epithelial tissues in an active form for prolonged periods, thereby leaving a residual antibacterial effect after each wash. This property, called "substantivity," fosters the build-up of an antimicrobial barrier against many common skin contaminants. If at all possible, hands should be dried with air or disposable paper towels, and not with reusable cloth towels.

EQUIPMENT ASEPSIS

All dental equipment that is heat resistant should be sterilized; all other equipment must be covered or disinfected. Thus, infection control should always be considered when new equipment is purchased. Office design, traffic flow, construction materials, and fixtures should also be considered. Examples of fixtures that promote better infection control in the dental operatory include sink faucets that are elbow or foot activated, wall-mounted antiseptic handwash dispensers that are foot activated, lined waste receptacles that are flush with the surface, office air exchange systems, and hard floor coverings.

The glutaraldehydes approved for immersion use should not be used on surfaces or large pieces of equipment, because they are not approved as environmental surface disinfectants and the fumes are toxic. It is recommended that disposable barriers be used to avoid the necessity of excessive cleaning for both environmental surfaces and equipment asepsis. Aluminum foil, plastic wrap, plastic bags, plastic-lined paper, or any other convenient item can be used as a cover or barrier on equipment and surfaces. For those equipment surfaces which cannot be covered, the spray-wipe-spray technique described previously is recommended. While the individual practice setting may affect specific protocols for dental unit asepsis, a suggested program is as follows:

Each morning Flush the water lines of the unit for three to five minutes and use the spray-wipe-spray technique on all "high touch" nonsterilizable surfaces and equipment, with particular attention to allowing at least ten minutes for the disinfectant to air dry.

Between patients Flush the water lines for at least 15 seconds, sterilize or disinfect (whichever is more appropriate) the handpieces and three-way syringe, remove all disposable covers and disinfect all "high touch" areas with an approved surface cleaner/disinfectant, and siphon an appropriate solution through the evacuation system.

At the end of the day Flush the waterlines for three minutes; evacuate a generous amount of disinfecting solution, disinfect floor around the chair, and use the spray-wipe-spray technique on all countertops and "high touch" areas.

Weekly Disinfect the inside and outside of drawers and cabinets, and disinfect the entire floor of the operatory and laboratory.

DISPOSABLES

Items manufactured and identified for single use only, such as needles, saliva ejectors and prophylaxis cups, are not to be reused. The availability of disposables continues to increase as manufacturers, distributors and office personnel recognize their usefulness. Examples of recently marketed items include disposable prophylaxis angles, rag wheels and evacuation line traps. These products present fewer cross-contamination risks since they do not undergo recleaning and recycling, but they must be disposed of properly. This is especially important for needles and other sharp items, which should not be recapped by hand and should be placed in puncture-resistant containers for disposal.[6,7]

LABORATORY ASEPSIS

Removal and insertion of prosthetic devices during patient treatment require frequent handling by the practitioner or the commercial laboratory staff. Many prostheses are coated with plaque deposits, saliva, or blood at the time of removal and can serve as sources of infection. In 1985, the ADA Councils on Dental Therapeutics and Prosthetic Services and Dental Laboratory Relations published guidelines for infection control in dental offices and dental laboratories. These guidelines were developed primarily as a result of efforts by dental laboratory personnel to protect themselves against infections, such as hepatitis B and herpetic whitlow.[25]

This area of infection control continues to provide research opportunities, especially in the consideration of dental impression and prosthesis disinfection. Table 12-3 presents information and recommendations, which are based on ADA guidelines, as well as recent scientific observations.[27] It should be noted that caution must be used and some distortion is possible with alginate, hydrocolloid, polyether, and compound. *Thorough rinsing of impressions under running tap water to remove any residual disinfectant is essential.* It is especially important to thoroughly rinse hypochlorite and glutaraldehyde-treated materials before processing.

CONCLUDING REMARKS

Effective infection control must occur as a routine component of professional activity. The use of universal precautions in

Table 12-3
Guide for Selection of Disinfectant Solutions*

	Glutaraldehydes†	Iodophors‡	Sodium Hypochlorite§
Impressions			
Alginate	–	–	+
Polysulfide rubber base	+	+	+
Silicone rubber	+	+	+
Polyether	–	–	+
ZOE impression paste	+	–	–
Hydrocolloid‖	–	?	?
Compound‖	–	?	–
Prostheses			
Fixed (metal/porcelain)	+	+	–
Removable (acrylic/porcelain)	–	+	+
Removable (metal/acrylic)	–	+	–

* A 30-minute immersion time is recommended. Thorough rinsing of impressions and prostheses under running tap water to remove any residual disinfectant is essential.
†Prepared according to the manufacturer's instructions.
‡Prepared according to the manufacturer's instructions. 1:213 dilution.
§1:10 dilution of commercial bleach. Must be prepared fresh daily.
‖Data not available. Alternative to spray models with iodophor spray.
+ = recommended method; – = not recommended.
From Merchant and Molinari.[26]

182

Table 12-4
Implementation of Infection Control Recommendations for Health Care Employees

1. Orientation and continuing education addressing:
    a. Epidemiology
    b. Modes of transmission
    c. Prevention of HIV and other blood-borne infections
2. Stress universal barrier precautions
3. Provide appropriate supplies
4. Monitor compliance to recommended precautions and procedures

Adapted from Centers for Disease Control.[7]

the management of all patients greatly minimizes occupational exposure to microbial pathogens by addressing the reality that most individuals with the potential to transmit infection are asymptomatic and therefore undiagnosed.

An organized, comprehensive program should be developed with input from all dental professionals in the clinical setting. Determine the infection control strengths and build upon them by integrating new knowledge into the practice routine. Communication of infection control measures to patients and newly employed personnel provides further positive reinforcement. Health professionals, patients and family members of treatment providers will appreciate the efforts. A few of the recommended measures are summarized in Table 12-4.[8]

Finally the necessity to remain current in this area is real, as developments in infection control continue to provide better products and advances in asepsis technology. Questions are being asked of the health professions. Fortunately, dentistry is showing a willingness to respond in a positive fashion.

REFERENCES

1. ADA Council on Dental Therapeutics: Viral hepatitis type B, tuberculosis, and dental care of Indochinese refugees. *MMWR* 1980;29:1-3.
2. ADA Council on Dental Materials and Devices, Council on Dental Therapeutics: Infection control in the dental office. *J Am Dent Assoc* 1978;97:673-677.
3. ADA Council on Dental Therapeutics: Sterilization, infection control methods offer defense against AIDS. *ADA News* Aug 9, 1983.
4. Centers for Disease Control: Acquired Immunodeficiency Syndrome (AIDS) precautions for health care workers and allied professionals. *MMWR* 1983;32:450-451.

5. Sterilization and asepsis. *ADA News* March 17, 1986.

6. Centers for Disease Control: Recommended infection control practices for dentistry. *MMWR* 1986;35:237-242.

7. Centers for Disease Control: Recommendations for prevention of HIV transmission in health care settings. *MMWR* 1987;36(2S):1-18.

8. Department of Labor/Department of Health and Human Services: Joint advisory notice: HBV-HIV. *Federal Register* 1987;52:41818-41823.

9. Whitacre RJ, Robins SK, Williams BL, Crawford JJ: *Dental Asepsis*. Seattle, Stoma Press, 1979.

10. Cottone JA: Infection control in dentistry, in Mitchell EW, Corbin SB (eds): *Proceedings National Conference on Infection Control in Dentistry*. Atlanta, US Public Health Service, Centers for Disease Control 1986, pp 34-46.

11. Molinari JA, York J: Cross-contamination visualization. *Calif Dent Assoc J* 1987;15:12-16.

12. Allen AL, Organ RJ: Occult blood accumulation under the fingernails: A mechanism for the spread of bloodborne infection. *J Am Dent Assoc* 1982;105:455-459.

13. Hales RH: Ocular injuries sustained in the dental office. *Am J Ophthamol* 1970;70:221-223.

14. Palenik CJ: Eye protection for the entire dental office. *J Ind Dent Assoc* 1981;60:23-25.

15. *Accepted Dental Therapeutics,* ed 40. Chicago, American Dental Association, 1984.

16. Council clarifies disinfectant use. *ADA News* Jan 2, 1984.

17. Molinari JA, Campbell MD, York J: Minimizing potential infections in dental practice. *J Mich Dent Assoc* 1982;64:411-416.

18. Molinari JA, Cottone JA: Considerations in developing an infection control program for the dental operatory. *Calif Dent Assoc J* 1986;14:14-19.

19. Crawford JJ: State-of-the-art: Practical infection control in dentistry. *J Am Dent Assoc* 1985;110:629-633.

20. Molinari JA, Gleason MJ, Cottone JA, Barrett ED: Comparison of dental surface disinfectants. *Gen Dent* 1987;35:171-175.

21. Favero MS: Sterilization, disinfection and antisepsis in the hospital, in *Manual of Clinical Microbiology*, ed 4. Washington, DC, American Society for Microbiology, 1985, pp 129-137.

22. Runnells RR: *Infection Control in the Former Wet Finger Environment*. North Salt Lake, Infection Control Publications, 1987.

23. Handwashing. *Clin Res Newsletter* 1985; 9:No. 12.

24. Scoulsby ME, Barnett JB, Maddox S: The efficacy of chlorhexidine gluconate-containing surgical scrub preparations. *Infect Control* 1986;7:223-226.

25. Council on Dental Therapeutics and Council on Prosthetic Services and Dental Laboratory Relations: Guidelines for infection control in the dental office and the commercial dental laboratory. *J Am Dent Assoc* 1985;110:969-972.

26. Merchant VA, Molinari JA: Infection control in prosthodontics: A choice no longer. *Gen Dent,* in press.
27. Merchant VA, Herrera SP, Dwan JJ: Marginal fit of cast gold MO inlays from disinfected elastomeric impressions. *J Prosthetic Dent* 1987;58:276-280.

13

Dentistry and AIDS:
An Educational Challenge

Barbara Gerbert

The AIDS crisis has confronted dental professionals with unprecedented challenges to their role as health care providers and to their diagnostic and therapeutic skills. Dental educators can help dentists meet these challenges by concentrating their teaching efforts in three areas that have been identified as deficient: the consistent practice of adequate infection control procedures, performance of thorough oral examinations with identification of oral lesions, and acceptance of all patients into the dental practice. Scrupulous infection control practices are crucial since the majority of people who carry the AIDS virus are not easily identified and many more are unaware of their infection status. Yet most dentists do not use all of the infection control procedures recommended by the Centers for Disease Control. A thorough oral examination can enable dentists to detect the first signs of HIV infection and refer patients for early medical treatment, but many dentists do not examine the oral cavity thoroughly and many cannot identify the lesions associated with HIV infection. Dentists are often reluctant to care for patients whom they suspect of carrying the AIDS virus, but only by accepting all patients into their practice will dentists fulfill their obligation to provide dental care for all who need it. Dental educators who address the needs in these areas will do much to help dentists meet the challenges of AIDS with confidence and improved professional skills.

In the last few years, AIDS has presented dentistry with a formidable challenge. Practicing dentists and dental students are encountering a life-threatening, communicable disease for which there is no vaccine and no effective treatment. No other disease has created such fear in the dental office. Yet dentists have a critical role to play in the AIDS epidemic. They must continue to provide professional services in a professional manner to all who seek dental care. They must also ensure complete protection from infection for all patients and dental staff. Dentists can play a further role in prevention by diagnosing early signs of HIV infection that appear in the oral cavity or on the head and neck so that patients can be identified and treated in a timely manner. Dental educators can aid dentists in meeting these challenges by helping them to understand AIDS, to cope with their fears and anxieties, and to learn the skills needed to provide appropriate diagnosis and referral services.

How are dentists responding to the AIDS crisis? From reports in the media, it appears not well. Dentistry has been publicly chastised for a poor response to the AIDS epidemic. Surgeon General Everett Koop has criticized dentists and other health professionals for unprofessional conduct in acting fearfully and refusing to treat people with AIDS.[1] A recent *New York Times* editorial pointed to dentistry as one health profession that was not responding appropriately to the crisis, and suggested that health professionals who refused to treat people with AIDS should find new professions.[2] Other newspaper accounts highlight the resistance of many dentists to treating people with AIDS; one reported that "only three dentists in Chicago will treat people with the disease."[3]

To date, organized dentistry has responded to the AIDS crisis using traditional educational approaches such as continuing education courses, lectures, brochures, and pamphlets. Moreover, a wide range of task forces and committees at the local, state, and national levels have been convened to examine the impact of AIDS on delivery of care in dental schools and on practicing dentists. Despite these efforts, dentists do not seem ready to render services to patients with AIDS. A recent survey of dentists showed, for example, that 74% would rather refer patients with AIDS, and those at high risk, to their colleagues.[4] Recent studies have also documented widespread deficits in AIDS-related knowledge and skills throughout the field.[4,5] One must conclude that dentists are not being affected by the educational efforts directed to them so far.

This report will present data that describe the extent of dentists' difficulties in meeting patients' needs during the AIDS epidemic. This analysis is offered as background for discussions of ways to help dentists respond to the challenge of AIDS.

AIDS PREVENTION PROJECT STUDIES

The AIDS Prevention Project for Dental Health Professionals (APP), based at the University of California, San Francisco (UCSF), has been studying dental professionals' response to the AIDS crisis and has been educating dentists about AIDS for several years. Much of the information in this paper was drawn from three studies conducted by the APP.

To avoid repetition, the methods of each of these studies are outlined here and referred to by name only in the text:

California Survey

A questionnaire was mailed to a random sample of 541 dentists in California. The questionnaire covered information in seven areas: demographic data, attitudes toward AIDS, beliefs about the role of the dentist in relation to AIDS, knowledge about AIDS, infection-control practices, respondents' means of learning about AIDS and infection control, and their perceptions about the need for further education.

Responses were received from 297 dentists (89 questionnaires were undeliverable) for a response rate of 66%. Thirty-one (12%) of the respondents were women; 234 (88%) were men (32 respondents did not indicate their gender). The average age of dentists in the sample was 45 years (range, 26 to 83 years). Of those who indicated the nature of their practices, 56 dentists (23%) were specialists; 14 (6%) were in a combined general and specialty practice; the remaining 171 subjects (71%) were general dentists. These demographic characteristics are representative of dentists in California.

A random sample of hygienists (N = 128) and dental assistants (N = 177) were surveyed.[4,6]

San Francisco Educational Intervention Study

Of 700 San Francisco dentists invited to participate in an AIDS education study, 107 signed consent forms (response rate,

15%). A questionnaire, adapted from our previous work, was used to collect information from participants at baseline. One hundred two completed pretests were received. Thirty-six participants were then randomly assigned to receive an educational intervention and the remainder (66) served as a control group, receiving no intervention. The three components of the intervention were bulletins, telephone conference calls, and individual, detailed analyses of performance on the pretest questionnaire. The questionnaire was again administered at posttest, six months later.[7] At posttest, 35 dentists remained in the experimental group and 64 in the control group. Ninety-one percent of participants were male, with a mean age of 41.4 years. Ninety-five percent were general dentists. Results showed that dentists in the experimental group had significantly higher scores than the control group on outcomes measuring knowledge about AIDS, identification of oral lesions, willingness to treat, and thoroughness of intraoral and extraoral examinations. We concluded that the intervention was successful.

Nationwide Educational Intervention Study

From an invitational mailing to a random sample of 2,400 US dentists, 185 completed consent forms (response rate, 8%) were received. Pretest responses have been received from 172 participants (study in progress).

THE RESPONSE TO THE AIDS EPIDEMIC

The AIDS epidemic has created a number of educational needs for dentists since the early 1980s. The APP has been assessing what dentists need to learn about AIDS. Three areas have been identified as needing improvement: (1) universal use of infection control following the Centers for Disease Control (CDC) guidelines, (2) performance of a thorough oral examination with timely identification of oral lesions, and (3) acceptance of all patients into the dental practice. Each of these areas will be discussed in turn with supporting data and identification of factors that appear to inhibit improvement.

Infection Control

The need for dental care providers to use appropriate infection control measures has been emphasized strongly by dental health care workers' associations and the CDC. Although the risk of transmission of HIV in the dental office may be low, the possibilities are real and the consequences are grave. The "Klein report" of one dentist who may have acquired HIV infection in his dental practice[8] and reports of other health care workers who apparently contracted the infection in their work settings[9] are harsh reminders that HIV can be transmitted to health professionals. While transmission of HIV through saliva is unlikely, most dental procedures have the potential to cause bleeding. Yet carriers of communicable disease are not always identifiable by history, examination, appearance, or readily available lab tests. All dental workers must assume, then, that all patients carry a communicable disease, and it follows that they must use appropriate procedures to ensure safety for themselves, their staff, and other patients. Although the importance of using infection control might seem obvious, it is not a matter of major concern for many dental professionals. As one observer aptly stated, "Dental practitioners are virtually the only health care providers who routinely place an ungloved hand into a body cavity."[10]

Part of the problem, perhaps, is that lax infection control has become a habit. Lack of adequate infection control precautions is not a new problem for dentistry. Though the use of infection control techniques in dental offices has been encouraged since the mid-1970s for controlling transmission of hepatitis B and other communicable diseases,[11,12] such techniques have rarely been employed in a consistent manner. In the last three to four years, with AIDS as the impetus, the American Dental Association,[13-15] the CDC,[16] and the American Association of Public Health Dentistry[17] have spelled out the most up-to-date infection control techniques and emphasized the importance of using them. Yet, even with the threat of AIDS, noncompliance with infection control procedures is common, both among practicing dentists and in dental schools.

Private practice. Through the years, researchers have periodically surveyed dentists to assess their use of infection control procedures. In one study, only 27% of the dentists surveyed were using gloves on a regular basis.[18] On a more positive note, the Academy of General Dentistry found 78% of dentists to be using gloves with all patients.[19] Findings from the APP's studies have been similar: 80% of dentists in the California Survey were using gloves, but only 58% of them were changing gloves after each patient.[4] In the Nationwide Educational

Intervention Study, 55% of respondents reported always wearing a new pair of gloves for each patient. Another 15% almost always did. Only 2% never wore gloves.

In June 1987, Klein and his colleagues reported the first case of a dentist who was infected with the AIDS virus, possibly through patient contact.[8] The "Klein report" was expected to increase dentists' perception of personal risk for AIDS and consequently improve their use of infection control measures. The APP tested these expectations in two separate studies. The first study compared data collected from dentists immediately prior to the publication of the Klein report with data from the same group collected four months after the report was presented. At pretest (June 1987), dentists in the San Francisco Educational Intervention Study who were given a list of eight infection control procedures indicated that they were using an average of 4.5 procedures. At posttest (October 1987), utilization had increased to 5.6 procedures. This was a statistically significant increase in infection control practices after presentation of the Klein report.

In the second study,[20] conducted in July 1987, 92% of 280 respondents had heard of the Klein report. Eighty-eight percent of dentists (up from 80% in the California Survey) now believed they would be at increased risk if they treated patients with AIDS. APP's assumptions concerning increases in infection control practices were also borne out. Fifty percent of respondents reported increasing their use of gloves; 30% increased their use of masks and eye protection. Even with these striking increases, only 73% reported using gloves with all patients and fewer than 60% always wore masks.

Both reports reveal that use of infection control procedures has increased since the Klein report, but not to the point where compliance with the CDC guidelines is complete. Private practitioners apparently are reluctant to adapt new routines into their practice, or they remain unconvinced of the necessity for using full infection control. Discovering the underlying causes of this problem will shorten the route to universal infection control among all private dentists.

Dental schools. Dental schools are no less obligated than private practitioners to provide patients, staff, faculty and students an environment with minimal risk of transmission of infectious diseases. Individually, dental schools are currently developing policies and procedures for assuring safe practice. The American Association of Dental Schools convened a panel to examine infection control in dentistry. But there are other difficult issues to be addressed. What should the policy be toward faculty and students who refuse to treat patients with AIDS; toward faculty and students who are HIV positive; and toward accidental needlesticks and instrument injuries?

Individuals and groups charged with developing guidelines for infection control in dental schools should first gather data to document the current state of asepsis. These data should be used to plan corrective programs, and additional data should continually be gathered to assess deficiencies. Without such data, plans to increase compliance will have less chance of success. Data regarding asepsis were gathered in a study conducted at UCSF. They are being used to help the dental school's task force develop guidelines to plan implementation strategies. The goals of such strategies are to bring compliance with infection control guidelines close to 100% and to increase faculty and student awareness of the effectiveness of infection control. Both groups were asked to rate infection control in the UCSF clinics on a 7-point Likert scale, from 1 (very bad) to 7 (very good). The current perception of both students and faculty is that infection control is mid-scale (mean = 4.5).

It is hoped that the implementation plan will improve both the use of infection control and students' and faculties' perceptions of its adequacy. But this is just the first step to formulating an overall policy with regard to AIDS. Other, more sensitive, issues must be addressed before the school can consider itself fully prepared to respond to the AIDS crisis.

Diagnosis of Oral Manifestations of HIV Infection

Many of the first symptoms of HIV infection are oral or extraoral manifestations and can be detected by dentists. These include unexplained oral candidiasis,[21] oral "hairy" leukoplakia,[22] and cervical lymphadenopathy as well as other head and neck manifestations of HIV infection.[23] A pathognomonic sign of AIDS is the presence of Kaposi's sarcoma (KS) in the mouth.[23] The incidence of KS in the oral cavity is rapidly increasing, and intraoral lesions are reported to occur in approximately 50% of patients with AIDS.[24] Because HIV-associated lesions may appear in or near the mouth, dentists should know what these lesions look like and be observant for them. By identifying the first signs and symptoms of AIDS, dental staff can contribute to early diagnosis and refer patients for timely treatment of AIDS or AIDS-related complex (ARC).

So far, however, dental professionals are unprepared to make this contribution. The data from recent studies indicate that many dentists are not ready to identify actual clinical manifestations. In one study, 41% of respondents among a random sample of Los Angeles dentists were not able to recall any oral signs of HIV infection.[5] Dentists who had attended two or more lectures on AIDS were able to name slightly more signs than those who had attended one or fewer lectures, but 30% of those who attended two or more lectures could name no oral signs of HIV infection.

Somewhat better rates of identification were found in the APP's San Francisco Educational Intervention Study. In that study, dentists were asked to match a brief description of an oral manifestation of HIV infection with its name. Before viewing photographs of lesions with accompanying descriptions, the sample matched an average of 5.1 of a possible 8 names with descriptions of the lesions. After an educational intervention, the sample matched 6.4 lesions with their descriptions. Even though this increase was statistically significant, effective clinical application would require that all participants be able to identify all eight lesions.

To find oral lesions associated with HIV infection as well as other disorders, dentists must perform a thorough oral examination. When dentists in the California Survey were asked to report whether they did a thorough oral examination, 55% said they did. The remaining 45% believed they did not do a thorough oral examination.[4] Until the former percentage increases, and dentists routinely examine the oral cavity thoroughly, they will not identify many oral manifestations of HIV infection.

Dentists' failure to examine the oral cavity for signs of oral cancer or systemic disease is not a new problem. For many years didactic courses in oral diagnosis have had a low priority in dental education. Schools have been accused of teaching students to look only at teeth and to ignore the rest of the patient.[25] As with infection control, AIDS highlights a long-standing educational problem in dentistry.

At their current level of knowledge and skill in identifying lesions and performing oral examinations, dental professionals cannot provide early diagnosis of AIDS. Dental educators' efforts must focus on creating behavioral change in the dental setting by teaching dentists to do a thorough oral examination and to identify lesions. The first educational task is to change the emphasis in dental schools toward examining the head, neck, and oral cavity. Practicing dentists must learn to do this routinely. Data thus far indicate that much more must be done to achieve these goals. Lectures or printed materials alone do not seem to solve the problem.

Barriers to Caring for People with AIDS/HIV Infection

There is no question that most dentists are reluctant to care for patients with AIDS and with HIV infection. And dentistry has received its share of criticism for this reluctance, whether it be for "dumping" people known to have AIDS[26] or for refusing to treat people with AIDS.

Dentists are scared. Some are considering leaving the professional practice of dentistry, as expressed by one dentist in APP's nationwide study: "I am seriously considering whether the risk of patient care is worth it. I have considered changing careers." Others are searching for help in coping with AIDS. Another APP study participant commented, "I want to increase my knowledge so I can stop rumors and the misunderstanding the general population feels about AIDS."

The APP survey of dentists in California revealed several major barriers to caring for people with AIDS.[4] These barriers concerned both the personal health of the dentists and the viability of their practices. Over 80% of those surveyed were afraid of losing other patients, perceived difficulty in managing staff, and expressed concern for their personal health and safety. Approximately half of the respondents believed they did not have the appropriate skills to treat people with AIDS. Finally, 45% felt that infection control would be a financial burden to their offices. Hygienists and dental assistants had similar opinions.[6] None of these fears is trivial or easily dismissed. Simply telling dentists about transmission mechanisms has not diminished these concerns.

Dental students are also fearful. Twenty-two percent of students at the University of Alabama School of Dentistry reported being fearful of caring for patients because of AIDS, and 60% were fearful of patients who were homosexual or intravenous drug users. Only 23% would provide dental care for a person known to be infected with the AIDS virus.[27]

Similar AIDS-related fears have been identified in physicians and medical residents.[28] For example, Cooke and Koenig found that 20% of medical residents had nightmares about AIDS, 18% had symptoms suspicious of AIDS, and 35% were preoccupied about giving AIDS to a family member.[29] (It is not known whether residents have similar reactions to working with patients with other infectious diseases.) On a more positive note, the researchers also reported that 65% of residents who had treated 10 or more patients with AIDS liked caring for such patients, while only 32% of residents who cared for 10 or fewer patients liked doing so.[29] This suggests that perhaps more satisfaction is derived when health practitioners have greater contact with AIDS patients. McKusick and colleagues reported similar findings in a survey of physicians who worked with people with AIDS. Although some of this group reported greater stress (56%), fear of death (46%), anxiety (44%), and overwork (39%), there were also increased rewards; 46% experienced greater intellectual stimulation and 45% were more satisfied with their careers.[30]

A positive side to dealing with AIDS was also evident in the APP's California Survey, where contact with people at risk or with the virus correlated with positive attitudes and improved behaviors. For example, dentists, hygienists, and assistants who perceived a greater percent of their patients to be at risk for AIDS were more likely to use infection control procedures. They were also more willing to treat such patients and were more likely to assess patients for AIDS by taking a thorough medical history.

Some have speculated that the main barrier for physicians and dental professionals to caring for people with AIDS might be their discomfort in treating people who are gay or who are intravenous drug users. A study of physicians by Kelly and colleagues addresses that possibility.[31] Physicians completed both a prejudicial evaluation and a social interaction scale on a male patient who was described to be either homosexual or heterosexual and who had either AIDS or leukemia. Physicians were more prejudiced against and wanted less social contact with the AIDS patient than with the patient with leukemia. In a multiple analysis of variance, the sexual preference was not a significant predictor of social interaction, but the disease of the patient was. Thus, physicians were more prejudiced against the AIDS patient than the patient with leukemia, but not more prejudiced against the homosexual than the heterosexual patient. This study suggests that AIDS-phobia or possibly a phobia about working with patients with life-threatening communicable diseases, not homophobia, may be the greatest barrier for health professionals.

Findings from APP's studies also point to fear of AIDS transmission as the major obstacle to complete care. In any number of ways, dentists have indicated that their greatest fear is the potential for transmission of infectious diseases in the dental office. For example, 32% of respondents in APP's California Survey did not believe that following the CDC guidelines for infection control for hepatitis B would protect them against the AIDS virus.[4] It can be assumed that dentists who do not trust the effectiveness of these measures are extremely fearful. They might be guessing which infection control practices guarantee safety and thus be afraid they are wrong. In the same survey, 47% of respondents believed that AIDS could be transmitted through saliva, although there is no scientific evidence for this belief. Dentists who have this opinion and who work in a saliva-wet field all day would be fearful. They might worry not only about current exposure but also about exposure in earlier years when their infection control practices were less adequate.

To design educational interventions that help dentists and dental students cope with the HIV epidemic, their fears need to be understood. This understanding of the barriers to caring for high risk patients will help us identify both the attitudes that need to be changed and educational methods that have potential for changing these attitudes.

THE CHALLENGE

The educational issues for dentistry in the age of AIDS are complex. Two behaviors that need improvement, infection control and intraoral examinations, are areas in which dental professionals have long been resistant to change. The third major issue of concern, fear of AIDS and the resulting barriers to treating people with AIDS, is a new problem for dentistry, but one that appears to be equally difficult to resolve.

Finding solutions to these problems will require a creative and committed effort. Conventional educational approaches have not improved dental health care workers' attitudes and behaviors, and the level of leadership to date has not been

196

sufficient to motivate change among most in the profession.
Part of the answer lies in finding new means of teaching skills
and in realigning beliefs about AIDS. Toward these ends,
research is critical. Dental educators have an important role to
play in guiding such research and interpreting its answers.

But the urgency of the HIV crisis demands immediate
action as well. One of the most effective paths to change available to dental educators lies in their leadership both as decision-
makers with regard to policy and as role models for students
and practitioners alike. From these positions of authority, dental educators can help to shape attitudes within the profession
and to formulate guidelines for behavior that are both practical
and ethically acceptable. Any action taken from these positions,
however, will be most effective if leaders understand the impact
of AIDS on dentistry, as illustrated in part by the issues outlined in this paper. It will also be helpful to address the distinction between acquiring knowledge and using it. While it is relatively easy to teach dentists the basic and clinical science of
AIDS, for example, it is another matter to have them apply the
information in their practices. Follow-through is central to
achieving results. A third useful concept is that of sharing information quickly and informally. The months needed to publish
data are often outpaced by the HIV epidemic; a rapid and critical exchange of ideas among colleagues can produce rewarding
results.

Although the problem of AIDS is an immediate one for dentistry, it will also need to be reckoned with for years to come.
Perhaps the greatest challenge for dental educators will be to
anticipate and meet the needs of those who will be dealing with
AIDS in the future. This will require careful planning and a
sustained effort over time.

REFERENCES

1. Boffey PM: Doctors who shun AIDS patients are assailed by surgeon general. *New York Times*, September 10, 1987.
2. When doctors refuse to treat AIDS, editorial. *New York Times*,
August 8, 1987.
3. Smith DC: AIDS and the Chicago dentists shines national spot-
light on CDC. *Chicago Dent Soc Rev* 1987;80:14-16.
4. Gerbert B: AIDS and infection control in dental practice: Dentists'
knowledge, attitudes, and behaviors. *J Am Dent Assoc*
1987;114:311-314.

5. Atchison K, Dolan T, Meetz H: Have dentists assimilated information about AIDS? *J Dent Educ* 1987;51:668-672.
6. Gerbert B, Badner V, Maguire B: AIDS and dental practice. *J Public Health Dent* 1988;48:68-73.
7. Gerbert B, Maguire B, Badner V, et al: Changing dentists' knowledge, attitudes, and behaviors about AIDS: An educational intervention. *J Am Dent Assoc* 1988;116:851-854.
8. Klein RS, Phelan JA, Freeman K, et al: Low occupational risk of human immunodeficiency virus among dental professionals. *N Engl J Med* 1988;318:86-90.
9. Centers for Disease Control: Update: Human immunodeficiency virus infections in health-care workers exposed to blood of infected patients. *MMWR* 1987;36:285-289.
10. The American Association of Public Health Dentistry Ad Hoc Committee on Infectious Diseases: The control of transmissible diseases in dental practice: A position paper. *J Public Health Dent* 1986;46:13-22.
11. Crawford JJ: New light on the transmissibility of viral hepatitis in dental practice and its control. *J Am Dent Assoc* 1975;91:829-835.
12. Council on Dental Materials and Devices, Council on Dental Therapeutics: Infection control in the dental office. *J Am Dent Assoc* 1978;97:673-677.
13. Infection control in the dental office: A realistic approach. *J Am Dent Assoc* 1985;110:969-972.
14. Council on Dental Therapeutics, Council on Prosthetic Services and Dental Laboratory Relations: Guidelines for infection control in the dental office and the commercial dental laboratory. *J Am Dent Assoc* 1985;110:969-972.
15. Council on Dental Therapeutics, American Dental Association: Sterilization, infection control methods offer defense against AIDS. *ADA News*, August 9, 1983.
16. Centers for Disease Control: Acquired immunodeficiency syndrome (AIDS) precautions for health care workers and allied professionals. *MMWR* 1983;32:450-451.
17. Silverman S: Infectious and sexually transmitted diseases: Implications for dental public health. *J Public Health Dent* 1986;46:7-12.
18. Rosen S, Mlakar L, Crawford JJ, et al: Comparison of infection control procedures in dental offices between 1985 and 1986, abstract. *J Dent Res* (special issue) 1987;66:162.
19. Academy of General Dentistry: Majority of general dentists use gloves, masks, and glasses, survey finds. *Dental News*, December 7, 1987.
20. Gerbert B, Badner V, Maguire B, et al: Perceived personal risk: Impact on dentists' infection control behaviors, abstract. *J Dent Res* (special issue) 1988;67:256.
21. Klein RS, Harris CA, Small CB, et al: Oral candidiasis in high-risk patients as the initial manifestation of the acquired immunodeficiency syndrome. *N Engl J Med* 1984;311:354-357.

22. Greenspan D, Greenspan JS, Conant M, et al: Oral "hairy" leuko-plakia in male homosexuals: Evidence of association with both papillomavirus and herpes-group virus. *Lancet* 1984;2:831-834.
23. Greenspan D, Greenspan JS, Pindborg JJ, et al: *AIDS and the Dental Team.* Copenhagen, Munksgaard, 1986.
24. Lozada F, Silverman S, Migliorati CA, et al: Oral manifestations of tumor and opportunistic infections in the acquired immunodeficiency syndrome (AIDS): Findings in 53 homosexual men with Kaposi's sarcoma. *Oral Surg* 1983;56:491-494.
25. Morris AL, Bohannan HM: Assessment of private dental practice: Implications for dental education. *J Dent Educ* 1987;51:661-667.
26. Raber PE: AIDS: Prevent its spread, treat its victims. *Dent Today* 1985;4:21-22.
27. Filler S: Report of a survey assessing dental student attitudes toward AIDS, abstract. *J Dent Res* (special issue) 1988;67:256.
28. Gerbert B: Impact of the HIV epidemic on medical education: Teaching doctors about AIDS. *Research in Medical Education, 1987: Proceedings of the Twenty-sixth Annual Conference,* Washington, DC, pp 283-290.
29. Cooke M, Koenig B: Housestaff attitudes towards the acquired immunodeficiency syndrome. *Third International Conference on AIDS,* Washington, DC, June, 1987.
30. McKusick L, Horstman W, Abrams D, Coates T: The psychological impact of AIDS on primary care physicians. *West J Med* 1986;144:751-752.
31. Kelly JA, Lawrence JS, Smith S, et al: Stigmatization of AIDS patients by physicians. *Am J Public Health* 1987;77:789-79

Panel Discussion: Session III

Dr Deborah Greenspan introduced the Session III speakers and welcomed three additional members to the panel:

Dr Enid Neidle, Assistant Executive Director for Scientific Affairs of the American Dental Association

Carolyn Gray, Assistant Executive Director for Educational Affairs of the American Association of Dental Schools

Dr Philip Swango, Epidemiology and Oral Disease Prevention Program of the National Institute of Dental Research

Dr Neidle discussed the position of the American Dental Association (ADA) on the treatment of HIV-infected patients. Dr Neidle noted that the ADA policy statement was the House of Delegates' initial best try at saying to the dental profession, "You should treat HIV-infected patients," but that the ADA hopes to improve the policy statement.

Carolyn Gray outlined initiatives undertaken by the American Association of Dental Schools. They included the development of curricula on ethics and professionalism in dentistry. A draft document should be ready for final review in the early spring. The Association is using the American Medical Association policy statement on AIDS as a model and has drafted a policy for dental education that will be presented to the House of Delegates at the next annual session. The American Association of Dental Schools is also attempting to establish funding to bring appropriate experts together to develop curricula on infection control and infectious diseases for predoctoral education. She noted that we have to begin to introduce concepts of compassion and sensitivity into the dental curriculum. We have to begin to train students to develop an ethical standard that they can defend themselves, in a rational manner, and we have to begin to integrate into our curriculum concepts of human sexuality. These educational changes applied not only to dentistry, but to dental hygiene, dental assisting, and dental laboratory technology.

Dr Swango asked for further discussion on some of the ethical issues related to the conduct of research in HIV-infected individuals. These issues included the question of when we acquire the obligation to treat individuals who are subjects in an observational study. Dr McCullough replied that it was essential to make sure that the subjects in the trial understand that it is a purely observational trial, and that treatment provision is not part of it. This can be handled through informed consent. Rules should be established to indicate to subjects when treatment becomes appropriate and where they should seek such treatment. It is an ethical obligation of any research group to make sure that referral networks are in place, and that you don't just throw the people back out in the community to fend for themselves, but rather have dentists already identified who are skilled and qualified to care for these patients' needs.

Dr Swango asked whether in a study in which one of the objectives was to document occurrence of hairy leukoplakia, one might want to perform biopsies on white lesions on the tongue to ascertain that they were, in fact, leukoplakia. The results of that biopsy may not help the individual at all. It may put the individual at some degree of suffering. And yet, if you don't do the biopsy, you're not collecting adequate documentation of the condition.

Dr McCullough replied that the questions would be: What is the nature of the pain and discomfort the patient would experience? Is it going to be a permanent pain and discomfort or is it something that will pass very quickly? Can the pain and discomfort be managed effectively through medication or other means? If those are all thought to be manageable and transitory risks, then the risks should be explained to the subject. One of the worrisome areas of AIDS research is that there may be an overeagerness on the part of subjects at risk to accept risks that ordinarily we would not let subjects undergo.

Dr Pindborg observed that the question of a biopsy is not an ethical one at all, because you take a biopsy to improve your diagnosis. As long as what you are doing to the patients is part of a diagnostic exercise, the biopsy is not an ethical issue. Such is especially true for hairy leukoplakia, for which a biopsy is essential for final diagnosis. Dr Scully agreed and noted that in the case of white lesions it may be unethical not to biopsy.

Dr Fox noted that in the view of clinical review panels, to simply say you are doing something for diagnosis is no longer sufficient. You have to look at the consequence of that diagnosis. If you establish a diagnosis with your biopsy for which there is no therapy — and this touches on the issue of HIV testing in the general population — most review panels would consider that a worthless exercise.

Dr McCullough noted that defining treatment options is not the only reason to establish a diagnosis. Telling patients what their problem is oftentimes is a very important part of health care. The question, "Why do I have this pain?" is very often more important to the patient than what you are going to do about it. Is it something I did wrong? Am I not eating right? Is this a heart attack or not a heart attack? So you do a diagnostic intervention to give patients information, to provide them reassurance, or to let them know that maybe they ought to be concerned, that their fear is a rational, not an ungrounded, one. There is care to be given to patients for whom cure is not possible.

Dr McCullough expanded on the concept of informed consent. Any invasive diagnostic procedure, including biopsy for hairy leukoplakia, must have the consent of the patient, even if it's done strictly for diagnostic measures. The patient has the right to refuse. Anytime you are performing a routine diagnostic test that is also going to be used to accumulate scientific knowledge, you're obligated to explain that fact to the patient, and the purposes of the research. Not because the patient is being subjected to additional risks to gain the knowledge but because the patient may object to the purposes of your research, and to being used as a research subject. Mary Logan added that informed consent issues have legal as well as ethical implications.

Dr Melnick raised a question relating to oral manifestations being a precursor lesion to HIV-associated disease. She said that in conducting nearly 600 screening examinations of male homosexuals in a community-based clinic in Seattle, it was determined that an individual with one of a constellation of oral manifestations is about 4.5 times as likely to be subsequently found to be HIV seropositive as someone without those lesions, with the risk of an individual with certain oral lesions being as high as 8 or 9 times as likely for HIV-seropositivity. In extrapolating that to clinical practice, Dr Melnick asked for comments regarding the responsibilities of the practicing clinician who is *not* plugged into a research protocol, with the attendant medical and counseling support, to inform such persons of their risk.

Dr McCullough discussed the problems in telling a patient, "What I'm about to tell you will be possibly very frightening, it might be psychologically destabilizing, and might lead you to become depressed and even suicidal." He wondered if we need an informed consent for the risks of disclosure of the information, and worried that dentists do not have much training in the psychological dimensions of health care.

Mary Logan observed that another approach is for the dentist to say to the patient, "I'm uncomfortable with some of the signs that I see in your mouth. I'd like to refer you to your physician or to a specialist. And when that person has looked at you and has told me that it's OK for me to continue, in your best interest, to provide care, then come back to me and we'll continue working." I don't think a dentist should ever say, "I think you have AIDS," or "in my opinion, you have AIDS."

Dr McCullough: But suppose the patient asks, "Why are you sending me to see these people?"

Mary Logan: "Because I see oral symptoms of some kind of an illness in your mouth, and I'm not qualified to tell you what those oral symptoms mean, but I'm concerned for your health and I think you should have somebody take a look at that."

Dr McCullough: Then they say, "Do I have AIDS?"

Dr D. Greenspan observed that the answer to the patient's question depends on the experience and training of the dentist.

Dr Goodson asked the panel to address establishing ethical and legal "stopping" rules for clinical studies involving untreated patients. Dr Goodson noted that studies of the natural history of periodontal disease at Forsyth Dental Center have attempted to establish cut-off values that were related to what was considered to be the minimum dependable or detectable significant change in disease. The patient would be told as part of the informed consent, "when we have measured half a millimeter of bone loss radiographically, or if we measure two and a half millimeters of attachment loss on repeated probing, then we feel that this is significant evidence of disease advancement; hence, we will intercede."

Dr McCullough discussed an example of stopping rules for studies of pediatric heart disease. The standard used to stop the trial was that, even if you assume that all the experimental arms failed at that point, you could still show statistically that the experimental arm was more effective and safe, especially safer, than the standard arm. For diseases that are not life-threatening, greater flexibility may be possible using a clinical judgment standard rigorously derived such that the dentist is sure that the patient is not being neglected into irreversible harm.

Dr Wright asked whether long or short sleeves in dental protective clothing were more appropriate. Dr Molinari replied that the rationale for short sleeves for scrub suits or scrub tops or clinic garments was that when you wear long sleeves, as evidenced by repeated spatter studies, you can drag those sleeves through areas of high concentrations of spatter in and around the patient's mouth, and transfer those from patient to patient.

Dr Neidle discussed the ADA guidelines which call for long sleeves. The rationale was that long sleeves, tightly covered by a glove which comes part way up the sleeve, will provide better protection for broken skin. All of the ADA recommendations call for discarding any gowns that are noticeably wet or soiled.

Dr Rosenberg asked what the ADA was doing to provide positive leadership for the practicing dentist. Dr Neidle replied that the ADA has spent literally hundreds of thousands of dollars and is committing hundreds of thousands of dollars to educational programs and development of guidelines for treatment of patients with HIV infection. The ADA message has been consistent: the dental profession has the responsibility to treat HIV-infected patients.

Carolyn Gray observed that one way to influence the leadership of an organization is to participate and become the leaders. There is no alternative to the effectiveness of that kind of commitment in the long run.

Dr Lucente noted that the triumph over the AIDS epidemic will come through educating both those in risks groups, and those who are really not in risk groups. He raised the questions, Do health care professionals have an ethical obligation to become effective educators, and how do they fulfill that obligation?

Dr Gerbert responded that there is great debate about whether dentists are appropriately qualified to educate patients about reducing their risks. Do we counsel every patient, or do we counsel those who we know have an oral manifestation, or who we know are HIV positive? Are we in a position to counsel patients about reducing risk to their sexual partners or to those with whom they share needles? She noted that many dentists are concerned they will chase patients away if they attempt such counsel, and that patients are being surveyed now to find out what their true attitudes are about these issues.

Dr D. Greenspan thanked the panelists and participants for a most stimulating session.

John Greenspan

UNANSWERED QUESTIONS AND FUTURE DIRECTIONS

I would like to go back to the issue of what future directions we and our colleagues should take, to talk about unanswered questions and action steps with respect to HIV infection. As far as the nature and significance of the oral consequences of HIV infection are concerned, there is little controversy about the knowledge that we have gained thus far. However, more work is needed on whether there are additional new and unconventional lesions yet to be described. The issue of geographic variation in the expression of HIV infection in the mouth was touched on but not really explored at this meeting because we confined our discussions to the United States and the European countries, neglecting Africa, South America and other areas of the Third World. We have reason to believe, from preliminary work by Drs Schiødt and Pindborg and their colleagues, that the situation may be very different in those places.

We have much to learn about the relationship of the oral features with the time since seroconversion, a key issue that was touched upon by a number of participants. Such information will become available from serial sequential studies of risk groups with known serostatus and with known times of seroconversion. Studies of this type are in progress at a number of centers, including San Francisco. The information they obtain will allow us to place the oral lesions in a rational staging of HIV infection. This issue is of great practical significance, not only in dealing with our own patients but also in the use of clinical diagnosis criteria as part of non-laboratory-based staging for HIV infection. Again I refer particularly to Africa, but also to much of the world where, as time goes by, the lack of availability and the cost of elaborate and expensive laboratory procedures will probably mean that more emphasis is placed on clinical criteria. There the oral lesions, with their sentinel function, will, I predict, become even more important.

There is another lesson to be learned from the oral lesions that we have not really begun to address. That is the significance of the tissue events in the oral lesions or the HIV-associated lesions elsewhere in the body. Reference was made to this as regards hairy leukoplakia and candidiasis, but it appears that the oral lesions are analogous to the fatal opportunistic infections that occur, for example, in the lung. Surely we can learn something from the way that opportunistic infection occurs in the oral mucosa that we can apply to the lung and other organs. Very little is known about the events going on within the oral lesions. We all take it for granted that *Candida* opportunistically colonizes the oral mucosa and that Epstein-Barr virus reactivates and causes epithelial hyperplasia in hairy leukoplakia. However, we really know nothing about the immunological processes that lead to those events. We have a big gap between the decrease or even ablation of the T4 lymphocytes and the colonization and invasion by microorganisms. As far as hairy leukoplakia is concerned, clearly there are a number of unanswered questions, particularly concerning a possible second virus as well as whether the findings we have recorded from San Francisco apply to other populations.

I think the biggest questions relate to the periodontal lesions — an area where the dental profession is uniquely qualified and trained to make a contribution. There is need for agreement on terminology. I did not sense from yesterday's discussion that everybody is talking about the same clinical entity. The people concerned should be encouraged to get together to agree on terminology, at least an operational terminology. To do that, as was hinted yesterday, there is need for calibration so that we are all at least making observations using the same tools. People do not yet agree on whether the HIV-associated gingivitis is a precursor lesion to HIV-associated periodontitis. Nor is much known about the tissue events going on in the periodontal lesion and whether the host response has a role in this lesion. Are the lesions entirely due to pathogenic microorganisms using the defenseless tissue like a culture medium, and thus destroying those tissues, or is host response also involved?

Little has been learned about the pediatric oral manifestations of HIV infection. We await confirmation of reports of embryopathy or dysmorphogenesis. Such studies will be difficult, for the populations concerned are not large, and are in different geographical centers. Furthermore, a variety of cofactors confound the issue, notably the drug abuse habits that lead to the transmission of HIV to mothers as well as the issue of fetal alcohol syndrome.

The treatment session was very exciting. This is the first time, I think, that attention has been focused on the treatment of the oral manifestations of HIV disease. I predict that this will be the next area for major development. I think it is clear from the panel discussion that studies of treatment will be complicated by the widespread use of azidothymidine (AZT). We need to plan studies that are large enough to be able to take account of the AZT factor, and still come to valid conclusions about the effectiveness of the anti-opportunistic-infection drugs. I propose that we plan for large-scale multicenter cooperative studies into the efficacy of antifungal and other regimes.

When discussing therapy for the oral manifestations of HIV, it is important to remember three issues. First, the lesions may be atypical or new lesions quite different from those considered in the usual oral diagnosis screening. Second, exotic microorganisms may be present. Third, the response to treatment may be atypical because of the underlying immunosuppression, because of the plethora of other conditions with which these patients are dealing, or because of the effects of other therapy. I would emphasize the need for competent oral clinical diagnostic and therapeutic skills to be applied to this problem. I am of the opinion, and I heard nothing at this meeting to convince me otherwise, that we have a serious problem concerning the availability of dental professionals trained in the fields of oral medicine, oral pathology and periodontology with an emphasis on AIDS care. I therefore raise the question, not for the first time, of whether new and specifically HIV-directed training programs are required.

I must digress for a moment and say how thrilled I was by Dr Pindborg sharing with us the possibility that *Candida*-immunized cows might be a source of colostrum with which to treat *Candida* a theme not entirely new to us from San Francisco, where patients use everything from boot polish to beeswax to treat hairy leukoplakia and oral candidiasis. To honor a much honored man, I have, therefore, written a limerick:

A jovial genius from Copenhagen
Was faced with an oral conundrum
Always in a great rush
Given one more case of thrush,
He cried, "What the heck, let's try colostrum!"

Today we received insight into the contentious areas of the ethical and legal implications of this epidemic. We are faced with the problem of communicating new information to dental health care workers and translating it into an agreed-on new standard of practice. We have also the dual problem of introducing curricular changes, so that we can bring about a new generation of informed practitioners, in a milieu of faculty colleagues who themselves need to be educated. I think Dr McCullough summed it up by saying that AIDS is going to be a major test of the professionalism of dentistry.

I will list some omissions that were not covered at this conference. The first involves implications of the HIV epidemic for dentistry in the Third World. We have an obligation to our colleagues elsewhere in the world. Also, there was a relative lack of attention during these discussions to the value of animal studies for AIDS work. Such studies have been commenced, but there is room for a great deal more work in that field. We said little at this meeting about saliva. Perhaps the issues involving saliva and HIV have been settled, but I doubt it. I suspect that there are many unanswered questions concerning relationships between HIV and other viruses, saliva and salivary glands. As far as infection control is concerned, a critical issue is occupational transmission because of needlesticks and puncture wounds from instruments bathed in saliva and blood. Infection control in dental practice must be directed toward hepatitis B virus, herpes simplex virus and other conventional pathogens. Dentistry has known that for many years and has neglected appropriate practices.

Finally, very little was said about the cost implications and the health services research implications of the HIV epidemic for dentistry. These include the training of personnel, changing of practice habits, and of course, the influence of the insurance industry on the ultimate expression of how we handle this problem. I suspect that to be a factor that will influence events.

I found this conference quite remarkable in the amount of information that I gained. I found it stimulating, at times depressing, but for the most part, exhilarating in terms of the number of questions, both old and new, that were raised.

Concluding Remarks 2

Paul B. Robertson

Two standards by which I judge the success of scientific workshops are the amount of new information shared by the participants and the number of questions raised for future investigation. On both points, this workshop has been a clear success.

John Greenspan gave an eloquent discussion of the epidemiology and virology of HIV. We gained a clearer view of why HIV's effects on lymphocytes, macrophages, endothelium, neuroglia, epithelium and Langerhans cells might favor opportunistic infections and neoplasms that take advantage of immunosuppression.

Robert Klein showed that while there is some occupational risk in treating HIV-infected patients, occupationally acquired infection is extremely uncommon. Moreover, the occupational exposures can be avoided by diligence with respect to infection control and other procedures that minimize the risk. Very well taken were his comments that risks are probably greater from those who have not yet been identified — the huge base of his iceberg.

Deborah Greenspan gave us a clear insight into the very unusual presentations of oral lesions in HIV infection, and Jens Pindborg presented a typically incisive discussion of oral candidiasis.

Jim Winkler provided a well-documented description of HIV-associated gingivitis and HIV-associated periodontitis. HIV-associated gingivitis was characterized by a linear band of erythema at the gingival margin, punctate and diffuse erythema affecting the gingiva and alveolar mucosa, spontaneous gingival bleeding, and failure to respond to conventional therapy. In addition to these features, HIV-associated periodontitis showed extremely rapid loss of attachment and, in some cases, pain and frank exposure of alveolar bone. I was most interested in the geographical differences in the nature and severity of HIV-associated periodontal changes, and I look forward to the next few months of exploration.

The relative contributions of oral pathogens and the host response to those pathogens was a topic of considerable discussion. The presence of high proportions of *Candida* and a variety of bacteria with proven pathogenic potential in the subgingival flora lent support to the possibility of direct microbial damage. The hyperresponsiveness of polymorphonuclearleukocyte function in Dr Winkler's patients raised many questions about modulation of the oral flora by a markedly altered host response in HIV-infected patients.

Charles Barr provided a concise overview of present and experimental treatment approaches to candidiasis, bacterial infections, viral infections, neoplastic diseases and miscellaneous oral manifestations. We noted his concern that routine dental care should be delivered to the HIV-infected patient, a theme which we heard throughout the conference.

The microbiological findings presented by Joseph Zambon and by Patricia Murray and Stan Holt were similar. Both groups listed *Bacteroides* species, *Candida* and, to a lesser extent, *Actinobacillus actinomycetemcomitans* as prevalent in HIV infections. And both groups also observed some unusual organisms. Dr Zambon saw an unidentified gram-positive spore-forming anaerobic rod, and Dr Holt a *Wolinella*-like organism.

Marcus Grassi compared conventional therapy (scaling, root planing and oral hygiene) with conventional therapy plus povidone-iodine irrigation and with conventional therapy plus chlorhexidine rinses. Conventional therapy alone and conventional therapy with povidone-iodine irrigation effected essentially no change in the clinical picture over a three-month period; indeed, patients in these two groups continued to lose periodontal attachment. Conversely, chlorhexidine all but eliminated gingival bleeding and both punctate and diffuse erythema. No further attachment loss occurred and, in some cases, severe lesions began to heal.

Laurence McCullough provided a most thoughtful discussion of the ethical considerations surrounding the reluctance of dental health care workers to treat HIV-infected patients for reasons of fear, self-infection, or loss of employment or income. He advanced a concise line of argument that no health care worker may refuse to provide such treatment, and we were challenged by his concern that there was a great deal at stake for the future of the dental profession in resolving that issue.

Mary Logan discussed the legal implications of communicable disease for dental practice and provided a careful analysis of the rights of HIV-infected patients to dental care, the liability

210

of providers for passing on HIV infection, the obligations of providers who are themselves infected with HIV, and government regulations for infection control.

John Molinari gave a well-organized overview of aseptic techniques, principles of sterilization and disinfection, laboratory and equipment asepsis, and use and disposal of needles and sharp items. I gained two critical points: the concept of universal precaution, which fit very nicely with Dr Klein's iceberg, and the importance of communicating infection control facts to staff and patients.

Barbara Gerbert outlined the substantial problems in educating the dental profession about HIV infection and the treatment of the HIV-infected patient, and suggested a number of approaches to changing dentists' knowledge, attitudes and behaviors.

This has been a most exciting workshop. I appreciated the open and frank discussion from all of the participants. Finally, I join the participants in thanking the Procter and Gamble Oral Health Group for the educational grant that made this conference possible.

Participants

CALIFORNIA

Gary C. Armitage, DDS
UCSF School of Dentistry
San Francisco, CA 94143

Jon F. Bauer, DDS
7060 Hollywood Blvd
Hollywood, CA 90028

William M. Carpenter, DDS
University of the Pacific
   School of Dentistry
2155 Webster St
San Francisco, CA 94115

Henry M. Cherrick, DDS
UCLA School of Dentistry
Los Angeles, CA 90024

James W. Formaker, DDS
10724 Riverside Dr
Toluca Lake, CA 91602

Barbara Gerbert, PhD
UCSF School of Dentistry
San Francisco, CA 94143

John C. Greene, DMD, MPH
UCSF School of Dentistry
San Francisco, CA 94143

Deborah Greenspan, BDS
UCSF School of Dentistry
San Francisco, CA 94143

John S. Greenspan, BSc, PhD,
   BDS, FRCPath
UCSF School of Dentistry
San Francisco, CA 94143

Robert Isman, DDS, MPH
Office of Dental Health
714 P St, Room 440
Sacramento, CA 95814

Penelope J. Leggott, DDS
UCSF School of Dentistry
San Francisco, CA 94143

Frank M. Lucatorto, DDS
UCLA School of Dentistry
Center of Health Services
Los Angeles, CA 90024

William P. Lundergan, DDS
University of the Pacific
   School of Dentistry
2155 Webster St
San Francisco, CA 94115

Patricia A. Murray, DMD, PhD
UCSF School of Dentistry
San Francisco, CA 94143

Michael G. Newman, DDS
UCLA School of Dentistry
Los Angeles, CA 90024

W. Eugene Rathbun, DDS, PhD
Loma Linda University
   School of Dentistry
Loma Linda, CA 92350

Morton Schiødt, DDS, Dr Odont
UCSF School of Dentistry
San Francisco, CA 94143

Sol Silverman, Jr, DDS
UCSF School of Dentistry
San Francisco, CA 94143

Jay F. Watson, DDS
UCLA School of Dentistry
Los Angeles, CA 90024

Cynthia A. Williams, DMD
UCSF School of Dentistry
San Francisco, CA 94143

James R. Winkler, DDS, PhD
UCSF School of Dentistry
San Francisco, CA 94143

COLORADO

Robert G. Schallhorn, DDS
11200 E Mississippi Ave
Aurora, CO 80012

212

CONNECTICUT
Warren R. LeMay, DDS, MPH
University of Connecticut
  Health Center
Farmington, CT 06032

DISTRICT OF COLUMBIA
Carolyn F. Gray, RDH
American Association of
  Dental Schools
1625 Massachusetts Ave NW
Washington, DC 20036

Lt C. John E. King, DDS, MPH
US Army Institute of Dental
  Research
Walter Reed Army Medical
  Center
Washington, DC 20307

Robert R. Rhyne, DDS
Veterans Administration
  Central Office
810 Vermont Ave NW
Washington, DC 20420

FLORIDA
Richard K. Ames, DDS, MPH
2421 SW 6th Avenue
Ft Lauderdale, FL 33315

Richard A. Cohen, DMD
University of Miami
1475 NW 12th Ave, Suite 2089A
Miami, FL 33136

L.R. Eversole, DDS, MSD
University of Florida
  College of Dentistry
Box J-414 JHMHC
Gainesville, FL 32610

Stuart Kline, DDS
University of Miami
Jackson Memorial Hospital
1611 NW 12th Ave
Miami, FL 33136

C.E. Stone, DMD
University of Florida
  College of Dentistry
Box J-414 JHMHC
Gainesville, FL 32610

Frank W. Stout, DDS
University of Florida
  College of Dentistry
Box J-414 JHMHC
Gainesville, FL 32610

GEORGIA
Thomas R. Dirksen, DDS, PhD
Medical College of Georgia, Room 103
Augusta, GA 30912

Edwin D. Joy, DDS
Medical College of Georgia
Augusta, GA 30912

ILLINOIS
William A. Ayer, DDS, PhD
311 E Chicago, Ward Bldg 9-207
Chicago, IL 60611

Kenneth H. Burrell, DDS
American Dental Association
211 E Chicago Ave
Chicago, IL 60611

John W. Davis, DDS
University of Chicago
  Zoller Dental Clinic
5841 S Maryland Ave, Box 418
Chicago, IL 60637

Mary Logan, JD
American Dental Association
211 E Chicago Ave
Chicago, IL 60611

Reza Mostifi, DMD
University of Chicago
  Zoller Dental Clinic
5841 S Maryland Ave, Box 418
Chicago, IL 60637

Enid Neidle, PhD
American Dental Association
211 E Chicago Ave
Chicago, IL 60611

Michael L. Perich, DDS
American Dental Association
211 E Chicago Ave
Chicago, IL 60611

Stephen A. Schwartz, DMD, PhD
Chicago Medical School
North Chicago, IL 60064

Wendy Wils, RDHB
Northwestern Memorial Hospital
303 E Superior
Chicago, IL 60611

INDIANA
Bradley Beiswanger, DDS
Indiana University
  School of Dentistry
1121 W Michigan St
Indianapolis, IN 46202

Chris H. Miller, PhD
Indiana University
  School of Dentistry
1211 W Michigan St
Indianapolis, IN 46202

Susan L. Zunt, DDS
Indiana University
  School of Dentistry
1121 W Michigan St, Room 106D
Indianapolis, IN 46202

KENTUCKY
Gerald A. Ferretti, DDS, MSD
University of Kentucky
  Medical Center
234 Medical Plaza
Lexington, KY 40536

LOUISIANA
Roland Meffort, DDS
Louisiana State University
  School of Dentistry
1100 Florida Ave, Box 138
New Orleans, LA 70119

MARYLAND
Philip C. Fox, DDS
National Institutes of Health
101 1B21
Bethesda, MD 20892
Matthew Kinnard, PhD
National Institute of Dental Research
Extramural Programs
Westwood Building, Room 509
Bethesda, MD 20892

Dushanka V. Kleinman, DDS, MSD
National Institute of Dental Research
Epidemiology and Oral Disease
  Prevention Program
Westwood Building, Room 6S250
Bethesda, MD 20892

Philip A. Swango, DDS, MPH
National Institute of Dental Research
Epidemiology and Oral Disease
  Prevention Program
Westwood Building
Bethesda, MD 20892

Carolyn Tylenda, DMD, PhD
National Institutes of Health
Bldg 10, Room 1B17
Bethesda, MD 20895

Joan Wilentz
National Institute of Dental Research
Bldg 31, Room 2C-36
Bethesda, MD 20892

William E. Wright, DDS
National Institute of Dental Research
Bldg 10, Room 6S250
Bethesda, MD 20892

Chih-Ko Yeh, BDS, PhD
National Institute of Dental Research
Bldg 10, Room 6S255
Bethesda, MD 20892

MASSACHUSETTS
Myron Allukian, Jr, DDS, MPH
Community Dental Programs
Boston Dept of Health and Hospitals
818 Harrison Ave
Boston, MA 02118

J. Max Goodson, DDS, PhD
Forsyth Dental Center
140 Fenway
Boston, MA 02115

Frank Oppenheim, DDS, DMD, PhD
Boston University Medical Center
80 E Concord St
Boston, MA 02118

MICHIGAN
John A. Molinari, PhD
University of Detroit
  School of Dentistry
2985 E Jefferson
Detroit, MI 48207

MINNESOTA
M. Bashar Bakdash, DDS, MPH,
  MSD
University of Minnesota
  School of Dentistry
388 Judith Ave
Minneapolis, MN 55113

Sandra Melnick, DrPH
Division of Epidemiology
Stadium Gate 27
611 Beacon Street SE
Minneapolis, MN 55455

MISSOURI
Sam V. Holroyd, DDS
4559 Scott Ave
St Louis, MO 63110

NEW JERSEY
Ernest Baden, DDS, PhD
Fairleigh S. Dickinson Jr
  College of Dental Medicine
140 University Plaza Dr
Hackensack, NJ 07601

Ann Goodwin
Fairleigh S. Dickinson Jr
  College of Dental Medicine
140 University Plaza Dr
Hackensack, NJ 07601

NEW YORK
Stephen N. Abel, DDS
St Clare's Hospital
415 W 51st St
New York, NY 10019

Mario Andriolo, Jr, DDS
St Clare's Hospital
415 W 51st St
New York, NY 10019
Charles E. Barr, DDS
Beth Israel Medical Center
New York, NY 10003

Alexander F. DeLuca, MD
Montefiore Drug Abuse
  Treatment Program
111 E 210th St
Bronx, NY 10467

Alan J. Drinnan, MD, DDS
SUNY at Buffalo
  School of Dental Medicine
Buffalo, NY 14214

Bruce Evans, DMD
530 5th Ave, #1856
New York, NY 10111

Catherine M. Gogan, DDS
SUNY at Buffalo
  School of Dental Medicine
Buffalo, NY 14214

Harriett S. Goldman, DDS, MPH
NYU College of Dentistry
345 E 24th St
New York, NY 10010

Robert S. Klein, MD
Montefiore Medical Center
111 E 210th St
Bronx, NY 10467

Frank E. Lucente, MD
315 E 52nd St
New York, NY 10022

John D. McKenna, DDS
SUNY at Buffalo
  School of Dental Medicine
Room 108Q, Squire Hall
Buffalo, NY 14214

Ronnie Meyers, DDS
Columbia University
  School of Dentistry and
  Oral Surgery
630 W 168th St
New York, NY 10032

Joan A. Phelan, DDS
NYU College of Dentistry
New York, NY 10010

Arthur Quart, DDS
3777 Independence Ave
Riverdale, NY 10463

Jack Rosenberg, DDS
310 West End Ave
New York, NY 10023

Edward Schlissel, DDS
SUNY at Stony Brook
    School of Dental Medicine
Stony Brook, NY 11794

James J. Sciubba, DMD, PhD
Long Island Jewish Medical
    Center Dept of Dentistry
New Hyde Park, NY 11042

Carol Sloane
SUNY at Stony Brook
    School of Dental Medicine
Stony Brook, NY 11794

Ahmed A. Uthman, DDS
SUNY at Buffalo
    School of Dental Medicine
Buffalo, NY 14214

Joseph J. Zambon, DDS, PhD
SUNY at Buffalo
    School of Dental Medicine
Buffalo, NY 14214

OHIO
George G. Blozis, DDS
OSU College of Dentistry
305 W 12th Ave
Columbus, OH 43210

William W. Briner, PhD
Procter & Gamble
Sharon Woods Technical Center
11511 Reed Hartman Hwy
Cincinnati, OH 45241

Robert D. Crawford
One Procter & Gamble Plaza
Cincinnati, OH 45202

Lawrence Farrell
One Procter & Gamble Plaza
Cincinnati, OH 45202

J. Paul Jones, PhD
Procter & Gamble
Sharon Woods Technical Center
11511 Reed Hartman Hwy
Cincinnati, OH 45241

Michael D. Manhart, PhD
Procter & Gamble
Sharon Woods Technical Center
11511 Reed Hartman Hwy
Cincinnati, OH 45241

Debra J. Moore
Procter & Gamble
Sharon Woods Technical Center
11511 Reed Hartman Hwy
Cincinnati, OH 45241

G.T. Terezhalmy
Case Western Reserve University
2123 Abington Rd
Cleveland, OH 44106

Cynthia A. Weeks
Procter & Gamble
Sharon Woods Technical Center
11511 Reed Hartman Hwy
Cincinnati, OH 45241

OREGON
Marge Reveal, RDH
7571 SW Bayberry Dr
Aloha, OR 97007

PENNSYLVANIA
John E. Fantasia, DDS
Temple University
    Oral Pathology Dept
3223 N Broad St
Philadelphia, PA 19140

Philip S. Springer, DMD
Hospital of University of
    Pennsylvania
3400 Spruce St, Box 654
Philadelphia, PA 19104

TEXAS
Edwin E. Cordray, DDS
1930 W Bell
Houston, TX 77019

James A. Cottone, DMD
University of Texas
    Dental School, San Antonio
7703 Floyd Curl Dr
San Antonio, TX 78284

David K. Dennison, PhD
University of Texas
  Dental Health Science Center
  Houston Dental Branch
6516 John Freeman Ave
Houston, TX 77035

Harry K. Hodge, DDS
4101 Greenbriar #215
Houston, TX 77098

Stanley C. Holt, PhD
University of Texas
  Dental School, San Antonio
7703 Floyd Curl Dr
San Antonio, TX 78284

Lt C. Edward B. Mandel, DDS
Wilford Hall Medical Center
Lacland Air Force Base
San Antonio, TX 78236

Laurence B. McCullough, PhD
Center for Ethics, Medicine, and
  Public Issues
Baylor College of Medicine
One Baylor Plaza
Houston, TX 77030

Dewey A. Newbold, DDS, MSD
University of Texas
  Dental School, San Antonio
7703 Floyd Curl Dr
San Antonio, TX 78284

Spencer Redding, DDS
University of Texas
  Dental School, San Antonio
7703 Floyd Curl Dr
San Antonio, TX 78284

VIRGINIA
RAdm Robert W. Koch, DMD
Atlantic Fleet Dental Office
Naval Dental Clinic
Norfolk, VA 23511

WASHINGTON
Timothy A. DeRouen, PhD
University of Washington
  SM-35, Suite B509
Seattle, WA 98195

Thomas H. Morton, Jr, DDS, MSD
University of Washington
Division of Oral Pathology
  SB-22
Seattle, WA 98195

Edmond L. Truelove, DDS, MSD
University of Washington
Dept of Oral Medicine, SC-63
Seattle, WA 98195

Mark M. Schubert, DDS, MSD
University of Washington
Dept of Oral Medicine, SC-63
Seattle, WA 98195

CANADA
Paul B. Robertson, DDS, MS
University of British Columbia
2194 Health Sciences Mall
Vancouver, British Columbia
Canada V6T 1W5

DENMARK
Jens J. Pindborg, DDS, Dr Odont
Royal Dental College,
  Copenhagen
20 Norre Alle
L2 Copenhagen 2L00, Denmark

GERMANY
Professor Dr Peter A. Reichart
Freie University
Fohrerstrasse 1000
Berlin 65, West Germany

SWITZERLAND
Markus Grassi, DDS, Dr Med Dent
University of Berne
  School of Dental Medicine
Freiburgstrasse 7
CH-3010 Berne, Switzerland

UNITED KINGDOM
Professor Crispian Scully
University of Bristol Dental School
Lower Maudlin St
Bristol BS1 2LY,
United Kingdom